1959

SISTER MARY CHRISTOPHER, GEORGE AND ALYCE LORE

1966

ELIZABETH ANNE LORE AND SISTER MARY CHRISTOPHER

OTHER BOOKS BY CHRISTIN LORE WEBER

FICTION

ALTAR MUSIC
GYPSY BONES
THE FARNEAR JOURNALS
THE BLUE SHAWL

NONFICTION

FINDING STONE
WOMANCHRIST
BLESSINGS
CIRCLE OF MYSTERIES
A CRY IN THE DESERT
CARING COMMUNITY

THE EDGE OF TENDERNESS

A MEMOIR OF MOTHERS AND SISTERS

BY
CHRISTIN LORE WEBER

Cyberscribe Publications
9700 Sterling Creek Road
Jacksonville, Oregon

ISBN 13:978-1505286953
10:1505286956

In Memory

Alyce Rose Lore
George Raymond Lore
Elizabeth Anne Lore Kensinger
Patrick Francis Kelly
and
Sister Marie Schwan

Sometimes in life, if you are more than usually blessed, a person will come quietly into your heart and never leave. Time won't make a difference, nor will place—physical presence of a beloved is overrated. Sister Marie Schwan died December 30, 2015 just a few weeks before my completion of this memoir, and I still hear her singing, like the lark ascending from what is deepest to what is highest as she makes her flight from realm to realm, from this earth, from this galaxy, from this universe, through the multiverse, into that totality of Being we try to utter in our feeble way, crying AH! Spreading wings and crying GOD! Dissolving in a burst of flame, in a song impossibly high, I hear her still in me as she soars.

All the Beloveds have sung this song:

I am not leaving.
This burst, this cry, this sweet flight, this surrender –
I am oneing with the All.
Never again will you NOT hear me, feel me, know me, love me
in the deep heights, in the farnear of pure essence
that you ARE.

AUTHOR'S NOTE

This story is true as I remember it. The interpretations are my own. The quotations from my mother's letters appear as she wrote them in her unique style.

The memoir's structure takes its form from the letters. Large sections of my convent experience are missing because she knew nothing of them, nevertheless, the spaces in our dialogue are as significant as our words.

I have changed the names of the sisters in the religious community to which I belonged unless an individual sister became a public figure. Family members and close friends retain their names as do public and historical personages.

The reader will note that I've kept the traditional distinction between those religious women who are called "nuns" and those called "sisters." Nuns live in monastic enclosures and spend their lives in prayer and contemplation. Sometimes I've heard people speak of nuns as the poems of God. Sisters are vowed women who dedicate their lives to God by way of compassionate service to the needy of the world—truly "sisters" to one another and to all of us they meet upon life's path. They are the story of God in the world.

Memoir is an act of bearing witness, feeling and tenderly holding life even as it passes. That past with all its voices, fragments of experience, ecstasy and loss, hopes, desires, dreams, each beloved person who occupied the heart—all of it transforms even as it slips into and inhabits the words written to keep it safe. To bear witness is not simply to watch, it is also to celebrate each fragment as it evolves, is held in a moment of silence and hope, then disappears. To remember is to reconstruct life experience that seemed lost and then to love that life anew, as in the words of poet and mystic, Gertrude von le Forte in *Hymns to the Church*:

I WILL LOVE YOU EVEN WHEN MY LOVE OF YOU IS ENDED.
I WILL DESIRE YOU EVEN WHEN I DESIRE YOU NO MORE.

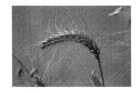

CONVENT REMEMBRANCE

Remember
The laws of cordiality and humility
The presence of the Trinity
In each of your sisters,
In each of their souls, see your bridegroom.

Remember
Our custom of greeting him there:
"Praised be Our Lord, Jesus Christ."

Remember
Modesty of eyes, of body, and of spirit,
Awakening your hearts to love of one another
And to the smallest things:
Wheat in the field behind our house,
Intricate miracle of each flake of snow
That glistens on your shawl in winter.
The longing in creation
For rebirth.

Remember
Your own emptiness.
Prostrate
Yourself before the infinity of Being
And let yourself become the conduit of tears
More than your own.

Remember
The rituals,
The practices.

The manner according to which the soul dies
And is reborn.

Remember
The drawing towards
The calling away
The sundered earth
The hands of the Beloved.

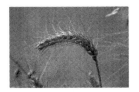

REMEMBER THE FIRST BELOVED

- Remember the beginning, the Mother torn away and lost. Where the mother had been was only hunger. The infant cried; she screamed, and another mother came with food. But the emptiness endured.
- Remember that she sought the Mother in the throat of a tiger lily. Still a child, she crouched beside a road where wilderness ran parallel. Lilies flamed against dark tamarack, enticing her towards a depth terrifying, irresistible. Deep within that throat, droplets of gold.
- Remember that she grew wings and soared, peering into swamps and bogs, Spruce islands floating on unmeasured deeps, illusions of stability. She called the Mother's name and a hawk's voice haunted the sky.
- Remember that Something set a fire in her heart; it leapt into her throat and then she could not speak. She tried to put it out with tears. She could not weep. Horses thundered through the sky. Their hooves burned up the stars.
- Remember that Something placed a drop of water on her tongue. The holy finger tasted of honey and orange. She swallowed. The drop was a rushing stream, a flood, a trilling of music over stones. She sang. Leaves of honey. Cascades of orange.
- Remember that her mother made a veil of ferns and spider webs to attract the Holy Breath. She wore it everywhere. Under the willow a bee mistook her for a flower and gathered nectar from her tears.
- Remember that she became an urchin, eyes endless and dark, face grimed with earth. Hunger wooed her mind to silence. She needed more than words. She went into the wilderness, lay

beneath the tamarack, and took nourishment from the tiger lily's throat.

- Remember that leaves, brown and dry, blew over her, snow fell. She was a leaf beneath it. She lay without dreams. She mingled with the earth deeper than abyss. And there remained the flame, remained the dark.
- Remember once again that the Mother had been ripped from her as though it were the larger being of her Self. Remember the abandonment she felt. Remember the extent of the wound. Remember that after seventy years had passed she would have only begun to understand.
- Remember that they named her Mary Jane.

MARY JANE

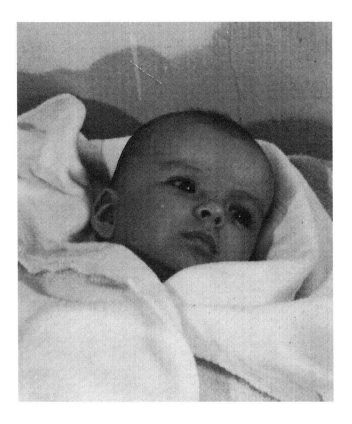

I wasn't yet this old when she was taken from me, the Mother. I don't remember that it happened. Only stories remain, stories I heard much later. She did leave me just that once. She tested positive for tuberculosis and returned to the sanatorium where she had been confined almost a year before she and my father married. After my birth she was gone six weeks. She needed twelve negative tests before she would be allowed to come home. In the meantime Daddy and my Grandma Klimek cared for me. The story is they had trouble making the formula for my feeding. It needed to be done just right or it would curdle, something it often did. While I cried for my bottle they started the process over once again. Mama insisted that she could feel me crying two hundred miles away.

I've wondered sometimes if this early separation from my mother gouged something out of me—the trust that people will stay or will come back if they leave. No matter how much I've learned about commitment, no matter how rational I try to be, and no matter how often people actually do return, I feel a suspicion and a fear of abandonment that rises from somewhere deeper in me than thought or words can reach.

I've wondered, too, if concealed in all these pre-verbal experiences of mine is the origin of a belief that my mother was a fragile creature who needed my protection, someone who required me to guard her existence by being who she desired me to be, by coming to her when she cried out, by offering her more in a daughter than she could have dared to ask. If I would give her all of this, she would stay with me and keep me safe. It was a contract impossible for either one of us to fulfill.

How they laughed, the storytellers, over my grandma and my daddy trying to make an infant formula that didn't curdle. How I cried with hunger until they got it right. How I howled as yet another batch was ruined. My poor sick Mama, gone, and her baby girl left behind six weeks or more. Hungry. I don't remember anyone speculating what effect that loss of Mother might have had upon the child. After all, eventually the baby always was fed, and afterwards she closed her eyes and fell asleep. If others hadn't told the stories, I never would have known.

TIGER LILY

Being—mysterious, ineffable, delectable and sometimes terrifying—beckons some persons from the moment of first consciousness. Yearning rises up and also fear. It is more than desire for mother's milk, the comfort of her body, and the beauty of her face, although the mother was preparation. It is more than fear of the dark or being left alone, though fear's chasms and personal fragility were foretastes. There are no words for this.

Throughout my seventy-plus years, people of all ages have shared with me their experience of this beckoning. I've spoken about it with children as young as six, and heard stories about children even younger. Artists, poets, other creative writers, actors, dancers, musicians have spent lifetimes honing their skills, hoping to represent it. Athletes strive towards it. Lovers open themselves to receive it. I sense that it is more common than we know. Ask them when they first felt this draw, this magnetism, and most will reply that it has been there always. Watch the old man and woman, finished with their work, gazing out at whatever they find in front of them, gazing inwards simultaneously, gazing with love. Monks and nuns of most religious traditions, in contemplation and compassion chisel the material most intimate to them—their very lives—risking everything to become unified with what is behind such experience, that ineffable Being.

A friend of mine, an accomplished poet, remembers her first experience of what she refers to as the "More." She was a toddler, standing in her crib, holding onto the rungs, when time and space opened up to infinity. That's the only a way to say it; who knows what it really was? It was More. It was the size of a pea, and it was also the ... I was going to write, "the everything," but it was more than the everything. It was simply More. It could have swept her away, dense and intense as it was, like a black hole at the core of matter. She couldn't think anything about it until later, but it left its mark on her, in her. Where do you go from something like that? You don't forget it. No matter how long you live, you don't forget. It came before words; surely it can last beyond them. You yearn for it. The yearning creates an imprint, and the imprint lasts. It defines your life. It forms in you a mystic soul, a contemplative mind.

At three-years-old, I became imprinted by a tiger lily. It could have been anything. Author, Petru Dumitriu, stopped in the middle of the stairs to clean his glasses and suddenly a chasm opened through the ordinary into... into what? He was filled with gratitude. But gratitude by its nature moves towards an Other. The supreme Giver. The Nameless. Something—again—More. More than any word, more than thought, more than all the perceptual world combined in a density smaller than a pea. Annie Dillard writes in *Holy the Firm*: "You fall on your knees. You cry, GOD." What are you going to do after that? Yearn. What else is there? "The drawing of this Love; the Voice of this calling," says the author of the *Cloud of Unknowing*. And T.S. Eliot, quoting that anonymous mystic, follows those words with the conviction that we can never cease our exploration into that Love— towards that ineffable Voice. No, we shall not—not ever.

Evidence of the breakthrough into More can show up in unexpected places. Remember Rawlings' novel, *The Yearling*? The boy, Jody, breaks through the ordinary in the experience of that day when he first glimpses the fawn. He reflects later in life: "A mark is on me from the day's delight, so much that all my life when April is a thin green and the flavor of rain is on my tongue, a wound will throb and nostalgia will fill me for something I cannot quite remember." Memory will not suffice because the experience is graced. Grace comes upon us; we cannot cause it. The experience cannot be repeated. Dumitriu could come down the stairs cleaning his glasses over and over and never again break through into the More. Nothing he could do could cause this to happen. But he would live his entire life unable to deny the certainty of the grace of seeing what he saw, of feeling what he felt, of knowing that for a moment he had been taken into the Unknowable, and felt that indescribable gratitude. It kept him on the edge of his life, waiting and yearning.

The tiger lilies still grow along the road, no more than tiger lilies. But I know that one day, against the wilderness, they were cups of fire flecked with gold.

WILDERNESS

The grace of yearning, the beginning of mystical awareness, was given against a backdrop of wilderness. This is the original chaos of most creation myths. Divine Breath drifts over the waters of chaos as a Word: "Let there be light." Some kind of primordial oneness of light and darkness existed before a fundamental separation took place. In the book of *Genesis* we read that once light came into being, "**then** God separated the light from the darkness." And there has been yearning ever since. The yearning, ultimately, is for the reunion of opposites, the realization of the oneness of all separated being with the One Eternal, Uncreated Being that we call by a sound or an absence of sound—depending upon the language of our spiritual tradition and our culture. In English the sound is "God." In the breakthrough-grace of mystic awareness, a person experiences a flame of that Eternal Oneness. In that flame, light and darkness once again unite.

The more powerful the breakthrough, the more intense is the yearning and the deeper the wilderness. This is the danger. We walk a blade's edge, the two edged sword of the Word of Divine Being. Slip off to one or the other side—blinding light or palpable darkness—and we could find ourselves in the inflation of presumption or in the lost lands of despair.

WINGS

A group of fishermen docked, bringing to shore a seagull chick they had found in the water off Gull Rock. One man put the bird into my little hands and asked me to take care of it. Johnny, the yard man, constructed a wire cage behind the laundry building for protection since the bird couldn't yet fly, and I supplied minnows and water several times a day. From time to time I let the bird out to waddle along behind me. Little girl and a seagull. I called him Peter after my uncle who was then flying Admiral Halsey from island to island in the Pacific. I cried when the gull's wings grew large enough and he flew off over the lake. From the end of the dock I cried to him, "Peter, Peter!"

He came back. Out of a flock of gulls one separated himself and landed at my feet. He followed me up the dock to the yard, played this game for a while, and then flew off again to rejoin his kind. "That bird was meant to be wild," my grandmother said. It was fine if he were wild, just so he kept coming back to me.

One day he didn't come when I called. I stood at the end of the dock and called, "Peter," over and over until my mother came to get me. She explained that Peter wasn't coming back. There were dogs that belonged to one of the guests at Grandma's resort. They didn't know that Peter was special. They thought he was a gull just like any other; not one with a name who was the friend of a little girl. And they attacked him. He didn't use his wings. He didn't know enough to be afraid. "Maybe it was wrong of me to let you tame that bird," she said.

At the end of the dock I waited. The flock came each sunset to dive for fish scraps that Johnny threw from his boat. I felt my own wings grow, and I waited. When the flock lifted into the sky something in me lifted with them. Something in me cried out. Something saw the earth from above. Something stayed wild, could never be tamed, must ride the wind, must never know a cage, must not exchange freedom for safety.

My temptation to safety was constant. I call it temptation not because safety is somehow evil. It is a necessity for productive life. Children need safety in order to develop a sense of inner security. It is mystic consciousness that requires the wild, and children often experience a foretaste of this truth.

16

There may have been a time for me before reason set in that I received an intimation of a larger world existing on the other side of the wild, liminal space that is more truly safe than anything this limited world can provide. It cried from within like the cry of a hawk. It felt like danger. It cried from within and from without at the same time.

FIRE

I woke from a dream and was covered in sweat. At first I didn't know I was awake. I thought the dream was real and that my mama was dead. I turned my head and saw the familiar slats of my crib and the big safety-pin holding my covers in place. I shivered. I had been standing by the road in front of Grandma Klimek's Lodge, right by the twin oaks that grew out of a green wooden box. Across the road the waters of Four Mile Bay glimmered. Suddenly, from up the road by McGuire's Resort, a dragon of a road grader—orange, with enormous steel legs—roared towards me. A laughing devil-man sat in the glass enclosed cab and drove the thing. He pulled a rope and fire snarled from the grader-dragon's head. Instinct told me where he was headed. I looked down the road. Behind a white picket fence and surrounded by flowers, I saw a perfect house, the kind that children draw, with windows like smiling eyes. My mother sat inside that house playing cards with her friends. If the grader-dragon got to the house the man would burn it down. My mother would die. I had to stop him. The dragon roared. I screamed. I couldn't stop the thing; I was too small. I screamed again. "Mama!" I woke. She came. She lifted me up and out of my crib.

Maybe I was two years old. If so, I might have been afraid that my fiery willfulness would destroy my world. But this dream haunted me throughout childhood. Once, trying in the dream to run, I fell out of bed. Finally I turned to God, and until well into my teens I couldn't go to sleep without the two-year-old in my mind whispering, "Please, God, don't let me have scary dreams, and don't let the house burn down for one-hundred-and-sixty-six years. Amen."

Maybe the dream mirrored the terror that humans experience when caught in something beyond human power to contain or to control, something numinous. It could have been a foretaste, even a prophecy of experiences yet to come. Or it could be simply that once, before memory, having lost the Mother, I couldn't endure such a radical loss ever again.

Fire and its threat of annihilation, forest and its confusing tangles, skies that could turn into tornadoes able to swallow the lake and boats upon it, water hiding blood-suckers: fire, earth, air, water.

These held the beauty of life and its wilderness. And maybe they were the same thing. This is the mystic's intuition.

In the beginning, though, it was the sky, the lake, fire, the woods, a bog, a spruce island—pathless, confusing, with dark swamps. And always just a step farther into the wilderness, another tiger lily, another possibility of More in which I had begun my life-long search for the Mother I had lost.

SONG

Girl with wide-set, dark brown eyes gazed at the sky where it met the water and trees, and tried to make sense of it. So far I hadn't asked anyone. I had no teacher other than my parents and grandparents who didn't know that the fairy tales they read to me had made me wonder. Where am I? I wanted to know. I must be something small living inside a gigantic orange. The world's sky was round, but the ground and lake were flat. I stood on a plain inside the orange. The stars were pin pricks in the skin of the orange. The orange floated inside an ocean of light. I felt great happiness knowing where I was. When it rained I lifted my head and caught the droplets on my tongue. Sweetness. When a drop hit the ground it either sank or splashed. If it splashed the rain would last all day. When my mama went to town for supplies I sat inside the lodge under the pendulum clock and watched rain through the big dining room window. My grandmother said that Mama would return when the rain stopped. I waited.

Life was big and I was small. I lived deep inside the small and pondered the big. Inside the small is another orange. I watched the rain from a place deep inside that smaller orange, a place that smelled like flowers and honey. I was a girl who lived inside. I was a girl who could get lost inside tastes and smells and the throat of a tiger lily. I looked inside myself for tiger lilies and saw that they grew everywhere.

I sat under the clock by the dining room window, waiting, watching the raindrops splash in expanding puddles, and all of it happened inside me. I began to sing. The song was "I'm Looking Over a Four-Leafed Clover." My voice emerged like a foghorn. Song must be thick to hold the orange that held everything else.

VEIL

Who was the mother who wove my veil? What threads did she spin fine enough to cover me yet be invisible enough that others, gazing, believed they saw all that stood visibly in front of them.

I was the girl who sat cross-legged under the hanging clothes in the wardrobe. They veiled me. Grandma's silk scarves veiled me. The drooping leaves of bushes hid a little den where I sat hidden, veiled. Night with its stars veils. Lace curtains veiled me, curled on the windowsill. One sheet pulled over a small body makes a veil that light shines through. Inside the veil I whispered to someone not myself but at the same time not other than myself. I loved being the one behind the veil. My heart almost cracked open with this love and released a thick yoke of orange-honey. I closed my eyes. I heard the sound of bees.

The contemplative personality begins to develop with a turn inward and the ensuing discovery of a world of the soul through which, afterwards, everything external is perceived. Of course, I didn't know this as a child and neither did my parents. I was seen as a shy and timid child. My mother, an active woman with great people skills, worked hard to socialize me by placing me in two different dancing classes, inviting children of my own age to the lodge and later to our house, encouraging me: "Put yourself forward more, dear." Crowds of children made me feel sick to my stomach. I didn't like birthday parties, and this distaste expanded to parties in general. She sent me to kindergarten with my cousin, Jack, and I became so sick that I vomited all over the teacher's piano keys. The first day of school when I was five became an occasion for a tantrum at the moment my mother decided it was time for her to leave. All of these reactions were deemed bad. Good children didn't act like this. I decided to work hard to become the child she wanted me to be. What is a parent to do? The child can't yet articulate what is happening within. The parent wants to raise a healthy child. I do credit my mother with having taught me skills I needed to get along in the world of people, skills I continue to use. And because I worked so hard at the development of these skills, I've often had the impression that I'm deceiving people about who I really am. Teacher, lecturer, performer, organizer—all of these roles

21

took great effort and energy to carry out because to be that, I needed to suppress my most fundamental self.

Once when I was in my early twenties I awoke to a stunning realization. I was acting. My life felt like a drama written by someone else, and I knew how to behave so long as I had a script to follow, but when left on my own there was nothing inside to tell me what to do. The truth was, I'd buried my original contemplative personality so well that I no longer had access to my real self.

The veil had become opaque.

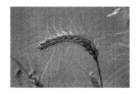

REMEMBER THE SECOND BELOVED

- That you would call her Mama.
- That she would come when you called, even in the middle of the night, even from the top of the icehouse, even from across the room, even from the end of the dock where deep water swirled, even from behind the glass partition at dance class, even twelve miles if you called from school, even one-hundred-fifty miles if you called from the convent, even from the realm past death.
- That you would adventure together: to the sand ridges to pick chokecherries, to the islands where blueberries grew, down the dark road to the outhouse, to the city with its streetcars and the elevator at the Foshay Tower, to the sky with your father dipping and whirling and stalling and plummeting, the engine restarting, and climbing towards the sun, to the church where God hid in bread locked behind a golden door.
- That she would read to you every single night, and sing a lullaby, and close the closet door, and kiss your face, and count your toes, and hold your heart in hers until both of you woke in the morning.
- That she would teach you to dance, to pray, to act in plays, to love the sound of words, to bake bread, to give the bread away, to be a friend, to be a daughter, to be loyal, and when the time came, to walk forward into a life of your own and she would say, "Go with my love; all I ever wanted was for you to be happy."
- That the two of you could dance and you could be still, that you could laugh and you could scream, that you could stand your ground or run away, that you could talk to yourselves in the mirror, that you could say terrifying things and follow them with words so loving as to melt your hearts, that you could lay

23

your heads against the rough bark of the cottonwood tree, that others might call you eccentric or weird and you could take it as a compliment.

- That when she cried out, that when she wept, that when the headaches came, that when she went to bed in the middle of the day, that when she tore at her clothes and prayed God to let her die, that when she wept, that when she wept, that when she wept...you would hear and take the pain inside yourself and carry it like your own child.
- That she would always love you. That you would always love her.

WORDS IN OUR FINGERS

After she died in 1993, I put my letters from Mama in plastic page-savers, organized them by date, and stored them in a black loose-leaf notebook. It's here, by my chair on the bottom shelf of my bookcase. If I begin to read a letter, my mind calls up her voice. I don't do so often, not because I don't want to hear her, but because I do, and the pluck of her words upon my heart vibrates a cord that was never severed.

Mama's old typewriter sits on a little stand against the wall in front of me, under a photograph of her from 1923. I've placed two dried red roses behind the corner of the frame, because of her name: Alyce Rose.

Her letters bear the personal marks of her now ancient Smith Corona. Some of the lines are skewed to the side. Some letters aren't inked as well as others. She used a ribbon divided between red and black so she could emphasize certain words not only by the pressure of her hands on the keys, but by color. I take the notebook out now, daring my heart to hear her voice, and see that on Good Friday, 1973, she typed her entire letter in red. All in caps she says that she's saved money for a trip south, but she must convince my dad. He thinks he can't leave his business, an airport and flying service on the Minnesota/Ontario border. She was sixty-two and he was sixty-four, and the furthest they had been from northern Minnesota were trips to Nebraska and Iowa to find better work during the Second World War. Vacation meant a three-day visit to relatives in Minneapolis.

Something makes me uneasy, and as I scan the red-print entry, I realize what it is. Each letter has a future and I already know it. She is excited to "go south next winter," but I know that my father will have a heart attack. She tells her dreams and they intersect my certain knowledge that they won't come true—that in a moment on a day in May those dreams will shatter when my father's heart seizes and he falls.

I'm older now than she was then and I've observed her future right through to her death and past her death over twenty years. But her letters—*the word*—connects us in a moment outside of time, a concept the poet T.S. Eliot explored extensively in *Four Quartets:* "Burnt Norton," moving toward his description of the locus of an eternal moment, the gathering of past and future into his famous "still point..."

"The words are in my fingers," my mother used to say, and her words collapse time. Instinct warns me that by following the trail of her words, I will walk the path not only of her life, but of my own, especially of the path I took into and out of a Catholic convent. Do I want to make that journey? Does it matter what I want? Must I follow it, regardless? The word is where the dance is. Maybe if I follow her, we can dance together upon this trail. I must remember that and fear neither her voice nor mine, despite the carefully hidden truths those voices can uncover and reveal.

MAMA

I can think neither backward nor forward to her, my mama. When I look at photos of her she isn't there. The photos have lost her. Surely her face was not like that, nor her smile; the very contours of her body are wrong.

What is she now that the living parts of her have slipped from her story? Even though her story was given me for safekeeping, the years have tampered with it, and what I knew of her is clay in my hands that I've formed first like this, then like that. Her face sometimes now is mine. When I open the letters she sent and run my fingers over the pages, when I read what she wrote when she was old but not so old as I now am, when I touch the words she touched and what they hold drains from her fingers into mine, when I take in her "I am alone, so all all alone. Please love me," I cannot tell whose tears flow out to stain the page.

She was born Alyce Rose Kathryn Klimek in Superior Wisconsin, August 31, 1910. The fourth and youngest. *"Das ist alles,"* proclaimed her father, Anton John. Thus her name, Alyce, no more, the end of it, enough, "that's all." She would later laugh over the story, how her mother, Elizabeth Kathryn Friesinger Klimek, past her due date, went shopping downtown that day. A policeman had to bring her home. She yelled out, "Anton, grab a pillow," and Alyce was born right then and there. My girl-imagination had her father catching her on a velvet pillow as she passed into this world from the invisible to the visible through the air. She was too quick for them, too much of a surprise. They weren't quite prepared. She lived with that as a myth of origin all her life. That's Alyce, and we can't do this again.

Before the woman is a mother she is someone her child will never know. How completely happy she looks in that boat on the Rainy River in front of her parents' resort, Klimek's Lodge. I just can't help it: I love that girl. Just a few years before this snapshot was taken, she had coughed up blood and written in her small brown leather diary, *Please God, don't let it be TB.* But it was TB. By then she loved George Lore. She could have lost him. He wrote to her every single day for the nine months she fought the disease. The day she said goodbye, though, she had to let him go because, clearly, she could die.

I grew up with the stories of that hospital stay: the younger woman in the next bed who died one night while Mama listened to her gasps for breath, the autobiography of St. Therese of Lisieux who battled the same disease, not with the "rest cure" but with faith in God, the weekly pneumothorax treatment which used a gigantic needle for the collapsing of her lung, the time George and her brother Peter buzzed the hospital in Pete's Travel Air plane, and Alyce broke all the rules about lying flat in bed to stand in the big window—a red-pajama-wearing girl waving and wanting to be seen.

Daring turned into courage early in her life. If not for this courage, I might never have been born at all. She wasn't strong, this mother of mine. She went through life with one lobe of her lungs permanently collapsed. And Dr. Mary at the "San" strictly forbade the bearing of children.

She bore me anyway.

My Aunt Edith once told me she suspected my mother was afraid of me. "You take her, Edith," she remembered Mama saying. "I don't know what to do. Make her stop crying."

"Poor Alyce," Edith crooned, "what did she know of babies? Youngest child herself. Coddled. You know what I mean? Timid when it came to being a mother."

One of the Sisters of St. Joseph remembered coming to Klimek's Lodge and leaning over my buggy where I lay sucking on the leather strap that held me secure. "Your mother would have had a fit if she'd seen you sucking on that dirty thing," she laughed in later years. "Your mother was the most persnickety woman I ever saw when it came to you. Why, if you dropped your bottle on the floor your mother had it up and out in the kitchen into a pot of boiling water. Sterilized. That's what your mother was when it came to you."

I don't remember her in either of those ways. I remember that she smelled like warm, buttered toast. I remember that I needed her close. If she left the room, I cried. I remember holding onto her leg, hugging, desperate for her to be still, to stay. When she went away without me I felt a sickness in the pit of me. I felt a loss like death before I knew of death.

Years later Mama would write, in what could only be called a prayer, about that daughter who was born anyway—Mary Jane, her forbidden one, the one who later would become a Religious Sister, this one, me. It was the eve of the day I believed I would cease being Mary Jane forever and became Sister Mary Christopher of the Catholic religious congregation of St. Joseph.

Tomorrow is to be her greatest—the gift of herself—not to a mere man—but to God—the Supreme Ruler of all, of everything, everywhere. My Lord has done great things to me! (Now is the time I can tell her— with tears of remembrance in my eyes—she was conceived in a great love on Valentine's Day—and little did I know then that it was really

*God's love and **for this purpose I was made to live**—On that day which glorifies LOVE, God created his child of love to be His Very Own and on this day I (we) give her back to him with all our heart and love.*

The question between Mama and me never was of love, unless it was of a love too much—love that risked death and loss and hands still reaching out to touch even when the possibility of touch existed no more.

LOVE'S CALLING

The call was still a whisper on a chill night in November, under the sign of Scorpio just as Venus crested the Iowa horizon. Snow, soon to develop into the great Armistice Day Blizzard of 1940, already was beginning to fall, covering the streets and sidewalks around St. Joseph's Hospital in Sioux City. It's vital to take such details into consideration, as each detail works its way through, a colored thread, a musical tone, a repeating theme.

Despite Mama's preeclampsia, I emerged into this world, one that teetered on the edge of war, several countries already engaged. My father, George Lore, an early barnstormer of county fairs around the country, by 1940 worked winters in the aircraft factories of Omaha, Nebraska, building warplanes. The Great Depression hadn't yet ended.

The first breath, the first cry, the first touch of air on skin, the first kiss—already I was moving outwards, expanding.

We lived in two worlds, each with a voice. The city, Omaha— The Minnesota wilderness at Lake of the Woods. The voice of the city was composed of fine dark wood and stairs. The yard broke off into a chasm that slid into nowhere. In the house lived four families. Grandma Hillie fed me food with stories and let me play with her telephone. Jacky Tomasi played walky-talky with me through the heat register in the living room floor. Little Judy taught me the "no no" of our bodies. She locked us in the bathroom—the water running in the tub—and my mother on the other side, her voice nervous, cajoling, "Judy, slide the key under the door."

I walked. I was pigeon-toed and needed special shoes. I fell. I needed dancing lessons. My mama sat behind the glass wall. Safe in her observation, I lifted my foot up to the railing. I looked back for her approval, and she was gone. My mind filled with lightning. My belly fluttered with moths. I cried out for her and continued crying until she returned.

Sundays we walked into the Catholic Church. A lady in a party dress slept in the back pew. Mama led me to the third row from the front. Soft light. Muttering voices. Clouds of sweet smoke. She whispered, "stay right here." I stayed. She walked up to a railing and knelt. The priest fed her. She returned and knelt again. Her head was bent. She didn't move. "Mama!" She still didn't move. "Mama!" Fear. "Mommy!" *If I should die before I wake.* "Mommy!!"

My daddy read the Sunday newspaper; he didn't go to church. He didn't hear the voice.

The voice of the lake world was formed of leaves, ferns, lilies of the valley, breezes and gulls. It echoed through the spruce bog. Wildflowers grew there, at my grandparents' resort on Wheeler's Point where the Rainy River empties into Four Mile Bay at Lake of the Woods. My life came from this place. Life in Omaha during the war consisted of snapshots. The resort was a motion picture. I felt my feet on the stones along the bank, on the planks of the dock. In memory my arms still reach out to touch the twin oaks that grew in front of the lodge. I watched the silver flicks of minnows in the tank and the rainbows of gas on the water's surface by the boats. I hid underneath the bed with Sparky, my dog, during thunderstorms. I banged the back of a kettle with a metal spoon, announcing to every cabin the end of World War II. I was four years old.

"Do not go into the woods!" One wild flower sang to the next. An old lady got lost, picking. Fishermen found her in water up to her waist. Three days wandering. Always at the edge of safety— wilderness. "Don't play in the reeds!" Blood suckers and leeches swam there. They stuck to your skin. They could cover your body. The boy who swam in the reeds to save my beach ball writhed on the grass bank screaming. All his skin squirmed with black. The grown-ups poured salt on him and the suckers fell, leaving his skin pocked with red wounds.

"Don't climb into the ice house!" But the ice gleamed amber in the sawdust and the air was cool. A child could fall between the ice blocks and never be seen again. I didn't fall, but my father laid me across his knees and spanked me anyway. You could have died. You could have died. You could have died. Did every beauty shimmer with danger? I held to my Grandpa Klimek's leg. My grandma's apron became a flag in wind. Over the Gap off Four Mile Bay a tornado chased our launch to shore. Water the color of gun metal. "Please, God. Please." The funnel broke and the dangling cloud poured from the sky.

Life at Klimek's Lodge feels timeless now, my few years there happening when my myths of the world were spun. This became Once Upon a Time for me, a tale of wildness and beauty, dangers and wonders, of endless time and vast spaciousness.

Two loves called me: earth's wild beauty and God's invisible wonders. God's face was every face. God possessed no name but drew me by wonder over everything earthly—night skies layered with stars, my earliest memory, seen through the rear window of my parents' Plymouth coupe as we drove from Nebraska to Minnesota, my bed the small shelf behind their heads. Winds and waves on Lake of the Woods at the border with Canada on the shores of which we lived. Wild flowers nodding and bowing behind the ice house in the forbidden woods that turned quickly into a spruce bog. And the face of Mama, the songs of Mama, the wild cries of Mama, her dances, her arms, her scent, her tears, her eyes that saw into me, saw through me, bound her to me in a way that never ends.

When I was four years old, Mama took me to a Lenten observance—the Stations of the Cross. I stood on the wooden kneeler in Baudette's old Catholic Church with its dark violet drapes behind the altar. The priest and altar boys carried incense, a large crucifix, and candles as they went in solemn procession from one station to the next. Though I couldn't read, Mama had given me one of the little ceremonial prayer books so I could follow the pictures. The priest droned the prayers. The choir sang of Mary's sorrow. And just before the priest moved on from one to the next of fourteen stations, he and the congregation recited Paul's words to the Galatians: "With Christ I am nailed to the cross, and I live, now not I, but Christ lives within me." I knew the words by heart from their many repetitions, but that evening something in my head said "What?" It might have been my first self-reflexive moment. Initially, confusion, and then something

33

like insight erupted in me, though at four years old my mind translated it immediately from words to images. I don't know what to call it. Before that moment Christ was Jesus and I was Mary Jane. God lived in a place called heaven and could see me praying in the little church. But at that moment, and only for a moment, heaven wasn't far away. The little person standing on the wooden kneeler surrounded by incense and song, watching the procession—who was that? The priest had said I was no longer me. Who was looking at the procession then? If I wasn't the one seeing, then the eyes looking out from inside me must be those of Christ. I remember feeling so light I could maybe even fly, and then something happened outside of me, probably the priest moved on to the next station, or someone sneezed, and there I was again, standing on the kneeler, resting my chin on the back of the pew in front of me, everything back to normal.

It was a moment strong enough to haunt me, call me, tantalize me all my years. The whisper from the tiger lily in the woods. The lake's many moods. Northern lights undulating across winter skies. The squinting eyes of my soul, searching the dark places. The vulnerable eyes of those I loved and who loved me. Through it all— that sense of Christ alive in me tugged on my heart, the cord of faith that never broke despite the years and everything that those years brought.

A WAY WITH WORDS

Words tantalized me, and Mama had a way with them. Among her books and treasured above all the rest was a thick red volume she referred to as Bartlett's. A veritable bible of words which she would retrieve from the bookcase often when an emotion gripped her or a memory surfaced. "This one I read to your daddy before he married me..." and then she would launch off into

I believe if I should die
And you should kiss my eyelids where I lie
Cold, dead, and dumb to all the world contains,
The folded orbs would open at your touch
And from its exile in the aisles of death
Life would flow gladly back into my veins.

Seventy years later, and I still can recite it by heart, along with snatches of Wordsworth (*My heart leaps up when I behold a rainbow in the sky)* and the mystical *Rubáiyát of Omar Khayyam* from which I imbibed a core lessen for all of life:

The Moving Finger writes; and, having writ,
Moves on: nor all your Piety nor Wit
Shall lure it back to cancel half a Line,
Nor all thy Tears wash out a Word of it.

When she first dazzled me with such lines I had no idea of their meaning. I drifted on the rhythm of them, learning their words like leaves floating on the lake. I lay beside her in bed, she with *Bartlett's Familiar Quotations* propped against her knees, and marveled at her magic ability to pick word-sounds out of the squiggles on the page and transfer them into my body. It was a dance of sound and sometimes a picture of the world. I began to hear the poetry in my head as I felt the wind coming off the lake or smelled the ozone brought on by the rain. I began to experience the rhythm of moments passing, a heartbeat in the earth and sky.

35

GROWING UP

In Baudette, after Grandma sold the resort and we moved to town, I was a street kid. There was nowhere else to play outside. Several children lived in apartments on Main Street—above the municipal building, above their dad's barber shop or hardware store. My friend, Nancy, had a back porch that extended above the alley. A clothesline stretched on a pulley from her porch across the alley. She and I ran up and down the alley and in and out of the narrow, trash-filled lanes between the buildings. No adult could fit. The boys wrote KILROY WAS HERE on the walls between Hartz Grocery and Windy Noble's hardware store. The feel of those tunnels between buildings was the feel of make believe, of being in a foreign land, a fairy place, invisible. I scraped the sleeves on my new deerskin jacket one winter day as I elbowed my way between the close-set stucco walls. It was leather from deer my daddy shot. Mama cried to see it so ruined.

Nancy and I played in the empty lot between the post office and the First National Bank where ivy covered the wall. We played horseshoes in the empty lot beside her dad's barber shop. It couldn't have been winter then. Spring or fall, maybe. Nancy's dad had a bench outside his shop where men sat waiting for their haircuts. They played or watched the others play horseshoes.

We played by the bay where the ferry docked in summer, but this was later, when I was older. The ferry dock was off limits before I was eight. We played behind my grandma's apartment. She had a wild rose bush and a bench for sitting. We played across the street next to Clay's Drug Store where rubble from a razed building was collapsed into a basement. The townspeople had the whole mess surrounded by a chain-link fence but it presented children recently released from threats of war with a playground for the imagination—it might be the ruins of Dresden or of Hiroshima. We climbed to the top of a shed behind Hartz Grocery and yelled at people; when they looked up we flattened ourselves against the roof.

Our town was child-sized. Every adult knew every child on the street. If anything went wrong you were whisked off to your mother almost before you could begin to cry.

36

Baudette, Minnesota is located on the United States border with Canada where the Rainy River backwashes into a bay making a "Y". Three towns once were located here, one at each point of land at the Y's center. Rainy River, Ontario is located in the cup at the top of the Y. It was connected to Baudette, to the southeast, by a railroad bridge. Spooner, which later became annexed to Baudette sat across the Baudette Bay, connected by a traffic bridge.

As a child I was told that Lake of the Woods County of which Baudette was the county seat was one of the ten poorest counties in the entire United States of America. I couldn't verify this for the 1940 era, and it certainly is not true now when it isn't even one of the one-hundred poorest. Many of the residents felt poor regardless of the statistics. I wasn't sure whether or not I was poor, but thought I might be. At Grandma's resort I had my own room, that was true, but in town I lived in a tiny apartment behind a bar where I didn't even have my own bed. From the alley entrance Dick's Place was weathered grey, unpainted wood with a tumbled-down look. Maybe Grandma wasn't poor. She had two houses and a fur coat. But not my family. Nobody who lived behind Dick's Place could be anything but poor.

Children in Baudette argued over whose family made do with less money. Bonnie insisted that even though her dad was the town doctor, she was not rich. "People don't pay him with money," she insisted. "They might bring a chicken or a sack of potatoes." But I knew she was not as poor as I. Otherwise how could she explain her mother's gold satin comforter and all of Bonnie's dolls. Susan said she wasn't rich even though her father owned the International Harvester dealership. But she had her own bedroom and a playhouse in her back yard. I figured I was poorer than all of them. You have to get your status somehow.

In 1948 we moved from the apartment behind Dick's Place Bar on Main Street to a little white house on Munson's hill above the Baudette Bay. It was ours. We owned it. It was more than a room in someone else's house. It wasn't Grandma Klimek's house. It wasn't Grandma Hillie's house. It wasn't Dick's Place. It wasn't Klimek's Lodge. It was my house, and my mother's and my father's. Ours.

I see it in memory as if for the first time. It is a child's house, the kind of house we children drew—a face with a pointed roof, windows like eyes, a door for a mouth. Mine had only one eye. Vines climbed up under, over and around the window, large-leaved vines, grape-like leaves that turned red in autumn. Three concrete steps led to the door and over it a canopy, pointed like the roof. There was a door exactly the same on the left side of the house leading into the kitchen. The front door opened directly into the living room.

We owned two lots. Daddy explained that the house was too small and we would build an addition onto the left side next to Johnson's. The neighborhood children grumbled. It had been their softball field. We owned a giant cottonwood tree right out front. We owned little trees, ash maybe, or box elder, which circled the lot. We owned a bushy berry tree to the left of the front door with "bird berries" on it, squishy red but poison for human beings. We owned a thicket of wild roses on the right side of the house and hollyhocks in the back. We owned a plum tree that produced hard red plums, tart, that Mama would turn into clear jelly. We owned a yard full of dandelions. Maybe we were rich after all.

I see it even now with child's eyes; its dimensions are the dimensions of the world. Its walls are safety. Its furniture, placed like stars in the night sky, is the order of the whole wide world.

My house had four rooms: the living room, kitchen, bathroom and bedroom. The basement was a pit filled with spiders in the summer. It extended under only the back part of the house. The living room was built above a crawl space where Daddy kept long pieces of lumber and broken things he might fix one day. At the foot of the stairs was a large coal bin that held the fuel for an octopus of a furnace which Mama had to stoke several times a day and night in winter. That takes care of three basement corners. The fourth corner held the washing machine above which a light bulb hung from a black electrical cord.

Why do I see the worst part of the house first? The basement was a place that might gobble me up in darkness. The enormous round and square arms of the coal furnace cast shadows where anything might hide. A spider might be hanging from its slender thread right in the stairs and land in my face when I walked down. Someone might be hiding by the washing machine. If Mama said to go downstairs and get the mop, she could count on my saying, "Come with me, Mama."

"If I had time to go with you, I could do it for myself! Now go!"

Mama didn't mind the basement. Sometimes she took off all her clothes and showered under a hose over the drain by the washing machine.

"Mama, the window!!" I worried.

"It doesn't matter," she laughed. "No one can see through it anyhow. It's too dirty."

The living room had three windows, two in front and one on the side closest to Munson's. They were covered with Venetian blinds and surrounded by wide oak casings. At Christmas time Daddy brought cedar boughs home to decorate each window and Jack Frost did the rest. I leaned over the back of the sofa and traced the crystalline designs with my finger. But the sofa wasn't always by the window. Sometimes it was on the other side of the room, the side by Johnson's. Mama switched the furniture. Maybe she needed the variety. Maybe she was never sure what looked best. This was what was in the room: the aqua blue fold-out sofa, Grandpa's piano, a large upholstered easy chair with fancy upholstery nails along the arms, a claw-footed chair from the lodge, a radio, and a lamp loaned us by Doc and Minnie Osborn when they moved from their big house at the lake. The lamp was like a lantern on a stand. Rosy-gold opaque stained glass doors on the lantern opened or closed depending upon how much light we wanted. It stood by the sofa and served both as a reading lamp and as a night light for me. I still didn't have a bedroom of my own.

At night Mama tipped up the seat of the sofa and pulled from the compartment beneath it a large goose down sleeping bag that smelled of earth and sweat and the lake. She pushed the seat of the sofa forward until it clicked and then let it settle into a bed. Over it she threw the soft sleeping bag like a featherbed and made it up with sheets and blankets. That was where I slept. I didn't feel deprived. I was in the middle of things and the sleeping bag was soft. Mama left the radio on to put me to sleep. I listened to "Lux Radio Theatre," "Mr. Chameleon," "Mr. Keen: Tracer of Lost Persons," "Pam and Jerry North," and lighter fare like "My Friend Irma," "Jack Benny," "Baby Snooks," and "Fibber McGee and Molly."

A door opposite the front door led to the kitchen. We closed that door on Saturdays when Sister Eleanor taught piano lessons. Mama's friend, Vi, arranged for two Sisters of St. Joseph from Rainy

River, Ontario, to teach piano in Baudette on Saturdays. Mother Adelaide, who taught the big kids, used the piano at Vi's house. Sister Eleanor used ours. Our payment for a full day of not being able to use our living room and of sitting in the kitchen listening to first, second and third graders plunk out scales was music lessons for me. My first recital piece was a Chinese sounding "Ming Toy" which I played with both hands—a big accomplishment. Sister Eleanor treated children like her own babies. She kept her voice soft, praised every accomplishment, and dismissed each mistake with "a little butterfingers today, humm?" When my friend, Bonnie, graduated to Mother Adelaide she confessed feeling deprived. "She's mean," Bonnie warned, "she never just says 'butterfingers,' she says 'repeat that phrase and this time, do it right.'" I wanted to grow up to be just like Sister Eleanor. One Saturday outside our house while we were waiting by the car for Mama to drive her over the frozen Rainy River back to Canada, I told her I wanted to be a Sister when I grew up. I could think of nothing finer than to be soft and gentle and wear that silky black veil and long dress for the rest of my life.

The kitchen was three-fourths as long and just as wide as the living room. Dark wooden cupboards reached to the ceiling. The counters were covered with mustard colored linoleum. A big white sink was right under a large window that looked out on Munson's Hill and the bay. The icebox (which was what I still called the refrigerator, a hold-over from the real iceboxes at the resort) had two doors that opened from the center out. It was bartered payment for some work my father did. It stood on one side of the kitchen door leading outside. The table and chairs were on the other side of that door. The gas stove was set against the back wall. It was a small kitchen by today's standards, but we spent a lot of our time there. I did my homework at the kitchen table. On it we laid out hot cookies, stirred fudge, ate popcorn, plucked the pinfeathers from the Thanksgiving turkey, ate our meals except for holidays when Mama pushed the living room furniture out of the way and Daddy carried the table in there to be decorated with a tablecloth, hand cross-stitched, which Mama had spent several hours washing and ironing for the occasion.

Off the kitchen in the back we had a hallway with a linen closet and the basement stairs on Johnson's side and the bathroom on Munson's. The bathtub, deep with little clawed feet, was just my size.

Daddy couldn't fit no matter what. Mama filled it with bubble-bath and I spent what seems now like hours soaking in it. Baths altered my consciousness. The feel of the bath water and the bubbles took me off into my imagination. I was a princess, alone in my bath, safe from the hubbub of the court. I was a fairy child entertaining elves and other fairies. Mama's voice, "Are you finished, Mary Jane? Did you wash between your toes?" startled me like a bowl crashing to the floor.

The bedroom at the back of the house, surrounded by hollyhocks, belonged to Mama and Daddy. Its closet, tucked in over the stairs leading to the basement, inclined from back to front at a forty-five degree angle that to a child's eyes became a perfect slide. I would climb up through my mama's blouses and slide down to land on her shoes whenever she wasn't in the house.

The house stayed this small for less than a year. In the Spring of 1949, Grandpa Lore arrived to help build an addition. Mama and Daddy needed a bigger bedroom and it was high time I had a bedroom of my own. Well, not completely my own. Mama was going to have a baby who would become my younger sister, Elizabeth Anne.

Here the four of us would grow into a family of our own.

BETSY

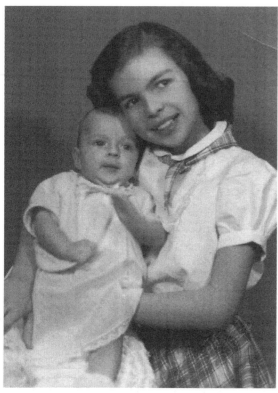

My sister, according to my mother, was conceived the night my Grandpa Klimek died. She was a creation out of compassion and tenderness, the life that arises from love reaching out to heal pain. Daddy hoped and Mama prayed all those years since I'd been born to have another child. It took that exquisite tenderness that my father brought to my mother's devastating loss; it took that breaking open of my mother's heart resulting from her father's death. Love and pain: they met in my sister.

I'd been hoping too. On my eighth birthday I wished for a sister when I blew out my birthday candles. Sometime during that winter when we were driving to Grandma Klimek's apartment downtown and my breath was emerging in white clouds, Mama said, "I'm going to have a baby." Her voice sounded bubbly with repressed laughter. "Oh, Mama; does Daddy know?" And her laughter broke through her restraint. I knew I had a part in it because of the birthday wish.

Her belly got big. We rubbed it with oil and it glistened. Her belly-button popped out like a nipple. She bought new clothes. We drove to Bemidji with Grandma Klimek. Mama wore her new slacks home. They expanded at the waist. She bought blouses that opened like umbrellas.

She lay beside me on the sofa when I went to bed and we talked in low voices about the baby inside her. I held my hand on her belly to feel my sister kick. She said she thought I shouldn't get my heart too set on a baby sister because this baby felt different from the way I had felt. It probably would be a brother. "He could help your father at the airport," she explained. "We could call him Frederick Anton after your two grandfathers." It seemed a terrible idea. An ugly name. If it would be a girl her name would honor the two grandmothers: Elizabeth Anne. Grandma Klimek would allow this so long as no one called my little sister "Lizzie." People called her "Lizzie" and she barely endured it. Mama said a girl could be nicknamed "Betsy." That was okay. Betsy Wood, a girl in high school, was nice. But why not call her Lizanne or Lizbet? No one I knew had either of those names. It would make my sister special.

We were eating corn on the cob in Vi's dining room when Mama went into labor. It was September 8, 1949, the feast of the Nativity of Mary. Mama thought her baby would come on the Feast of the Seven Sorrows of Mary on September 15th. I suspect she felt this because of the connection she felt between the conception and her sorrow over her father's death. She'd made a nine month novena to Our Lady of Sorrows that her baby would be healthy and safe. If Mary had anything to do with it, she must have considered her birthday a more suitable time.

Mama and Daddy took me home and called the teenager next door to sleep overnight with me. They drove to Warroad. Daddy called at dawn the next day to tell me I had a little sister.

Mama stayed in Warroad over a week. I sat in her closet and buried my head in her clothes to catch a whiff of her, and I cried with lonesomeness. In the middle of the week Grandma Klimek said, "Come on, Mary Jane, we're going to Warroad."

I knew I was too little to get into the hospital. You had to be twelve. I wasn't even nine. Grandma kept assuring me I'd see Mama. We climbed the wide stairs. So far, so good. We turned to the left down a long hallway. Just then two things happened simultaneously. Mama came out of her room into the hall. She was wearing her coral chenille bathrobe and looked yummy. When she saw me she said my name in a voice mixed with alarm, excitement and hope. At the same moment a nurse walked up to Grandma and me and said, "how old is that child?" My tongue was stuck. Grandma smiled and said, "She's—she's ten." That was as close as she could get in her lie. Anybody could see I wasn't twelve and she knew it.

"Children must be twelve years old. She'll have to leave."

"But her mother's right there. What would it hurt?"

"I'm sorry."

Mama had disappeared into her room. I can still feel the sharp slice of absence. Grandma led me back down the stairs. I was choking on tears. Grandma led me around to the side of the building and pointed up. "You see that window?" she said. I did. "That's your mother's window. You just stand right here. You'll see your mother. There's more than one way to skin a cat!"

I stood there. Grandma went back into the hospital. Pretty soon Mama came to the window. I stood looking up, crying. She talked. I listened, hungry for her.

I would need to wait to meet my baby sister.

I saw her for the first time when Daddy and I drove to Warroad to bring Mama and Betsy home. We took the bassinet with its soft yellow batiste flounces in the back seat. I waited in the car while he went into the building to get them. Mama hugged me. "This is your little sister." She smiled and set the bassinet beside me on the back seat. "You take good care of her."

I couldn't take my eyes off her. I thought she would look like me, dark. She was golden. She had wisps of strawberry blonde hair and blue-green eyes. I put my finger in her hand and she held on. I fell absolutely, completely and irrevocably in love with her.

And that would never change.

From here life winds outward in an even flow to my eighteenth year. Themes weave in and out. People. Places. All increasingly recognized as elements of home. Family, church, school, my mother's souvenir shop and my father's airport, the neighborhood, the lake, the places where I went to be alone and dream.

It seems now, looking back, that my sister opened the floodgates to this outward flow. I looked down into her tiny face. I stared at her all the way home from Warroad while Mama and Daddy talked to each other, a comfortable murmur, in the front seat of the car. I touched her soft skin and breathed in the powdery scent of her. Something spiraled out from me and into her and back again in unending connection. I stopped being merely me.

The curse of the only child is loneliness, a peculiar kind of loneliness consisting of absolute symbiosis with the parents that takes them in with each breath and recognizes no distinction. I was locked in an inescapable inwardness and all my world was in there with me. My mama's tears fell within me. My daddy's silence made a wide open space in my mind. Their emotions formed the boundaries for my own; the places I lived became the landscapes of my soul. Nothing was outside of me to comfort me and let me know I was just a little girl. I was the only offspring of my parents and contained everything they were. And they were heavy and mysterious.

I touched the small body of my sister lying in her bassinet in the back seat of the car bumping over the potholes in the road from Warroad to Baudette and I knew, somehow, that everything had changed. There were two of us. I no longer bore the burden of my parents all alone. She also contained them. She was their daughter and she wasn't me. The walls around my world crumbled, opened to infinity, and I was released.

These are adult words for what happened. Eight-year-old girls do not think these thoughts. I felt it. I looked into little Betsy's face, so unlike mine that she couldn't possibly be me, and my heart felt big. I talked to her. I sang "The Irish Lullaby." I glanced out the window and saw the world zip by. I leaned over and kissed Betsy's nose and said "I love you."

Daddy carried the bassinet into the house and set it on the kitchen table. He told Mama to go in and lie down. I wanted Betsy with me, in my new bedroom. That's where the crib was: my bed on one side of the small room and the crib on the other with a space of maybe two feet between them. Daddy said that for a while the baby needed to be with Mama. They would set the bassinet on its stand right beside her bed so she could hear Betsy if she cried at night, if she was hungry and needed to be fed. Later, when she'd grown just a bit, he would move her into the room with me.

She couldn't nurse. Mama's nipples went in rather than out and neither she nor Betsy could figure out how to remedy this. Mama squeezed and prodded herself; she tickled Betsy's tongue with her milk-wet finger and then tried to shove the soggy, full breast with its ill-defined nipple into the baby's mouth. Betsy cried. Mama cried. Mama used an aspirator and put her milk in a bottle. She cried some more. She had wanted to nurse her baby. She hadn't been able to nurse me because of the tuberculosis, but she had expected to be able to nurse Betsy. Betsy took the bottle. She got used to it. Mama's milk dried up and she put Betsy on formula.

I wanted to learn everything; how to change a diaper, how to feed her, how to bathe her, how to rock her and sing lullabies. Mama taught me. After that it seemed as though I did all these things constantly. Nine-year-old girls tend to be little mothers anyway. I was completely satisfied. When Helen Munson or Peachy Menke came over to babysit, they took care of me and I took care of Betsy. They sat in the living room listening to the Top Forty Songs. They talked on the phone to their friends. They kept the house safe from whatever danger the night might present. I listened for the baby's cry. I changed her diaper. I washed the soiled diapers in the toilet and left them in the bathtub to soak. I stood by Betsy's crib and sang her to sleep.

Each day I could barely wait to get home from school. My friend Susan and I banged in through the door. Mama frowned and asked how many times had she told us to be quiet and not to wake the baby, but we intended to wake the baby. "Can I hold her?" Susan always wanted to know, and Mama arranged her on the big rattan rocking chair and fit Betsy into the nest of her arms. Later, when Betsy began to crawl, Mama often kept her in a playpen. Susan and I climbed right inside with her and she cooed and emitted exuberant yells and offered us her toys.

I dropped her once. Mama warned me about the soft spot in Betsy's head and impressed upon me how fragile babies are. I was rocking her. I think I had her on my lap. Mama did that, laid Betsy on her lap, feet towards her belly, and Betsy waved her arms and looked up into Mama's face and cooed. Mama's lap was bigger than mine. I sat in the rocking chair with Betsy in my lap just as Mama had, and I rocked and Betsy cooed, and suddenly she slipped, head first, off my lap and down my legs onto the floor landing on her soft spot. My heart shook, turned over and thumped in my chest. For a few seconds Betsy was silent and then she let out a wail such as I'd never heard before. At least she was alive! I picked her up. By that time my heart was pounding like crazy. I examined her soft spot; it wasn't cut or anything, nothing was running out of it. Hopefully she was all right.

A photographer came to Grandma's house and set up equipment in her dining room. The living room had, by this time, been transformed into Lake of the Woods Souvenir Shop. Whoever could afford it made appointments to have their children photographed. Betsy and I had our pictures for free in just the same way that I got my piano lessons free. In fact, the photographer practiced on us. He took pictures of each of us alone and of the two of us together. I held Betsy. She was an infant. The photographer told me to look at her like I loved her. It was easy. He placed our portraits in the display window of the Souvenir Shop as an advertisement. I stared at our portrait. You might say that I contemplated it. I began thinking of Betsy as my baby. I became her little mother.

She must have been about four years old the day I walked through the front door and saw her sitting in the big black leather chair we'd inherited from Klimek's Lodge. She was doing something I'd told her not to do. I don't remember what it was. I told her "no." I told her she knew I didn't want her to do whatever it was. Her eyes gleamed with defiance. She didn't stop. I yelled at her. She didn't stop. I had a magazine in my hand. I threw it at her. It hit. I didn't mean to hit her, just to get her attention, just to let her know I meant business. I couldn't pitch a softball or throw a basketball with any accuracy at all. I didn't expect the magazine to hit its target. Neither did she. She looked up, startled, her eyes like little chips of broken glass. Then she got up and, without saying a word, walked out of the room and into her bedroom, the one that had been our parents', then mine, then ours, and by that day, hers alone. She closed the door. She didn't slam it, just closed it quietly. I waited a few moments and didn't hear anything. Fear began to seep out of my heart into my whole body. "Betsy?" I called. Nothing. "Betsy?"

What to do? She was supposed to obey me. It was wrong of her to defy me. But I shouldn't have thrown the magazine. Maybe I had broken something that could never be repaired. Fear increased. I needed her.

I went to the closed door. "Betsy?" Nothing. I opened it. She sat cross-legged in the middle of the bed holding the magazine I'd thrown. Her cheeks were streaked with tears. "I'm sorry," I said. She looked at me. "Even if you don't love me, I love you," she whimpered and all my sharp edges dissolved.

Another time—it was summer; she was about the same age—Mama was working at the Souvenir Shop, and I was taking care of Betsy at home. Susan burst in through the front door. "Let's go to the cemetery by way of the river." She'd just realized it might be possible. Go down Munson's hill, south past Menke's, take the shoreline around Menke's woods, the cemetery ought to be right there at the top of the embankment. "Let's try it." Off we went. Adventure. Exploration. We were twelve years old. Just below Menke's woods I remembered Betsy. Where was she? Was she playing with Maralee Forney? Susan said she probably was. Susan said she had to be okay, probably in Maralee's house or playing in her yard. Let's go, Susan urged. In my imagination I saw Betsy hit by a car; I saw her playing with the kitchen knives; I saw her leaving the neighborhood and getting lost; I saw her falling from the tree with seven trunks. "I'm going back."

We ran. It felt to me that I'd never run so fast in all my life. The frightening images pushed me. I got a stitch in my side and my lungs burned but I kept running. Past Menke's, through the river grass, up Munson's Hill. There she was, running towards me, arms stretched wide. "Sissy!" I caught her up and hugged her. "Were you lost?" she asked.

"I told you," Susan grumbled.

She called me Sissy. She called Susan, Tutu. We took her everywhere. She straddled the back of my bike and held onto the seat for dear life. Her long blonde hair (it lost the strawberry color of infancy) blew in the wind. She got scared one day when I was going particularly fast down Thompson's hill and tried to control our speed with her bare feet. She stuck them in the spokes of the back wheel and toppled off the bicycle. She screamed. I dropped the bike and ran to her. Again I almost killed her, I thought. Her legs and toes looked a mess, all scratched and bleeding. I carried her home and somehow, I think, I refrained from saying "I told you to keep your legs out wide. I told you not to get caught in the wheel. I told you, you could get hurt. I told you."

It's a wonder she survived.

For Mama these were difficult years of the sort that wove a pattern through her life. She yelled a lot. She cried. She threw a cast iron skillet at me one day to call my attention to her anger or frustration over something I can no longer remember. Betsy was right there beside me. The handle broke off the skillet. She threw cups, plates, glasses—whatever was at hand. She slammed out the door, climbed into her car and spun the back wheels in the gravel as she floored the gas pedal to take off from a dead stop. She ran down into the basement screaming and tearing at her hair. Once I followed her and found her with her clothes torn open in front, her breasts bare. She was kneeling and crying, pounding her breasts as we did when we said "*Mea Culpa*" at Mass. She spent afternoons in her bedroom, her head under the pillow, the blinds drawn; in a pitiful voice she begged me to turn off the Hit Parade.

Mama may have had good reason for outrage or whatever this was. Grandma Klimek's mind was slowly deteriorating and my uncles and aunts all expected Mama would take care of her. In addition to that responsibility, Mama had just been diagnosed with uterine fibroid tumors, and Doc Brink wanted her to undergo a hysterectomy. He must have told her it could be malignant because during one of her tirades she finally collapsed, exhausted on her bed and sobbed. I might have been twelve or thirteen-years-old. I put my arms around her and begged her not to cry. She blurted out about probably having a cancer in her belly and had I seen how big and bloated her belly always was and the doctor wanted her to have an operation and she was afraid that she would die. Sometimes she wasn't home in the morning because she had hemorrhaged during the night and Daddy had taken her to the hospital. The early stages of menopause were upon her and her hormones were misfiring like crazy.

Mama had her reasons—more, no doubt, than I've listed here, reasons a daughter couldn't see. And Betsy may have felt she had to choose between her mother and sister, but who knows what that means or how it's done in a child's mind and heart? And what choice did she have? A mother suffering from something no child could be expected to understand, something that transformed her into a danger, that made you want to run and hide. A mother who, even when happy, was unpredictable. And, on the other side, a sister, not yet grown-up, not dependable, often afraid, lost in fantasy and books much of the time, adolescent selfish and not all that much the mothering sort—a sister who up and left for good when she was seventeen. I left Betsy with the menopausal mother whom she may or may not have chosen and probably did not. I left and never knew until twenty or thirty years afterwards just how much of an abandonment that leaving was for the little sister that I loved. It wasn't until then that she would refer to my leaving for the convent as "the time you left me alone with that crazy witch!"

CHAOS AND CONTROL

Betsy's legs bristled with coarse little hairs and were smudged with earth and the scent her body gave forth was sharply metallic. In direct opposition to Mama's attempts to produce an angel—the long ringlets, dresses made by Aunts Eva and Eleanor, constant corrections in language: "Sissy and I, Betsy, not ME, not Sissy and me." Betsy seemed determined to be a tomboy. One of Mama's favorite stories is of looking out the kitchen window towards the new neighbor's place. The Farrells. Farrells had two little boys, twins, named Doug and Roger who were a year older than Betsy. That day Mama caught Betsy wrestling with one of the twins; I think it was Doug—called "Dougie." She sat, straddling his chest, hitting him with her little fists. Mama opened the window and called out to her, "Betsy, stop that. Act like a lady!" Betsy stopped only long enough to look up, a face that I can imagine filled with her victory and power, and said with Amazon disdain: "I isn't a lady, I is a tough girl!"

She developed a complex form of resistance, unexpected in a child. There was the time, already mentioned, that she chose silence as a resistance to my outburst when I threw the magazine at her. Kath, who was her companion whenever she was not with our little neighbor, Maralee, relates that Betsy was the only one of her friends who, when a fight erupted during play at Kath's house and Kath gave that imperious order, "GO HOME", actually went home. It was a resistance by compliance, doing exactly what the "enemy" requested as if understanding that compliance was the precise behavior unwanted and unexpected. As an adult, Betsy often told of her somewhat different response to another of Kath's attempts to...what? Gain power over her? Turn her into a less difficult friend? Kath, who must have been physically stronger, pinned Betsy down on the ground and dug her fingernails into Betsy's flesh until it hurt like a branding iron. "Say Uncle!!" Kath insisted nailing her gaze into Betsy's eyes. "Say Uncle!!!" But Betsy wouldn't. She just stared back making her own eyes hard, impenetrable. She concentrated the pain away. She resisted by refusal when (maybe because) Kath expected her to comply.

Mama never could figure her out. She tried what she called reverse psychology, "Don't eat your potatoes, Betsy," a ploy that Betsy quickly untangled and twirled in concentric circles of *don't eat* means eat and *eat* means don't, then back around again to where she could do whatever she did by settling on what might most hide her true feelings.

Daddy was her champion as well as her teacher in the arts of silent resistance. If Mama yelled in frustration, giving forth a barrage of words usually expressing all she had to do and how she didn't get the help she needed and no one listened to her and "why not?" Daddy just looked up, if he <u>did</u> look up, with the same impenetrable eyes that Betsy developed, and said, if he said anything at all, "What the hell's going on around here?" and left. He walked out. He never slammed the door. He walked down the sidewalk to his car and drove away. He did what Betsy did when Kath tried to pin her down. He went "home," wherever that home was. One didn't get the impression that his home was the house where we all lived. He was hardly there. He never seemed to work there, to mow the lawn, to fix the corner by the kitchen where rough wood and two-by-fours were exposed and "someday we'll have a breakfast bar." Mama even shoveled the snow or got a boy from the neighborhood to do it.

We always said that Daddy was busy at the airport or running the projector at the Grand Theater or driving the school bus and all of these things were true. He did need to work hard, at three different jobs, to keep enough money coming in to put food on the table and clothes on our bodies. It was pretty clear though that the airport was his real home. When he left our living room during our mother's outbursts, during the expressions of her rage, he left us with the impression that he was the sane one and our mother was crazy.

What does one do with a crazy mother? Too immature for compassion, we chose pity or disdain. I chose pity and I think that Betsy chose disdain. Also there was fear. I know that Betsy wasn't the only one who withdrew from her rage. I often went into my bedroom and took out a book or turned up my phonograph so that I couldn't hear her. I learned that she would yell louder and louder but that nothing would follow; she would not hurt me. She would hurt herself instead. If I didn't watch I wouldn't see the hurt. I didn't want to see the hurt. If I became frightened for her and followed her through her rage I might see her, like the time I found her naked and crying in the basement or the time in her bedroom that she sat on her bed wailing that she knew her belly was filled with cancer and she most probably would die.

My sister remembered being downright mean to her sometimes. I don't remember a hurtful Betsy so it must have been after I left home. She once told me she used to hide in the coat closet behind the winter coats, jackets and overshoes waiting for Mama to come in from outside. All unsuspecting, Mama opened the closet door to hang up her coat and Betsy popped out screaming like a banshee. She remembers that Mama gasped, staggered back with her hands over her heart, "and she never learned!" I've wondered if that was so, or if Mama came to expect the bloodcurdling scream but went along with the game. Perhaps she was such a good actress that her little Betsy never realized that the game had been turned around on her by an even more proficient player. I don't know. It wasn't until Betsy was a teenager that Mama began to express questions regarding her ability to relate to her. By the time she was a young adult, twenty, and living in Minneapolis, Mama really struggled to find a way to relate. She wrote to me: "I wish she could understand how much I love her and want to help her to be happy but it seems it always ends up like criticism and she shuts me out—except occasionally she takes me into her confidence."

It was easy to take Mama's attempts to help as criticisms. Her attempts blazed. They could consume you like a grass fire. Maybe she was mostly right in both her analysis and her prescriptions for a better way of living. Maybe it was only her timing that was off, but something was wrong. Her excitement over a project equaled her rage in its intensity. She wanted everything for her girls. She wanted me to dance—no, more than that—to be a prima ballerina. She wanted me to sing—no—to be an opera star. She wanted me to act—go to Hollywood or New York. She had wanted to act. She'd recited the monologue "Madame X" and won a prize when she was in high school. She felt certain I could do better. She started teaching me monologues before I could read. I always memorized the longest poem in the Sacred Heart Christmas Program. She drove me to drama contests, singing contests, band contests. She drove me all the way to Minneapolis one year. She told me I could write, she was certain of it; she could, so obviously I could do better; she might have been a journalist, she said, had it not been for Grandma's hotels and the resort

53

and then the Great Depression and the tuberculosis. If I didn't write well enough she did it for me; change it here, she said, write the sentence this way. I simply couldn't remain myself and do anything well enough.

My analysis now is that I attempted to comply with Mama's schemes and failed. Failure is built into a system like this. I couldn't become my mother; I couldn't attempt it and continue to develop my own self. Betsy attempted to protect herself by creating a barrier strong enough to resist Mama's intensity. The barrier held other things out as well. Each of us was formed by our attempt to deal with Mama's repressed creativity: I developed in compliance with her need and Betsy developed in resistance to her need. Neither of us was free.

I resisted, too. It was just too much. I had enough to do with living a life of my own. I still feel her love coming through the words of her letters. Her hopes for me emerge like blossoms from every sentence, her need for me to be happier than she had been, her insistence that I succeed where she felt she did not measure up. I read her letters and my heart bleeds. I feel something essential being drained from me. There wasn't enough of me for her. No matter what I did, I would not have been enough. No matter how large my heart became I could not have contained all the yearning that her love produced.

WHERE NO STORMS COME

I grew older. My awareness of myself and the world surrounding me increased. All the time, morning and night, my heart felt large and on the verge of cracking open. I wanted life bigger than I saw it and what I saw was already enormous. I walked home, nights, my head tipped back, staring at the stars. I stood under the pines gazing as silver-green curtains of northern lights waved across the sky. The night I menstruated for the first time I walked home in snow glittering under old fashioned street lamps. I walked slowly listening to the scrunch of new snow under my stadium boots, feeling the pom-poms on my new red and green knit cap bump lightly against my cheek. My edges were dissolving, I could feel them turn to mist. Mama had said don't get cold. She treated me like a miracle.

I wanted ruffles on my bed. Mama crawled around in the attic and opened a box filled with linens. She ironed a white bedspread appliquéd with the image of a girl carrying a basket of flowers. Her dress was made of ruffles.

I wanted music all the time. Mama and Daddy bought me a portable phonograph. I closed the door of my bedroom and listened to love songs until they made me cry. Then I felt relieved. I played the piano and sang. I sang with my records. I sang "Serenade" with Mario Lanza. I sang "Indian Love Call" and "Ah, Sweet Mystery of Life." We visited the Delaney's in Minneapolis and Alice gave me all of her World War II sheet music. I sang "When the Lights Go On Again All Over the World," and "I'll Be Seeing You." I went to see *The King and I* and I sang "Hello, Young Lovers." I saw *Carousel* and sang "You'll Never Walk Alone" and "If I Loved You." I sang at the big player piano in our expanded house where Sister Eleanor once gave lessons. I sang to the moonlit river from the top of Munson's hill. I sang walking home from school. I sang to the stars from Pine Island one summer night. I sang for my boyfriends and for the school chorus and for contests and for the county fair and for weddings and funerals at church, but mostly I sang for myself. I sang because song was the only effective way of releasing the fullness inside. When I sang I felt a sonic boom inside my head, I felt an explosion in my chest, I felt completely free.

Apart from band, chorus and my friends, school had little meaning for me. I wanted to get good grades because I was ashamed of receiving anything lower than a C. I wanted my name on the honor roll and managed to keep it there throughout high school but the connection between good grades and actual learning escaped me. I found most of what was taught in high school supremely irrelevant. I definitely was not on a college track; I never even thought about college or its requirements. I was going to be a Sister of St. Joseph. These sisters ran the local hospital by then, and how could I ever forget Sister Eleanor? I learned to cut out a pattern and sew a straight seam. I learned all the various stitches one can produce with a needle and thread. I learned to cook and to set a proper table. I learned to type. I learned to perform on stage—singing, acting, giving speeches. I learned journalistic writing. I learned the titles and authors of great pieces of American and English literature. I learned to dance, to chair a meeting, to organize a project, to give a party, to design an attractive bulletin board, to play volleyball. I didn't learn anything that I retained about mathematics, physics, world literature, politics, earth sciences, history—all the things one would suppose school is supposed to teach. No one, including my parents, thought it strange that an intelligent young woman could complete high school as an honor student and know next to nothing about everything.

I enjoyed philosophy, ethics, metaphysics, theology, cosmology, spirituality, the arts, and psychology but those were not subjects taught in Baudette High School. I read the lives of the saints, the *Confessions* of St. Augustine, the *Bible*, and every book of poetry and all the novels I could find. Baudette had no book store. Mrs. Carlson, who taught English, was really a history teacher and didn't have a clue as to how to teach literature. At home we had a copy of Steinbeck's *Of Mice and Men* but I didn't know who Steinbeck was and Mama said this was not a book for good girls. The Baudette Public Library was poorly funded and I didn't use it much after I finished all the Nancy Drew Mysteries in Sixth Grade. I read the novel of the month in *Redbook,* all the stories in *Seventeen, Saturday Evening Post, McCall's, Ladies' Home Journal,* and *Good Housekeeping.* By chance I picked up some real literature. *Death Comes for the Archbishop* and *Ethan Frome* are all I remember. My true academic education needed to wait until the convent years.

School also made me sick to my stomach. I couldn't eat breakfast. I ran out the door leaving Mama's carefully buttered-to-the-edges toast and precisely cut grapefruit on the table. Three times a week I left early to sing the Mass of the Angels for Father Clemens. Sometimes when I walked to school from the church I glimpsed my dad through the window of the Rex Hotel Cafe and ran in to sit with him for a moment before I hurried the last two blocks to the school. If he was there it meant that he'd already finished his school bus route and I didn't have much time.

Even now, in dreams, I can't find my school locker or I don't have the right combination. I've forgotten to attend a class and it's time for the final tests and I don't even know where the classroom is. These dreams take place in Baudette High School where the classrooms smelled of teenaged bodies, chalk dust and dry radiator heat. Chaotic energy hit me in the face when I walked through the door. It silenced me. I hoped Mrs. Carlson would not call on me in history class. I never wanted to go anywhere alone. "Wait for me after class," became a common request asked of my friends.

I felt caught between nausea and excitement, imminent failure and tantalizing possibility. School challenged me not by its academics but in its people. I hadn't noticed before how much power everyone possessed over something inside me. I hadn't realized before that all these people were essentially strangers. Most of us had been children together, sat next to one another in the old flip-top school desks, played games during recess, and I thought we were friends. Now I realized they didn't know what I thought or what I felt. I wasn't sure of it myself. I felt vulnerable to self-theft. With Senia I felt Senia-like. When Georgine stayed at my house I judged myself by her judgments. With Bonnie I became aware of my inferior-to-her intellectual abilities.

In the middle of eighth grade I had dropped out of the school's social conventions. All I remember from this time, a time of complete turning inward, is that I wore what we called "boys' jeans" and a red plaid flannel boys' shirt, tails hanging out, every day for six weeks. I sat, holed up, in my desk hoping no one would notice I was there. The teacher, a forgettable blond man, played his own form of baseball with a ruler and a piece of chalk. If the chalk hit you it was your turn to answer his question.

If I just could get away from there, I thought—go to the convent—just maybe there, with people like Sister Eleanor, I would be safe.

57

About this time Mama gave me an autograph book and on the first page inscribed the first written message that survives from her:
I love you more today than I did yesterday,
And tomorrow I shall love you more than I do now.
I treasured even the ink with which her letters were formed, even the loops and lines of her cursive penmanship. I would open the little book and read her words over and over, gleaning their warmth, leaning my soul into the endless expanse of time, all the tomorrows she promised with love increasing as each one came and went forever.

With high school came my turning inward years, the years of hiding the convent dream. I stored up gifts for sacrifice. I shook life, forcing it to relinquish its treasures and I hid them because when I had enough I planned to give them all away.

I constructed and played a role of being popular, of being talented, active, alive, knowing—a role of leadership, competence, and determination. I designed myself to look normal. I wanted everyone in Baudette presented with this dilemma: "How could such a normal, popular, everyday girl end up in the convent?" I wanted people to witness the ultimate *Seventeen* magazine girl, then to see her sacrifice herself into the larger life of God. Never once did it occur to me how self-serving all this fantasy might be.

Deeper in me than my adolescent role-playing lay my realization of never having felt at home in the world. I liked sanctuaries. I liked the choir loft in the clean smelling knotty pine church where I went on stained glass afternoons to sit by myself at the organ and sing my way through the *Gregorian Hymnal*. I liked the knoll of trees by my lake. I didn't like most parties because they were loud and frenetic with intoxicated people who claimed to be having fun. Even now, having left the convent forty years ago, I create my own cloister at the end of a mountain road in the shelter of giant pines.

A TENDER EDGE

On August 15, 1958, both Mama and I woke with the knowledge that this would be the day into which we would try to cram all the days we'd ever had together. We would fold our years like hankies; she'd keep mine and I'd take hers with me. As time went on each of us would cry into the soft receptivity of those years, tell the stories to whomever would listen, sing the songs to ourselves that once we sang to each other. I was off to join the Congregation of the Sisters of St. Joseph at their convent in Crookston, Minnesota. I was seventeen years old. There had never been a moment I could remember in my life that I hadn't wanted to surrender myself to God, the Christ within, and for a Catholic girl in the Forties and Fifties, a convent was thought to be the place, the life, in which unconditional surrender and total dedication in love of God could be achieved. "How could you have known?" people ask me now. Or, "How could you have known at such a young age?" I knew with a knowledge that I couldn't resist or call imagination or a childhood fantasy of veils and long dresses. I knew somewhere so deep in myself that when I touch that place now it seems the background hum of Being itself. Even today I have no doubt that I was beckoned by this Being to do as I did, when I did it, and for as long as I continued as a member of that religious community of women.

Mama called me that morning to wake up and come into the kitchen for my favorite breakfast, strawberries and strips of light toast with melted butter. We would be leaving at noon. I'd packed my new steamer trunk with the required articles of clothing, linens, blankets, plus pictures of family and friends. How did Mama feel that morning? I came into the kitchen and sat down at a breakfast prepared and arranged so beautifully that tears filled my eyes. What had it cost her to fix what she must have thought would be the last breakfast I would ever eat at home? I stared at it. She stood looking down at me. "You have to eat something, honey." Her voice, soft, maybe on the verge of tears. "Just a bite of toast? Try dipping a strawberry in some of that powdered sugar. How about a little sip of tea?"

I'd foiled her plans to block this calling, to make me forget. My first campaign to leave home for life in a religious community began when I was eleven years old and about to begin seventh grade. A recruiting book from the Franciscans informed me that any twelve year old Catholic girl with a vocation could join them as an aspirant. I begged with her and begged. Being a faithful and religious woman herself, she didn't want to do the wrong thing, but to allow her little girl to leave home at such a young age felt inconceivable to her. She sought advice from a friendly priest and then presented me with a compromise. No one could tell yet if I were ready for such a life, and it would be unconscionable for her to allow me to leave home if I were not ready. So if for two years I could live according to strict rules (and he'd given her a list), then she would know I was mature enough to observe a holy rule, and I could leave for the convent during the summer before my Freshman year in high school.

I declined the compromise. If I had to stay home, I reasoned in my adolescent way that validated her concerns, I'd live the same sort of life as all my friends. I'd play drums in the high school band, sing in the chorus, cheer for the home team, join the civil air patrol, work as a clerk in my mother's store, go on hay rides, ice skate on Baudette Bay, date several different boys, fall in love, and share secrets with my girlfriends. What was the use of living as though I were in a convent if I didn't have any of the perks of the convent? What those perks might be I had no idea.

The morning of my departure, I looked at Mama and at the strawberries, tea, and toast and was stunned to realize that leaving her would be impossible. Tears began to drip onto my plate. "I can't," and the words rode a sob.

"Sure you can, honey. Or not, if you change your mind. You can do whatever you want to do." She remained strong. How could she do that? Why didn't both of us just break down then and there? "Maybe you can try this food a little later," she crooned as she removed my full plate.

If I didn't leave her right that minute, I wouldn't do it. Something deep inside me said, go and go now. "I think I'll go downtown and get a haircut." I pushed myself back from the table and broke away from the compassionate look in her eyes. Walking, almost running the five blocks to our small downtown, I tried to chase from my mind the thought that I'd left her before I needed to, the thought that she might have begun crying when I let the screen door slam, the thought that her grief at this loss might be so much greater than my own.

Later that afternoon we stood inside the convent of the Sisters of St. Joseph in Crookston, Minnesota. My father—his workingman's body out of place in the dainty parlor, his grey eyes holding back tears. My mother, gregarious, trying to please the sisters, trying to do the right thing. My little nine-year old sister, standing back, wide-eyed. I faced my father and removed my graduation ring, my diamond ring which had been my grandmother's, and my new wrist watch, placing each into his open hand. "Keep these for me..." knowing that if the future had its way, I would never wear them again. I remember a fleeting sense of symbolism, that these items represented a connectedness that I was severing from family and friends. The watch meant a shifting of time, a disconnectedness from the present and a shift backwards in time towards antiquity. "I'll keep them safe for you," he said.

We were not aware when the sister led us to the stairway that we wouldn't have a chance to say goodbye. The sisters thought it more kind to conceal the actual moment of separation by leading the new postulants to the front of the chapel for the induction ceremony and seating our families towards the back. I feel even now the pull of attachment on my heart. All through the prayer service and the sermon of welcome I felt that binding of myself to the little family seated rows and rows behind me. Just before the last hymn I heard shuffling sounds. We rose and sang "Holy God We Praise Thy Name," and I listened for the voices of the fathers in the back rows, but the priest's was the only male voice singing an octave below the voices of the sisters. The other men, our fathers, had been led out with our mothers and siblings just as the hymn began.

"Stand up," something in me urged. "Turn around." Where were they? Probably the sisters took them back to the parlor so we all could say goodbye. I tried to reason with myself. I thought that any moment one of the sisters would lead us from the chapel back to our parents. But we sat there. And sat...

In the meantime the cars in which the five of us postulants had arrived were driving off, and the severance from our former lives quietly and efficiently done. Years later my mother told me that she still felt a ripping inside her at hearing that Holy God hymn.

So do I.

I was seventeen years old. Unlike many of the other young women who entered convents that year I had never attended a Catholic school. The sisters had not watched me grow; they had not nurtured my development. I was no one's protégé. I had not yet learned the acceptable reasons for a young woman to devote her life within a religious community. A wordless, urgent desire led me there. When I filled out the entrance form question: "Why do you want to be a Sister of St. Joseph?" I copied my response from a pamphlet on religious life.

I came open, aching, lonely, determined. I came, not knowing what I would find, but ready for any deprivation, any sacrifice—committed to do as I was told in order to become a sister and be permitted to remain with these privileged women. I took literally the metaphor "Brides of Christ," and yearned to be among their number. These women seemed to me to embody a mystery, a secret unknown to anyone else, and I longed to share it.

So I would tell Mama nothing of the difficulties I soon would encounter. On the surface the requirements seemed small: read no newspapers, never listen to the radio or watch television. John Kennedy was elected president without any of us having even heard his name. We were novices with more important matters to consider. We were learning to be without fault and constantly warned that "one who ignores slight faults will infallibly fall into those that are great."

I took the training seriously, never purposely breaking a rule, trying to live up to every expectation, never able to do so well enough. The maxims suggested: "Never say anything, whether good or evil, about yourself without great necessity. Have no esteem for yourself or for what you do, since what you are or what you can do is nothing at all before God, and in every respect you are full of imperfections sufficient to make you despise yourself utterly, if they were known to you."

Adolescent as I was, and uncertain anyway what kind of person I might be, such admonitions struck forcefully at the roots of my still fragile sense of self. I began to pray to be nothing, to recognize my nothingness before this God whom no one could please. This surely was a jealous lover to require that there be no love for anything but him—that only if I became nothing and despised might I finally be received, could I finally become perfect. If I could be nothing, God could be everything. To be the bride of Christ I would need to disintegrate. Dissolve. Only then would I no longer stand in the way of God's will. If I could be nothing, then Christ would be the only one present wherever I happened to be. I would be a true Christ-bearer.

This is what happened during the novitiate training to Mama's daughter. In religious life I chose to be called by the name that meant Christ-bearer, and to me indicated that of Mary Jane nothing would be left:

Stepping over the edges of myself, I would be new-named, Sister Mary Christopher.

THIS IS FROM YOUR MAMA...

Five of us made first vows in the Congregation of St. Joseph on May 15, 1961. That day we left the novitiate and Mother Celine's direct supervision to begin our life in the community of professed sisters. Then, before I could adjust to the change, I found myself in summer school at Viterbo College in LaCrosse, Wisconsin, where I began my "secular education," preparing to be the English teacher in the congregation's academy for girls. My future profession as well as the particular classes I took that summer had been chosen for me, and I'd not been consulted on the matter, but I couldn't have been happier with the choice. This summer's fare was "Modern Philosophy" and "Contemporary Drama." Fresh from the convent novitiate, a new twenty-year-old religious sister, I was studying Kant and Hegel alongside O'Neil's "Great God Brown." I loved every minute.

The first extant letter from Mama, dated July 4, 1961, is still with its envelope, sandstone yellow with an institutional return address: *St. Francis Hospital, Crookston, Minnesota.* That address disoriented me when the sister placed the envelope in my hand. My stomach lurched. What was Mama doing at the Crookston hospital? Her hand looked steady.

That day we'd just completed our mid-term exams. The sisters were celebrating. Sister Florence played something classical and intricate on the recreation room piano, and followed it with a rollicking boogie. She was from my same community, but scores of religious communities were represented there that summer, a strange fashion show of veils and bonnets in blacks and browns and greys and various shades of blue, all trimmed in white.

"You may want to go outside to read this letter," said the sister. She'd been contacted about it by Mother Celine, my former Mistress of Novices, who'd been given authority in this case because of her extensive knowledge of me. She told the sister to keep the letter from me until after exams.

Maybe I was alone when I read it; maybe Sister Florence stayed with me. I don't remember. I do remember dusk and a long walk with her through neighborhoods bordering the college. I remember lighted windows of houses where families carried on their lives in what I thought must be the safety of the ordinary.

My mother wrote in pencil. Someday this letter will simply fade and disappear. She wrote on letterhead stationery belonging to Fr. John O'Toole, but crossed out his name and printed above it, *"This is from your Mama."* I noticed all these things the first time I read the letter as a sleuth might notice. She wanted to tell her daughter something, the daughter I was before I was a Sister of St. Joseph, and so she began *"Dear Mary J...,"* then inserted *"Sr."* at an angle before the *"Mary,"* and pressed a *"C"* over the *"J"* to finish up with *"Christopher."* She began by printing her words, but as the story emerged the writing turned cursive. She spun the narrative as though she didn't want to tell me the ending too soon. But what I remember is the mix of dread and empathy I felt along the way. I knew that if all had turned out well, she wouldn't be writing like this. She'd be home at her typewriter, and she'd tell me the happy outcome first.

July 2nd, there had been a storm on Lake of the Woods in Minnesota where my dad was a bush pilot and member of the Coast Guard Auxiliary. He'd flown rescue missions all day long—to Portage Bay, Flag Island, Alexander Island. He'd picked up two local people in Winnipeg, and thought he was finished for the day. But at suppertime a call came through. Some Indiana fishermen had a mishap on a lake north of Kenora, Ontario. Their small plane had blown over and was resting, floats up, on the rocks. Would Dad fly out, land, right the plane and fix the engine? Of course. Just as he was about to leave, another call came in, this time from Smith's Resort, that two of their guests were stranded on Burton Island and needed supplies. Would dad drop them on his way to Kenora? He would. He took two other men along, while Mama and Betsy remained at the airport. It was 8:46 PM. She kept in contact by radio. She described it in the letter:

"Cessna 4688 Alpha to Baudette Radio—We're halfway there. Do you read me?" (George's voice from the plane.)

"Baudette Radio to 4688 Alpha. ROG—ER!" (Mama in office).

"What do you mean 'ROG—ERRRRRR?" (Laughter at both ends of the connection).

"8:57: Cessna to Baudette Radio—We are over area—will circle and size up situation and call you back in <u>one</u> minute!"

SILENCE!
SILENCE!—SILENCE!
"9:05—Calling Cessna 4688!
CALLING—Cessna 4688!"

SILENCE!

At this point in Mama's letter I didn't know whether my father was still alive. I could feel her desperation, and my guilt that I wasn't with her, and a growing anger that I was reading about this incident a week late. Why hadn't she called me immediately? Only later would I learn that she had tried to reach me but had been rebuffed by Mother Celine. As I read the letter, I had my first experience of the chasm that could open between family needs and convent authority, and I suspect this was the moment I began the long but mostly unconscious detachment from convent life with the mythic world view and dualistic moral code that then supported it. Ten years later realizations that sprang from this and subsequent experiences would result in my exodus from that way of life.

Mama goes on chronicling, minute by minute, the events of that night—the calls she made to resorts, the boats that took up a search. Finally at ten o'clock:

Wigwam Resort called—Russell had just come in from Burton in a 16 ft. boat—almost drowned—to tell them that <u>no one</u> was killed but the plane had crashed.

Betsy told me later how shaken Mama was. It was clear to my sister that our mother was unable to drive the car, so even though Betsy was only eleven years old, she asked Mama for the keys, got into the driver's seat and drove the car through fog the twelve miles to the lake.

At 1:30 A.M. the Wigwam launch came in and Ted and Mutt—with George. He was hurt in the face—I went with him in Paul's ambulance to town—got to the hospital at 2:00 A.M. Dr. Brink said broken jaw and nose. Poor George—lots of pain—and remorse.

Dad was alive. Reading the letter I felt ill—the nausea of impotence. Mama continues for three more pages, both sides, with a narrative of the transfer from the small hospital in Baudette to the trauma center in Crookston. She wonders if he should stop flying now. She'll never stop worrying about another crash. She reports on the surgeries to fix a once handsome face that had not been simply broken but pulverized by slamming into the instrument panel in the cockpit of his 180-Cessna. She ends, *This is the last of the paper. Don't worry, dear. Maybe send him a note.—Oh yes! 2 Masses at the motherhouse this morning for him. It's glorious to be related to the St. Joseph family of Sisters. Love and prayers, Mama.*

I walked with Sister Florence up and down the sidewalks of LaCrosse that evening. I'd put Mama's letter back into its envelope and slid it beneath the folded bodice of my religious habit, next to my heart. Sister Florence told me it was normal to cry, but I didn't want to cry in her presence, only with my mother.

Now I read in Mama's last line her insinuation that all the sisters were interchangeable and could substitute for each other, and I am stunned. At the time I must have accepted such a notion also. If I had not, then this incident could have become an immediately effective challenge to the life I'd chosen. Despite my acceptance my mind whirled with contradictory thoughts: I ought to have been told; I ought to have been with her. Mother Celine had been wrong to forbid this.

Mama must have suspected that I'd be feeling lost while reading about everything my family had endured in my absence, and that I might feel betrayed by Mother Celine's refusal to allow her to talk to me. Years later she admitted to me that she, herself, had felt betrayed. But she widened herself in that letter, including all my religious sisters in her family. She must have thought that otherwise I would have left the convent on that day, that I would have gone to her.

But despite the nausea, the sense of betrayal, the belief that my family had been wronged, I could not yet even think of leaving. It didn't enter my mind. The novice mistress may have been wrong, but God makes no mistakes. This was my conclusion. I would surrender as I had been taught to do. I would kneel and pray until I could freely offer this sacrifice that I then believed God, through my religious superior, had asked of me.

67

REMEMBER THE THIRD BELOVED

- That he would be strong, reliable, steady, but distant as a silhouette against the sky.
- That he would protect you from any danger except that emerging from your mother, and then he would not protect you.
- That you would yearn for him, run to him, hope for a word from him, wait for him, watch for him, wonder what he felt and what he thought.
- That he would remain a mystery.
- That his language was silence.
- That you created the words he might use to say he loved you, if ever he might be inclined to speak.
- That he could do anything, fix anything, make broken airplanes fly again, radios emit sound, dead engines fire up.
- That he could look at you with his grey-green eyes until you believed there would be nothing you couldn't be or do.
- That he had weaknesses he hid from the sight of everyone for as long as he could.
- That for most of your life you would measure every other man by his dimensions.
- That he became for you almost an idol which God alone was able to surpass.

THE FATHER'S DAUGHTER WALKS A THIN LINE

I thought my father the handsomest of all men. Tall for a man of his time, maybe 6'2", he had stunning grey-green eyes, slicked back black hair, and a moustache like Clarke Gable's. And best of all, he wasn't like other fathers, those with a normal job. Aviation continued to be rare in small towns during the 1940s and 50s when I was growing up. He projected an aura of romantic ruggedness when he stood on the windswept field beside his Piper Cub or down at the ramp on the Rainy River by his Cessna 180. As a child of nine or ten I'd hear the roar of my father's engine and run with my girl friends into the center of the yard where we could be seen, and all of us would lift our arms in sweeping waves as though we ourselves had wings. Daddy's plane would swoop down over us, dipping its wings to return the greeting.

I knew him by intuition. He seldom spoke, keeping his counsel. I'm aware now of the way I spun my stories and created him, silence by silence. His females whirled around him like planets round the sun. He could still us with a word, probably because there were so few of them. We came to count on him for the stillness he brought.

Later in my life, studying psychology, I would learn about women whose personalities develop as "Daughters of the Father," and I would recognize an aspect of the complex dynamic motivating my life and choices. I would feel compelled to fill his silence with my words.

An airplane in the sky seems not to move over the earth. I looked down from my father's Cessna 180, and the ground appeared almost still as we inched along, our shadow like a meandering cloud. We had forever, it seemed, to view the tiny houses below, the roads that slithered over the countryside like wet spaghetti noodles. It wasn't until we came in for a landing that I realized how fast we had been moving all along. One barely can imagine it until then, or until the plane unexpectedly falls. This juxtaposition of far with near contributed to the paradox at the core of my father.

I guess you'd have to say that while my first memory of my mother is connected with my fear of losing her and my need to prevent that loss, I have no first memory of my father. I see him sitting in a chair by a window in the Omaha apartment. He's behind a newspaper. I see him with two other men sitting on his haunches in the grass by the gas pumps at Klimek's Lodge. They are talking. I am wearing a sundress and running towards him. It is morning; I just got up. He holds out his arms and I run into them. He lifts me on his knee. In a minute he puts me down on the grass and tells me to search for a four-leaf clover. I was older then, three or four.

There is nothing distinct about my early memories of him. I don't know how often he was a part of my world. Just a few years ago my mother's sister, Eva, told me he spent much of every summer in Omaha during the war while my mother and I spent that time at Klimek's Lodge in Minnesota. I thought he was with us. I thought my memories of him in his captain's cap, climbing out of the launch, lifting up the day's catch of walleyed pike were of everyday events.

His name was George Raymond Lore and he was the second son in a family of six children—my aunts and uncles Lore. Uncle Harvey, Auntie Eleanor, Auntie Edith, Uncle John and Auntie Barbara. His father, Fred, was more than anything else a lumberjack. Grandpa Lore was tall and craggy. Slender, with dancing legs. He laughed a lot and called me Sunshine. Daddy's mother had died before I lived.

Daddy didn't tell me stories of his boyhood until the year before he died, one week when I was home and the television went on the blink. He couldn't get out; he'd had a heart attack and spent most of his time sitting in his black leather recliner staring at game shows. He was developing cataracts in his eyes and didn't read books. Reading never was a habit of his anyway. He was always too busy. The television repair man came and took the set to the shop. Mama was in the hospital recovering from a mastectomy. Daddy and I sat in the living room. There was nothing to do but talk. He told me he never completed high school. Some kid insulted his mother and he ended up in a fist fight. The math teacher broke it up and blamed Dad. He just walked away. It was his Junior year. He quit school to get even. Never said why. Never told anybody why. He never went back. It was a point of pride with him that he was asked each year to give a lecture on aviation to the seniors in the same high school he'd quit so many years before.

My memories of my father are almost all from later in my life and even then I can't be sure I knew him very well. He always said, "I don't need to tell Mary Jane. She knows how I feel." I didn't though. I had to guess. Maybe I made it up, figured he must feel the way I hoped he felt. I figured "she knows how I feel" meant "I love her."

After the accident Mama described in her letter, Daddy didn't look at all like himself. He looked simply awful. I feared I would reveal how shaken I was to see him like that, his face inside a cage of wires to hold his teeth in place and purple bruises on the skin over his lost cheek bones.

My first glimpse of him took place later the same summer. My family joined me under gigantic pines beside the prayer bell at the sisters' rustic vacation cabins beside a tiny lake outside Bemidji, Minnesota. Both my parents and I had hoped I could visit them at home for the week after summer school. We petitioned my religious superiors, including Mother Celine, but to no avail. They judged that I needed this time to relax with the sisters, and I had no say in the matter.

But of course I had no say. We all knew this. I'd chosen this. I'd made a vow of obedience, surrendered myself to the will and wisdom of the elected superior. I believed—we all believed—that God infused her will towards me with a tender grace that would bring about good for all. Still, we wanted a waiver. Certainly God would be just as satisfied if I went home. It was not to be. A concession was made, though, for Mama, Daddy and Betsy to drive the considerable distance from Baudette to spend a few hours with me at "The Pines."

I tried not to stare. Something in him was different from before, and it wasn't confined to his wounds. He seemed softer than before, almost apologetic. We made small talk for a few minutes. Betsy scuffed her feet in the pine needles. She felt nervous. Mama talked about the sisters; how gracious we all were to open our home to them at this extraordinary time. Finally Dad pointed to his wounds and the cage around his face. "I can't feel much," he said. The nerves were injured. Probably they would heal, but maybe not. It wasn't bad, he assured me. The pain, if you could call it pain, was the numbness itself. You just had to get used to it was all. A human being can adjust to anything.

I invited them down to the lake where we stood on the dock. Probably on the way down the hill I pointed out the poison ivy that grew thick among the red sumac. I kept trying not to cry. Daddy sensed my feelings and told me he was already so much better. I wanted him to be the same as always, but he was not. He was wounded, fallen from the sky. I wanted to touch his face, but I did not. I wanted him to hug me; he did not. In the future many years from that day he would take me into his arms and hold me close, but it would be when I was no longer a sister. "I can hug you again," he would say. Although we had no rule against hugging, he'd felt restricted during all my convent years.

72

Probably it was Mama who did most of the talking. Probably it was a hot August day, humid, the air buzzing with mosquitoes and colorful with dragonflies. Likely I could feel the itch of my woolen clothes and the sweat running down my neck underneath my finely woven wool veil. Maybe I concentrated on all of that rather than on my father's face that made me want to cry. But I would not cry.

Before long Daddy would be strong again. He would fly again. His character would shine out through his new face and, recognizing him, all three of us would finally believe that he looked better this way. Rugged, but gentle too. More stable even than before. From that time on, though, each of us realized that the center could give way and suddenly, in the time it takes to gasp, our world could stop its whirling and everything could fall and shatter on the rocks.

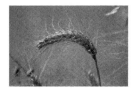

REMEMBER THE FOURTH BELOVED

- That you would call her Mother Celine of the Holy Cross.
- That you would polish her shoes and carry her sewing box.
- That you would humble yourself, that you would kiss the floor to honor the earth on which Jesus walked, that you would lower your veil and confess your infractions of the holy rule, that you would lower your eyes, that you would lower your sleeves, that you would bend your knees, that you would kiss her shoes as she stood on the threshold, that you would sit on a child's chair, that you would back out of her presence and bow.
- That you would whip yourself with chains every Friday night unless you were in the period of blood, and then you would not whip yourself with chains.
- That you would appreciate the power of words, that you would love the stories she told and learn from them, that you would not be surprised when words drove her to laughter or to tears.
- That you would allow her to bind you to herself by virtue of holy obedience, that she could tell you when you sinned or when you didn't sin, that she could tell you to pronounce your vows or not to pronounce them, that she would take the consequences of your sins upon herself. That therefore you would obey her.
- That you could make mistakes because those who don't risk falling never reach the mountaintop.
- That you would set your eyes and heart "neither on Lancelot nor another, but the King."
- That you would never really know her.

WHAT COULD THIS OLD WOMAN DO TO ME?

Just after my graduation from high school in 1958, I had been interviewed at the convent by the Provincial Superior, Mother Martha Mary, and by the Mistress of Novices, Mother Celine of the Holy Cross. We waited in the parlor—Mama and I—to be summoned. I felt more excited than nervous, and had brought pictures of my high school graduation to share. Prom pictures. Pictures of me with my boyfriend, John Weber. Pictures of the graduation ceremony and the party afterwards. I knelt beside Mother Celine as she went through them, one by one, and I pointed out my friends, naming them for her as though she might someday meet them and would want to recognize them when she did. She sat stiffly upright in her chair, her feet upon a little stool. Her veil covered what I now realize must have been a quite severe scoliosis. Her shape was that of a pillow pulled together in the middle by the rope of her cincture. Her hips sat at an angle and I later saw that she rolled from side to side as she walked. Her face was a theatre masque or the masks of all the Buddhist gods—terrifying, ecstatic, joyous, impassive, dissolved by tears, wrinkled with laughter. As she looked at my pictures that day, her face was cordial but dismissive.

Mama had more experience reading people than I did, and as we walked to the car after the interview she quizzed me. "Does it bother you that Mother Celine is so old? Do you think that will be a problem for you?"

I felt too excited that day for anything to seem a problem. And anyway, I thought, what could this old woman do to me?

"She's sixty-seven. What if she won't be able to understand your generation?" Maybe Mama picked up something about Mother Celine's reaction to those pictures, the dismissiveness, perhaps. Maybe she was clairvoyant. Maybe she caught a glimpse of the future when my novice mistress would tell me to get rid of them.

When I remember Mother Celine, I always need to remind myself that I was seventeen when she took hold of and chose to keep me. How could I possibly have mined the treasure within her? From the beginning of my tutelage, she demonstrated a confusing complexity that drew and repelled me. When I tried to read her expectations, I virtually always failed to get it right, and the guilt I incurred dogged my heels throughout my novitiate. Her rolling walk ahead of her novices down the cloister hallway elicited both pity and fear. She held her head high above that off-kilter body. Her eyes could pin you to the wall or set fire burning in your heart.

She read to us every afternoon in a voice and with inflection developed over years as a teacher of English literature. She quoted Tennyson often, and each year on All Soul's Day we heard Newman's haunting "Dream of Gerontius." She read biographies of saints and books of poetic reflections such as *A Woman Wrapped in Silence*, which went straight to the heart of Mary the mother of Jesus. I can see now that during these times I was taken in spirit and emotion back to Mama and her own daily readings when I was a child. The rhythm of words sank deep into me and I walked to them, breathed them, fell asleep with them pulsing in my blood.

These were the last years of the pre-Vatican II church when every doctrine and article of faith, every demand of the holy rule and custom of the congregation remained certain, and all I needed do to become pleasing to God was to be told, to learn, to internalize the rule, and to live it. Once the barrage of rules was leveled against me, I forgot that God had been pleased with me already enough to have called me to this life. The rule added a new level of responsibility and of doubt. Rules and the orders of superiors sometimes contradicted each other. What certainty did I have that my observance of the rule was perfect enough? In fact, I was pretty sure it was not. Mother Celine's face most often appeared stern. Thinking she meant I needed to try harder to be observant, I pushed myself, bringing on headaches and anxiety at which she shook her head. I'd become scrupulous, she told me, something she could not permit. And so by trying harder, I'd failed again. Just use your common sense, she insisted, but the rule often precluded common sense. "If your superior tells you to plant a cabbage upside-down, you must do it if you are truly obedient," Mother Celine explained. I worried I wouldn't know what to do. She nicknamed me "Worry Wart," and called me that in class whenever I asked a question about the seeming contradictions. In my notebook that first year I wrote: "Jesus, forgive me my lack of trust. Strengthen me, good and most sweet Jesus. I resolve from this moment to regard all worry as coming from the evil spirit, and will treat it as a temptation. Help me by Thy grace." Despite prayer, my obsession with being imperfect in

THE EDGE OF TENDERNESS

obedience and lacking in common sense became worse as the novitiate continued. I didn't yet understand that by focusing on worry, I would become more worried.

One evening at recreation the conversation in the community room was unusually lighthearted and we still were laughing when the bell rang for silence. Mother Celine's voice rang out. *"Benedicamus Domino,"* the sign for an immediate transition from levity to solemnity. We all swallowed our laughter, picked up our sewing boxes, and proceeded from the community room to our dormitories where we would put them away before the evening study hour. Sister Innocent and I walked together trying to keep silence. It wasn't easy. I could hear little bursts of air from her nose and giggles threatened. Once in the dark dorm, she hid as I put my sewing box into the cabinet. Everything was completely quiet when I turned to leave, and I thought I was alone. Suddenly she jumped out at me and I yelped. As luck would have it, Mother Celine was just walking past our dorm on her way to her room, and my yelp brought her to a halt. "Sister?" It was her most stern voice. "Which of you sisters just made that noise?" So I stepped out into the hallway.

"I'm ashamed of you, Sister Christopher," she accosted me. "I will see you in my office."

On the way down the hall I thought of the rule forbidding self-justification. The idea was that when a sister found herself accused of something she didn't do, she should not attempt to defend herself, but just take the consequences. After all, there had been many times in her life that she had offended and not been caught. Humility demanded that she admit her universal sinfulness and not expect to be found innocent even on the occasion that she actually was.

Mother Celine motioned for me to sit on the child's chair across from where she sat in an adult chair at her desk. "Why did you yelp like that?" She wore her stern face.

"I don't know." I said as my eyes began to tear up.

"Certainly you must know. You were being frivolous, were you not?"

"Yes, Mother." A sob escaped.

"And it was during our rule silence, was it not?" Still the stern face and voice.

"Yes, Mother." Another sob and tears began to fall down my cheeks.

"So tell me: what was so funny?" She handed me her white handkerchief.

"I don't know, Mother." I took it and blew my nose.

"Of course you know, Sister. Tell me what was so funny."

I must not justify myself. I must not blame Sister Innocent. I began to sob harder.

"Why on earth can't you tell me?" She said.

Now I was sobbing so hard I was gasping like a little child. The handkerchief was soaked. She went to her dresser and got me a clean one. I accepted it and continued to sob.

"For heaven's sake!" She exclaimed. "One little yelp isn't worth all these tears. What on earth is wrong?"

How could I tell her how trapped I felt? The rule effectively ordered me not to tell her. She was ordering me to tell her. If I told her she would accuse me of justifying myself. So I just kept sobbing. After four handkerchiefs she gave up. She shook her head and with pity in her tone sent me back to the study room. Maybe she decided to chalk it up to adolescent hormones. I don't know, but she never brought it up again.

As the two remaining years of my novitiate went on, my attacks of scrupulosity worsened despite Mother Celine's best attempts to relieve me of my worries. "Stop nit-picking!" She ordered me in private, but in class she reminded all of us that every jot and tittle of the law must be fulfilled. In private she recommended that I pray for humility, and in class she told us we were entering a "state of perfection," and that if every holy rule book were to be destroyed that night, tomorrow it should be able to be reconstructed by observing our lives. I took literally every word she spoke. The smallest infraction of the holy rule had the power to plunge my mind into a state of anxiety from which only Mother Celine could free me. She pushed me to my knees before her and told me she would take every bit of my guilt. Since I could not seem to let it go, she would wrest it from me and give it to the all-forgiving God. Then she commanded me to forget my worry and go in peace. If it threatened to come back I should remind myself that Mother Celine had given it to God, and tell the worry devil to be gone. This small imperfect woman took on the dimensions of

Moses on Sinai. Lightning flashed around her. I obeyed. For the moment, for a day, sometimes for as long as a month I felt freedom. But it didn't last.

In the meantime, in the aura of freedom and peace, I lived and studied with the other novices. Our convent was not in the city but on one hundred fifty acres of prime farming land bordered by woods in which lived a herd of deer. In winter we hunkered down in the bushes, our black wool shawls held tight against the cold, and watched for them to venture from the trees into the sugar-beet field. Each season presented us with its own wild beauty that moved my spirit and my heart. I felt normal then. I felt free then. Then I felt close to God. Nature had its own rules, spacious rules that could be read in one's heart. In summer we picked gooseberries, sought out wildflowers—the Jack-in-the-Pulpit, the yellow Moccasin; we swung on thick looped vines, built bonfires to roast hot dogs and corn, sang as the fire became embers and the stars hung deep overhead. Mother Celine could not accompany us during these times. For practical learning and for fun she entrusted us to Sister Emma Joseph, a middle-aged daughter of truck farmers, who could do anything from planting and harvesting a field to refinishing furniture, from cleaning a barn to collecting fresh water clams, from keeping the financial records of the community to fine-hemming a delicate veil. Mother Celine counted on her both to teach and evaluate us. Her expectations were as down to earth as her skills, and although I seldom excelled at waxing and buffing a floor or darning a hole in my stocking, it was far easier to accept her criticism of my work than to accept Mother Celine's critique of my soul.

I wanted Mother Celine's love and her acceptance, but never felt it in a way I could recognize. She pointed out my vanity, a sin common to superficial souls. Great souls might be troubled by pride, a sin she promised wouldn't trouble me. And don't worry about the *real* devil coming after you either, she mused. Why would the devil bother with someone like you? There are great souls far more worth his time. Just do your duty. Finish your studies. Complete your chores. Don't look in the mirror. Keep the silence. Lie on your back in bed. Keep your hands at your sides. Don't lean over your plate; you look like a nibbling rabbit. Volunteer to iron the linens. Don't let your eyes stray to the newspaper under the potatoes you peel. Spend your time with sisters who annoy you. "If you love those who love you, what reward will you have?" Keep your sufferings a secret from your family; why should you make them suffer also? A little soul like you can do only little things: no sugar on your cereal, no butter on your toast, no salt on your egg. Examine your posture—are you standing straight? Do you still lean against the pew in chapel? Kneel upright without support. Posture alone could be all God asks of you. Can you accomplish even that much?

It is wrong to characterize her as one-sided though. Even as an adolescent novice I could see that she was more complex than that, and I loved the mystery in her. In the spring before I was permitted to make my first year of vows, Mother Celine turned seventy. She thrived on celebrations, and in our attempts to please her, the novices strove to make each major feast more creatively artistic than the last, with music, decorations and special events. Though we could do nothing without her permission ("yes, you may plan a celebration for...") all of us hoped that with this birthday party we could surprise her. Sister Innocent, our artist, would design a card—though she was not permitted to draw without permission. Sister Emilie and Sister Paulette would play a duet—though the piano was forbidden to them during the year of canonical novitiate. I would write a narrative poem for all of us to perform—though creative writing was forbidden to me without permission. I think now that we must have had someone's permission to have a surprise party.

I wrote the poem in the lavatory. In my pocket I kept small scraps of paper, and when a line came to me I would ask permission to "circulate" (a euphemism for a visit to the lavatory, though its more accurate meaning was to interrupt the stillness of the classroom in order to go wherever one needed to go). I would hurry down the hallway, lock myself in one of the green institutional stalls, sit on the toilet, take out my scrap of paper, and write the line or lines. In a few weeks I had the entire poem. It lauded a wise woman who took five virgins into her life to be her daughters, and she brought them to God. Now, equipped with her love and her teachings, it was time for them to leave her. I no longer have the poem, and I suspect it was quite sentimental. Mother Celine cried when we performed it. Then she called us to her side and put her arms around each of us. We received her smile. She told us how proud and pleased she was with what we had become. Then she recited:

My life has been a wild surprise
Of kindnesses unsought,
Taking from others' hands and eyes
Much greater than it brought.

Throughout my novitiate I had watched her in the chapel, her arms outstretched in the form of a cross, not leaning against anything despite her twisted body. I had determined to be perfect in everything she required, but the harder I tried the more I continued to fail.

It didn't occur to me that I might be meant to fail. Pray, she said to me. Repeat over and over, "Jesus, meek and humble of heart, make my heart like unto thine." All along she might have been trying to teach humility rather than perfection. Remember what Jesus said, she continued: "Learn from me for I am meek and humble of heart. Take my yoke upon you, for my yoke is sweet and my burden is light." Only years later, after she had died, did her meaning come to me. I stood in the chapel looking down at her where she lay in her simple casket. Her scripture verse popped into my mind. "Give up your harsh illusions of control over your life," she seemed to be saying from somewhere on the other side of death, "and be yoked instead with the sweetness of Christ. Give up the weight of your self-imposed burdens, and exchange them for the lightness of His, and you will finally realize that the burden of God in your life is Light itself. It's a paradox, Sister. What I wanted you to learn was a divine paradox." Tears came and then gentle sobs of gratitude.

I remember overhearing a conversation between Mother Celine and Mother Martha Mary only a few years after I'd made my vows and was at the motherhouse for the summer. They were discussing Sister Innocent who had just left the religious community. The wall between the two rooms was made of cinder-block and I could distinguish both their voices. "I was too hard on that girl," Mother Celine confessed.

"Her spirit was too delicate for this life. How could you have known?" responded Martha Mary.

"I should have known. I fear that I overstepped, pushed her too hard, did not let up even when it was clear she wouldn't benefit. The sorrow over what I've done..." her voice became low, inaudible.

"We do our best. We are not God. Forgive yourself now, Mother, as God forgives. And we will pray for her."

I heard the door open and the two mothers left the room.

I remained where I was, in silence and the realization of how little I had understood of her during all those years.

"SHE'S NOT YOUR MOTHER, I AM."

During my two years and nine months as a postulant and then a novice under Mother Celine's directives, my own mother, father, and sister, Betsy, visited me for a few hours one Sunday a month. They drove from Baudette to Crookston, arriving mid-morning. We ate dinner together in the guest dining room, spent several hours talking in the guest parlor, and said goodbye mid-afternoon at which time I answered a bell to attend community prayer, and they let themselves out the front door to make the trip back home. The occasion always gave me a stomach ache.

First came nausea from anticipation. I remember only one time they didn't come. Mama called several times that morning and spoke with Mother Celine's associate, Sister Emma Joseph, who relayed the news to me. A winter blizzard made the highway impassable. Yes, I could see the blizzard out the third floor window of the novitiate. Blowing snow obscured the ice covered road. But the plows were already out. Mama wanted Emma Joseph to assure me that they would do everything in their power to make the trip. I stood staring out the window, up the highway, as though my concentration could open a gap in the storm through which they would appear. Mama called again to say they had started out, only to be stopped. Even the plows were mired in drifts. Around noon they stopped trying. "We'd need to leave the moment we arrived," she mourned, referring to the community prayers from which I could not be excused.

Second came the confusion of concealment. Under no circumstances could I allow myself to worry my parents with difficulties I might be having in my training. Under no circumstances could I reveal details of convent life my parents were not equipped to accept or understand. They had been called to a different state of life. Did they share with me the secrets of their marriage vows? No, they did not. Thus went Mother Celine's directives. You must be kind— loving. Your parents have made a great sacrifice in surrendering you to this way of life. Never forget that. Do not make them question their gift. Remember that although you are their daughter, you are no ordinary daughter. You are their daughter who is also a Daughter of the Church. Make them proud of you. Make them grateful to have given such a precious gift to Our Lord.

83

I did my best. There was no relaxation in it. Over the months, what had Mama come to think of her daughter who sat with perfect posture on a straight-backed chair, who spoke with modulated voice about things she'd never before found interesting, whose every movement appeared (and was) stylized, who looked ill with her face full of stress-induced acne.

One acute memory still haunts me. On a day during my novitiate, I was regaling my family with whatever stories I could about my life since their last visit. Many times I mentioned Mother Celine, the stories she told, the teachings I felt my parents could accept. Suddenly Mama stood up and yelled at me. "STOP IT! Mother Celine, Mother Celine, Mother Celine! SHE'S not your mother; **I** am!"

Then she dashed out of the room and into the guest lavatory, locking the door behind her.

I looked at Daddy who wasn't moving. Betsy also sat very still, looking ashamed.

"It's a hard time for your mama," he finally said.

If there were further explanations, I don't remember them. I don't remember if she'd been crying when she came back into the room. I don't remember if, after that, they stayed or left to drive home. I remember a lot, but I don't remember that.

Thirdly was the ripping when they left—the essence of each of us torn away, or each of us torn from it, the true being of what we were. The story of ourselves was being rewoven, though only Mama came close to pointing that out with her "She's not your mother. I am your mother. I am."

I think now that there are no stories until we weave them. Until we tie them together in a meaningful way, the moments of life are individually spinning atoms without identification. It has been said that story has many layers. We can weave a story from any perspective and it will mean something different—a little bit different or profoundly different. I wonder now if I've been too afraid of the story being a falsehood, something that makes it a mockery.

If I'd woven differently, chosen the colors and yarn textures differently, if I'd caught hold of that wispy thread thin as a spider spins, if I'd even seen it hanging from the ceiling of consciousness, lifted on currents I could not then feel and barely can feel now, would I even yet be able to put into words the frightening suspicion that eluded me—that I left her to make her love me more. I left her so she never could leave me. I left her to bind her to myself by a goodness, a cry of God himself in me to rise and go. How after such a sacrifice could she see me as anything but good? The paradox overwhelms the mind, the present glimpse of it disintegrates as I reach to catch its wisp on the currents of the soul. By taking myself from her I'd bound her so close she could never get away. The binding and releasing and binding yet again, this motherhood of hers, would become her destiny.

If we are the makers of the stories, there is no false story. In fact, the more ways we can tell it, the better. We weave and weave until we know who is doing the weaving. Then we can cut it from the loom.

SHALL I CLOSE THE DOOR?

In the spring of my third year in the convent I stood behind the barn watching as the Red River of the North thundered, ice floes crashing against each other, and I screamed. What I thought I went to the convent to find seemed not to be there. I'd gone to the only place I knew that a door might be opened into the mysteries of the Divine more-than-ordinary, and each month I found less. A powerful vise had closed all around me. I didn't know what it was or why it was happening, and I blamed myself. I tried harder. But the harder I tried the more insane I felt. Fear oozed up worse than quicksand in the forbidden bogs back at Wheeler's Point behind the lodge. "Don't go there," warned the mother-voice from within me. "You'll be lost."

It couldn't be the convent's fault. These women were the chosen ones of God. My fault. My fault. My most grievous fault. At night I heard the scream of a rabbit in the woods and thought it was a woman. If she died it would be my fault. In the kitchen I peeled a beet that looked like someone's heart. I plunged a knife deep into it, then terror rose up into my throat, the taste of metal. Had I killed someone? I lost weight. I knelt in the chapel and my heart beat out "crazy, crazy, crazy—if this keeps up I will go insane."

Mother Celine told me I was scrupulous, a shameful thing to be. Didn't I trust God? Everything she said chipped away at the small part of me that still remained. Maybe this was the meaning of that fool-hearty request I'd made of God to "take everything; I surrender all." I wasn't thinking about the common, ordinary things like space, like time, like privacy, like making choices of my own, like knowing I could love, like believing I could learn, like sensing what was right and wrong. When she told me I was vain, I thought she meant I looked too often in the mirror. I couldn't know yet that she meant I grasped "in vain" for what could not last, even if what I grasped to hold was my own idea of God.

It didn't occur to me to leave that place. It did occur to me that I must fight even my own soul in order to stay.

I had a terrifying intuition that I had lost the very God I had come to the convent to find.

For two years I lived like this. No one taught me that I might be reacting to a normal contemplative experience. In the Carmelite tradition it would be called the Dark Night of the Senses. If I'd entered a contemplative community, I might have been counseled differently when the loss of the sensate experiences of the More seemed to me to be the real loss of God. Instead my sisters were trained to serve an active role in the church, as teachers and nurses. Prayer would support that mission. Our Novice Mistress discouraged any inclination I showed towards a mystical or contemplative life, telling me I tended towards too much vanity for that. The less I understood what she probably meant, the more I turned away from my natural calling which resulted in a life that grew smaller until it almost disappeared.

I stood in the novitiate hallway looking like all the others, a small young face swathed in white linen, head veiled in black wool, body clothed in black robes. Inside, a gaping emptiness. Instinct insisted no one was to know about this. God knew, if God existed. I wouldn't give up belief. God must have cloaked himself. All of this must be for my own good--could I keep a secret between us? Wasn't I to be the bride of Christ? This could be a wedding game. How well could I convince the others I felt joyful, calm, loving, prayerful?

I straightened my back and lifted my head. I would walk like a queen.

What can we do when life confuses us? The life of the spirit has its own process that can move at odds with the life of the mind or even the life of the soul. At the same time that I felt confusion in spirit, I was growing intellectually and felt excitement over my discovery of some creative abilities in myself—advances in understanding of literature, philosophy, music, and a delight in writing both poetry and prose. A similar blossoming seemed evident in my sisters, and I felt drawn to them to share our ideas, our talents, our hopes and dreams. We wrote poetry to one another.

We had classes in scripture, spiritual living, the holy rule, Gregorian chant, philosophy, logic, metaphysics, but we became to one another like runes carved in stone, a forbidden language. On a summer afternoon another novice and I knelt in the long rows of string beans, picking and filling our aprons. We were talking about some topic from one of our classes, and I asked her if she, personally, had ever experienced God that way, or prayer that way, or whatever the topic had laid out before us. "We aren't permitted to share that sort of thing," she reminded me.

I didn't realize it then, but I needed a teacher who could pull it all together for me, could unite rather than separate, could find for me a binding thread. There is an orthodox icon of Mary's annunciation celebrated these days by the Sisters of the Red Thread. Mary is holding a spindle of red yarn when the angel encounters her. The red thread trails from the spindle up through her other hand and points to the God Child in the womb of her heart. I needed someone to show me that the solution I'd hit upon—to close the door of my heart—could never work in the realm of the soul or of the spirit. It could never be my calling. Openness, unity had to characterize my spiritual path, and many of the novitiate rules and practices might have set me on a lonely, rocky and even dangerous detour.

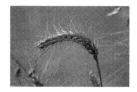

REMEMBER THE FIFTH BELOVED

- That you would call her "Joy," and she would call you *"Deo Gratias."*
- That she would call you to her side and you would go to her.
- That she would be a visionary, that she would whisper her visions in your ear, that her descriptions would be vivid and beyond the wild of nature or the invisibility of God, that she would smile and tell you to see.
- That she would open Thomas Merton, Gerard Manley Hopkins, Gertrude von le Forte, Emily Dickinson, and T.S. Eliot, and drop their words into your soul; that you would catch your breath and love her for the gift of them.
- That she would dissolve the rules and extol wisdom, the knowledge gleaned from love.
- That she would carve a path away from that of the Second Beloved, and you would walk that path gladly for three years. That she would plant you in the future before the future could come true. That you would begin to live in her dream.
- That when you needed an even deeper dream, she would send you away.
- That you would lie on the floor of your little convent room and weep with what you feared might be the loss of her.

YOUR WORDS FOUND AN ECHO IN MY HEART
AND I FOUND MYSELF SAYING INTERIORLY
"YES — AMEN."
                                        -Sister Marie Schwan

Sometimes these days, when I write of my convent years, I dream of returning. I imagine myself, not back with the Sisters of St. Joseph, but at the Redwoods Monastery on the Lost Coast of California where the Cistercian women worship with their lives, their prayer, their study, their work of gardening and spinning honey, their mysticism. These nuns remind me of Sister Marie.

If not for her, I would wonder if I had simply joined the wrong group of religious women. I knew nothing of the differences in religious orders when I was seventeen. I went to the Sisters of St. Joseph who served in Baudette, an active congregation of teachers and nurses. Contemplative nuns, on the other hand, devote their lives to prayer. The Cistercian is a living prayer, a poem of God in a silent space where each woman is one clear word. If one of them were to read that last sentence, she would probably laugh at my romanticism. "Christin Weber knows better than that, she would say. It's her nostalgia speaking."

I look out my window at the mountains, the woods. I feel my solitude and realize that right here I already have a hermitage such as Thomas Merton, the famous contemplative monk, mystic, and writer from Gethsemane Abbey in Kentucky, hoped to build on the coast not far from that women's monastery I regard with my romantic turn of mind. Have I returned to my beginnings already? When I do think of the beauty of convent years, I don't think of my professionally active years as an educator; rather, I remember those more nun-like, cloistered years of prayer and study at the motherhouse with Sister Marie.

Finding a teacher for the mystic journey is never easy. Most often the teacher isn't found at all; the teacher appears. Her name was Marie. She was an opener of doors. The doors she opened finally led me out of the convent, but she would not like knowing that. Her dearest wish was for me to be a spiritual daughter to whom she would pass on a spiritual legacy and maybe even the destiny she foresaw for herself. It was her own, that destiny, and she has fulfilled it.

The teaching began with metaphor. She pointed out the daisies blowing in the field above the river, the red leaf caught in an ice flow, a thorn bush with red berries, and she wove these natural experiences together with the poetry she taught, the philosophy, the theology. She gave the words a tone of her own experience and mine, and of the mind itself. My sense of mind changed, my sense of the word's power changed, and the world within and around me was transformed.

That autumn all the whispers around the motherhouse were of her return. Few of our sisters went on to post graduate education in those days, but she was so intelligent, the superiors had sent her on for her Master of Arts degree at Notre Dame. Now she was to become the director of education for the newly professed sisters.

"I'm glad of it," one of my classmates, Sister Mary Francis, told me. We had our veils tied back and our aprons on over our pinned up habits while we worked outside in the yard. She went on to say that if the novitiate had lasted any longer she wouldn't have been able to tolerate it. "I hated the way Mother Celine picked on you. Why didn't you stand up to her?" I remembered how Mary Francis had done just that one day, not for herself, but for me.

Maybe I told her that all of us got picked on. Maybe I told her I was scared of the woman. Maybe I shrugged. Mother Celine had only a short time to transform us from post-war rock 'n roll teens into young women dedicated to a mid-seventeenth century way of life. How could she do it? Barring some seismic shift she would have succeeded as she had with numerous classes of novices over the years.

No one expected anything to change. But change came. The old Pope Pius XII died and the now sainted John XXIII was elected by a consistory of cardinals who, it is said, thought him old, an interim pope, harmless. But he was an earthquake. Mother Celine's time really had been too short before church renewal would toss us, unprepared, into the midst of the twentieth century where our duty would be not to keep our eyes off the newspaper, but rather to "read the signs of the times."

Sister Mary Francis said she was looking forward to having Sister Marie as a teacher. I wasn't. She was too young (27), too pretty, and too modern. She scared me in ways diametrically opposite to Mother Celine's. At least Mother Celine's directives were clear even when they seemed impossible or simply ridiculous. But I had no idea what Sister Marie expected of us—no idea at all.

I did what I still do when I'm not sure of someone. I took a step back and watched. She taught classes both in the novitiate and to the newly professed like me. The black veils of novices and young professed fluttered around her. I took another step back. She sat at the head of our table in the refectory (dining room) and would ask us afterwards for critique of whatever book was being read while we ate. Often she disagreed with the author. One evening after supper she took me into the library and handed me a copy of Thomas Merton's *Seven Storey Mountain*, saying that she sensed I disagreed with the more pedestrian author of the table-reading just as she had. She opened this book (forbidden reading according to Mother Celine, but she was no longer my superior) to the elegant and intimate section at the end:

You will be praised, and it will be like burning at the stake. You will be loved, and it will murder your heart and drive you into the desert.

You will have gifts, and they will break you with their burden. You will have pleasures of prayer, and they will sicken you and you will fly from them.

And when you have been praised a little and loved a little I will take away all your gifts and all your love and all your praise and you will be utterly forgotten and abandoned and you will be nothing, a dead thing, a rejection. And in that day you shall begin to possess the solitude you have so long desired. And your solitude will bear immense fruit in the souls of people you will never see on earth.

The words fell hot on my mind. I took a deep breath. "How did you know?" I asked.

Know what? Probably I didn't know, myself, except that the words fit into a strangely shaped hollow in me where nothing had ever fit before.

Her knowledge of me began to feel more dangerous than if she'd had none. I fell back a greater distance. The farther in the distance I stayed, the closer I felt. One day I was dry-mopping the

92

hallway outside her office, and she called my name. I pretended I didn't hear, so she stepped out and told me to lean my mop against the wall and come inside. What is wrong? She wanted to know. Nothing is wrong, I lied. Something is wrong, she lowered her voice and smiled. "Kneel." she said. Is this kneeling a thing with superiors? Does it always come to this? I knelt. She was sitting in her chair. What she said is lost to memory, but the theme went something like this: It's not just okay to love, it is the fundamental law of God. She knew I loved her, and she loved me, too. This love was happening in God for God. I should not fear it.

Then she unpinned her profession crucifix from her habit and held it out for me to kiss. I kissed the feet of Jesus. She kissed those same feet and returned the crucifix to its place as part of her habit.

I returned to my mopping. What had just happened? Some momentous shift had taken place, a fundamental change that had no words but felt permanent. What had no word then now has a word I recognize. The word is *erotic.*

Only much later in my life would I be introduced to C.S. Lewis's treatise on *The Four Loves.* And even later than that would I experience a lecture by Brian Swimme and Matthew Fox in which the entire universe would be presented as erotic, drawn into further and further creation by a fundamental and irresistible attraction. Only by a false reductionism in popular thought and language would eros be limited to sexuality. In mythology, when Eros visits Psyche (the soul) in the night, it is not literally for sex, but rather to awaken what is limitless in the soul. Eros is the son of Aphrodite, goddess of love and beauty, of art and creation. Eros sets the soul searching even the most barren of places, even the desert, for the Source of Life itself. Eros is what prompts the cry of the mystical author of *The Cloud of Unknowing* as she awakens to God through "the drawing of this Love."

Sister Marie and I began to live vicariously through literature, drama and music the various human relationships. She was the Mother and I was Amahl when we listened to Menotti's opera. She was Violaine to my Mara in Claudel's *Tidings Brought to Mary.* She pointed me towards Hopkins's poetry, especially his sonnets which articulated his own desire and despair. They felt like mirrors. In this way Sister Marie opened an inner door that I'd locked with a key of fear in the novitiate, and she restored the gift of love and freedom for creation to my soul.

She reconnected me with the beauty and wildness of the natural world. Our motherhouse was fronted by fields of wheat and barley and set against a small wooded grazing land. Alongside ran the Red River of the North. In summer the wind raised clouds of dust blowing in from the Dakotas and the fields sang the song of crickets. Wheat waved like golden surf on a prairie lake and heat shimmered at its tips. The chrysalis of the monarch hung from milkweed plants, and meadowlarks accompanied with song the flight of swallows over the fields.

At first, for all its abundance and beauty, the prairie was barren for me and God seemed absent from its vastness. But after walking through those fields with Sister Marie, I would be claimed by that prairie-god so strongly that years afterwards—now, today—the memory of that wide sky and rolling wheat opens in my heart a wound left over from a time of yearning for the wideness of everything that exists and for a time of believing that eventually, if I could be true enough, would be the mirror of my own soul.

We met in small rooms or in pathless woods where stinging nettle grew along the river by the ancient linden and the fire-hollowed elm. Words connected us, not touch. She asked me if I understood the cost of love. I knew she hoped my answer would be no.

Sister Marie also reconnected me with the beauty of religious community life—with the religious "house" itself. I wrote:

"Golden home, proud home rising from the prairie, our blood and tears made mortar for the shaping of your body, and our singing, the whisper of your soul. Before the dawn the music fills your heart and as the sun rises, melody flows from you to drift above the waving wheat and mix with the breeze. I walk your halls and can identify the voices in your walls. They laugh and cry and whisper secrets only nuns can understand. Our bodies coexist; your open rooms and hidden corners parallel the spaces and the crevices of our selves. I realize that your voices have become the voices of my heart, my tears the distillation of your longing, my cries your frustration over longings unfulfilled. In the twilight I stand beside your door. A cooling breeze lifts my long veil. Across the field where the wheat has ripened and been harvested a full moon rises and the meadowlark sings her final song of the day."

Sister Marie and I wrote poems to one another casting me as John the Beloved and her as John the Baptist. Out of this came my barely veiled poem to her titled, "John."

THIS MAN CAME AS A WITNESS...
I loved you:
> *Younger than a tender blade of wheat in spring*
> *I laid my life within your hands*
> *And with a tenderness born out of discipline*
> *You formed me*
> *And I grew.*

I loved you:
> *You were my soul's father and its mother:*
> *You touched me with a little water*
> *And I was plunged in God.*
> *You were a burning lamp*
> *And the Light within you drew me.*

I loved you:
> *I had to follow you*
> *Although I somehow felt you feared this thing;*
> *"I am not the Christ," you said,*
> *But your eyes spoke of the Desert,*
> *Of the wonder of the Desert.*
> *You sang*
> *Of one who would come after you,*
> *Yet set high above you.*
> *Joy held your heart in peace*
> *In knowing He would take your place . . .*
> *I did not know, could not know, but*

I loved you:

> *One morning*
> *At the silent elevation of the Sun*
> *That day when most I loved. . .*
> *Day when I saw you,*

Lamp of the Light,
Day when I heard you speak,
Voice for the Word . . .
"Behold. . . Behold the Lamb,"
Day
Day when
I left you
For Him,
And your joy was made full.
From your hands and your "Behold"
To His word "Come"
And for the Love-Fire of His Heart
I left you.

There is a desert in His eyes.
You live in Him more wholly
Than in your very self.
There I found you.
You who taught me love by sending me away:
Because of the nets on a white beach
Because of a storm and a light on the sea
Because of a vineyard, a wine-press, a ripe field of wheat
Because of a mountain
Because of a valley
Because of a rock in a desert
and a child made a man at the foot of a tree
Because of midnight
Because an old man died on an island
Because of these things:

I love you.

The wisdom of the Father
Becomes a Word:

JOHN BORE WITNESS CONCERNING HIM, AND CRIED,
"THIS WAS HE OF WHOM I SAID,
'HE WHO IS TO COME AFTER ME

HAS BEEN SET ABOVE ME,
BECAUSE HE WAS BEFORE ME.'"

AND WE SAW HIS GLORY
GLORY AS OF THE ONLY BEGOTTEN OF THE FATHER
AND WE SAW HIS GLORY
FULL OF GRACE AND OF TRUTH,
AND WE SAW HIS GLORY
HIS GLORY
HIS GLORY!
                    -John

No longer were there restrictions on my reading, and I began to explore the works of Therese of Lisieux, and Elizabeth of the Trinity. Both of these women had made special offerings of themselves to God, and I felt compelled to do the same. The intimacy of this offering or opening of my soul to God felt on a different plane from that of my vows—far more personal. I would completely surrender myself to the divine love of God, to be used however God wished, even as a substitute for those who could not bring themselves to love or who refused love altogether. Granted, I had no idea what this implied. It was such a leap, completely counter-intuitive. In later years I would discover its corollary in the Buddhist practice of tonglen: breathing in the suffering of the world, surrounding it with spaciousness and compassion, and breathing out the gift of peace. In those early years, though, I had no awareness of Buddhism, and only the slightest realization existed in me of a connection between this offering and my first spiritual experience: "With Christ I am nailed to the cross, and I live now, not I, but Christ lives within me."

My training had taught me that such an offering required the permission of my spiritual guide and superior—now Sister Marie. The wisdom of centuries recognized the dangers inherent in such an act because it would form the mind, the psyche, the soul and spirit of the person. It would affect the identity for good or ill. Spiritual pride could result, so an act of humility would be needed to counter that tendency and assure that the inspiration came from the Spirit of God and not simply from my own imagination or worse, from a hidden need to be exalted.

It was winter, just past my birthday in November. I was twenty-one. Sister Marie and I were driving through the snow on the way from the motherhouse to St. Joseph's Academy in downtown Crookston. I chose this moment to ask her permission. The atmosphere in the car was one of "Are you sure?" She may even have said those very words along with other, more specific, questions. She didn't say yes. Her questions probed and my spirit felt bare and vulnerable. She couldn't say yes; not yet. Wait and pray.

How long did I wait? A week? Two? Time enough to weave hope and surrender into one. Perhaps Sister Marie consulted others; I don't know. The snow continued to fall on the fields and in the woods. We walked the paths where red berries clung to thorn bushes, and she spoke to me of God's love and how it transcended human love to a point that we sometimes didn't recognize it as love at all. Whether I remember all of this, or whether it is an understanding that evolved in me over the years, I don't know. But I associate with her the belief that divine love, by our human standards, isn't always kind. The love of God enters our suffering not to remove it, but to suffer along with us. Look at Jesus on the cross. "When you see me, you see the Father," he had said. The fullness of God as divine love hung on that cross. The Trinity cannot be divided. This was not the Father sacrificing the Son; this was divine love in the fullness of the Trinity surrendering to human suffering, living it to the utmost in the humanness of Jesus, so that forever-after we would never be alone.

One day close to Thanksgiving she called me into her office and gave permission for me to make the offering to divine love. "I thought you might want to do this at Mass on Thanksgiving Day," she smiled. It would be November twenty-third, the day before my anniversary of baptism on what was then the feast day of St. John of the Cross.

The choir had practiced psalm 107 as a communion hymn for that day, and Sister Hildegard had asked me to sing the cantor's part. I'd written out my offering and made a cloth pouch in order to wear it close to my heart. The choir filed down from the loft to receive communion first and then we made our thanksgiving in prayer while the other sisters approached the communion railing. My offering to divine love became my thanksgiving on that Thanksgiving Day. Then we all stood. I stood at the front of the choir loft so that my voice would not be lost, but would carry out into the large chapel. "Oh give thanks to the Lord for He is good..." I sang, and the choir responded, "For His great love is without end."

We do things when young, when innocent, that later we might not dare to do. What I did that day in response to what I believed was the call of God, still works itself out in my life over fifty years later. Although it wasn't pure, wasn't perfect, lacked humility, contained a yearning for something in my life I knew no other way to find, still God used it in ways beyond my imagination and even my faith. It is to this day a central mystery, a question put to all my life experience and to every choice. How is love calling now? What must I surrender?

The possibility that Marie presented for continuing in this way of yearning and love was somewhat paradoxically contained in the intellectual life. We read the philosopher, Sertillanges—

Begin by creating within you a zone of silence, a habit of recollection, a will of renunciation and detachment which puts you entirely at the disposal of work; acquire that state of soul unburdened by desire and self-will which is the state of grace of the intellectual worker. Without that you will do nothing, at least nothing worthwhile.

Here was a container open and strong enough to hold the emotion, the desire for The Holy, the mystery of the fire lily, and especially the often meaningless rules. Perhaps here was an overarching rule that could absorb all the rest in a silence and divine knowing that could bring me to God.

To the intellectual life, Marie linked the brilliant spiritual writings of Elizabeth of the Trinity, her hymns to silence, and her profound offering to the "Trinity Whom I adore." She gave us Gerald Vann's *Eve and the Griffin* that opened my eyes to the sacredness of the feminine, Gertrude von le Forte's *Song at the Scaffold* and *Hymns to the Church* that in their beauty amazed my soul. She delivered into my mind the spiritual/theological poetry of T.S. Eliot which has haunted me all my life. She read poems from ee cummings that fascinated me with his mysticism of image and language structure, and Emily Dickinson, who captured my soul with deceptive simplicity.

Was the intellectual life my new path to God? At the time it seemed so. I read the poets and philosophers, linked my emerging identity to their thoughts and words, began to believe in a unity between those thoughts and my own being.

She told me she'd been pinned to a fire-charred tree to still her heart while a silver lark drew from her throat a chant of exploding stars and brandywine. She pointed out the tree, an old creature the loggers of the last century had allowed to stand. Its roots clung to a riverbank eroded by each spring's breakup. Its insides were exposed. Its secret roots, the large taproot and tangle of vine-like clingers wrapped around whatever they could find: large stones, the roots of younger trees. Life requires a creature to remain standing. Above ground, seen from the path, the tree's heart also was exposed, blackened by fire. "I've seen myself hanging there," she told me.

I think now of the Madonna of Czestochowa with her sword-scared face also blackened by fire. If I could hear her song, what would it be? And what, over the years, has become the song of Marie? To what has she clung while her heart smolders? To what is she pinned as the song is extracted from her throat?

The image of the Black Madonna tree fascinated me at the time. I imagined Marie pinned there, singing, while stars flew from her mouth, new stars to adorn the heavens. I saw her crucified there, drunk with the bitter wine of failed love. Love that does all it can and is no more than an icon trampled underfoot, speared with the soldier's lance.

We all are there. I didn't understand that then. We all are pinned upon that tree, the Black Madonna, insides exposed, heart charred, face scarred, mouths open, silent, awaiting the arrival of the lark.

Sister Marie eroded outdated traditions with the persistence of rain. She believed in us even when the Mothers thought us incapable. Ordinarily on the Feast of Holy Innocents, December 28th, the youngest sisters would present an entertaining skit for the recreation of all the professed nuns. That year she wanted to present a completely different kind of play—the complex drama created from Gertrude von le Forte's story, *A Song At The Scaffold,* about a community of

100

Carmelite nuns who were guillotined during the French Revolution. The superiors tried to dissuade her: It's too difficult for such young women. It's too painful. It has a depth of spirit they haven't reached. You'll fail. It could hurt them, throw them into a spiritual crisis for which they aren't prepared. You don't have the resources and equipment to put on such a performance. You'll make a fool of yourself as well as of them. But in the end, Sister Marie prevailed.

She typecast us. As the years passed some of us would marvel at the way we were living out the script because we possessed the personality of the roles we played. I'd hoped for one of the major roles but was given only a bit part along with the job of assistant director. Years later Sister Marie would confide that she had intended to form me into a vision she had for me, and I would follow her footsteps in the religious community as she had followed in the footsteps of her own beloved teacher, Sister Agnes. I think I sensed her intention even at the time. And although years later I would chaff at what seemed too controlling, at the time her intentions made me happy.

My heart sang all that year with a sense of freedom enhanced by memories of its opposite—the strictures imposed by novitiate life under Mother Celine. No sign of my obsessive scrupulosity remained, and I began to delight in the cloistered life as I had dreamed I would back when I was a child. I delighted in my sisters and their talents. Sister Innocent came to the door of my room with her art—a face of Jesus done in pastels—and placed it in my hands. A gift beyond words, she offered it a bit shyly. I could disappear into those eyes of the Christ, deeper than an icon's. I gazed on her artwork. The silence of those eyes went on forever. I would never reach the end.

What were my faults back then? Jealousy. Greed. I wanted all of everything that bore the marks of love. All of Sister Marie's time. All her insight and dreams. Everything she knew of God. Paradoxically I wanted a spirit of surrender, to give it all away, to give *her* away—a gift that large to present before God. But when I looked out my window to see her walking down the path with another sister, I wanted to BE that sister just to hear what holy secrets they might be sharing. I tried to welcome my heart's hunger, offering it to the Beloved Lord, to the Divine Love incarnate.

After a few months Sister Innocent knocked again at my door and asked me to give back the picture with the eyes of Christ. "It's too painful," she explained. "I need to destroy it. No one should have to look into those eyes." I argued, but she won, and the image was lost to something secreted away in her heart. As Sister Marie called me *Deo Gratias*, and herself Joy, she called Sister Innocent *Agnus Dei*, or Lamb of God. In doing this she named an essential part of that young woman's soul.

Spring arrived. The Red River of the North broke and crashed past the motherhouse, gigantic plates of ice upended, uprooting trees and carrying them off with a deafening roar. Sister Marie and I walked along the path in the woods where a pond was fed by a little stream running under clear ice towards the churning river. A red maple leaf had caught on bright green moss, spotlighted by a ray of sunlight through the ice. She would later write:

There is a pond, my heart,
Arteried in crystal, holding
Sky and earth in fragile glass.

Sun-soul breathes tears
That glow, grow and gather
To a giving...given.

It is early April.
        -Joy

...I just returned from a walk, and now there is no trace except for a little hollow—full of a prayerful memory that lives in gratitude and joy in Him.

Rest in Him in simple trust. You belong to God.
        In Him,
                Sister Marie

On that original visit we stopped to gaze. I felt we shared a common heart, saw every minute wonder of creation in the same way—as filled

102

with God. A drop of water holds mystery, I thought. A song I sang while in high school came to mind, a Celtic love song with a beautiful melody. New words began to form to fit that melody. At first I meant them only for Sister Marie, but later realized that they expressed a wider experience. All of us. She'd brought all of us together into a sacred time. We sang it together many times over the following years.

Together we walked through a daisy field,
We've known the wind on a hill,
A drop of water holds mystery
God lives in the silent and still.
Together we sought Him in everything,
Together we found Him, until
We've known peace and joy
In His love which unites us,
We've known peace and joy in His will.

The following year I was sent to college in Wisconsin. Sister Marie wrote every week. One letter in particular moves me almost to tears, now as I write, fifty years later:

Home . Eve of Our Lady of Lourdes
1963

Dear Sister in Christ,
	Tonight I have just reread "John"—and it is as new and as dear—no, more so—than it was a year ago. Tonight—and tomorrow— is the anniversary of its writing, as somehow it seems especially appropriate to be near you in Spirit this evening.
	I hear my little Sister saying, "Speak to me about God." That does bring joy. Reread "John." I have never wanted to do anything but that— to speak to you of Him, or rather—daring as it might seem—to somehow let Him speak to you, through me when it was His Will.
	Again tonight... "Behold...the Lamb of God," the Heart of Christ. Sister, when those waves of darkness come, know that He is asking you to rest in His Heart—to know something of His poignant pain of love for souls. Receive Him without the consolations, without the spiritual pleasure. In other words, receive Him. I know you accept all. Accept your

103

weakness, too—and offer it lightly and with a smile (!)—because if He did not love weakness, He would surely never have become human, never let Himself become a fragile bit of Bread. Let your desire carry you to Him.

The thought that comes to me now as I write this is, "I will to be one who holds nothing back." (I think it is from [the novel] JOY.)But Sister, only He can accomplish this total openness in each of us. "Bend the rigid; melt the cold." And I have confidence that He will. This is really joy, too high for laughter, too deep for tears —and how near we are to each other.

. . . Tonight, I will renew a gift—the only one you have ever asked for—as I offer to Him (and in and with Him) my Gratitude.
In this is my joy—and yours—made full.

With love in His Heart,
Sister Marie

The way she educated my mind, opened my heart—How did she do that? Later, when I read Rilke's *Letters To A Young Poet*, I wondered if she'd taken her style from him. She defined wisdom as love-knowledge, and as years have passed life has taught me slowly what this means. She hadn't quoted Rilke's recommendation to "love the questions themselves," but by the time I read Rilke, I recognized the truth in what he said. It's not even that Marie could do this for herself. She lived, as I did, tangled in her many thoughts. But she stopped with me to gaze at the field of daisies or to stand in the blustery wind unable to look away from the red leaf caught in a gleam of ice. She put the thorn I gave her at the feet of Mary's statue on her desk. In these ways we had a beginning together in the art of mystery, in the practice of contemplation, on the road to wisdom.

Love. Love the questions. Love the wind. Love not knowing what lies behind a person's eyes. Love the wide space of mind, the yearning heart. Love having nothing or holding something. It seems it shouldn't be difficult to learn these things, but it is, because thoughts, however sure of their position, keep slipping away.

Soul, could you love your face in the mirror the day of your betrayal? Could you love your hands slick with the blood of your dying love? Could you love the blood itself? Could you love the echoes of "why" through empty spaces? Could you love the knife that cut? the last note of the final song? Beyond "could," should you?

Eliot calls it "a lifetime's death in love." Only when there is nothing left to hold can you know what it was that once you did hold, because now you've loved it well enough to let it go.

Into her hands I placed
A bird with a broken wing,
A basket of daisies from the field
A thorn shaped like a cross,
A piece of flint the color of her eyes
A poem in which I said goodbye.

I buried her in a box of driftwood and shells
I sprinkled rose petals and holy water
I drilled a little hole in my heart to release what still remained
I walked the road of trees and vines alone
I wrote her words on stones and dropped them along the way
I said a prayer as I went: I will not miss you...
I will not...

New students came to her. We saw one another for an hour now and then, when she visited all the young sisters enrolled in the university or when we took the train back to the motherhouse for a holiday. I kept the letters she wrote to me, letters filled with ideas because although we spoke of love-knowledge, neither of us yet knew the degree of sacrifice and surrender implied in that wisdom-path.

But now, I do.

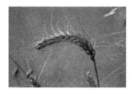

REMEMBER THE TIME OF SOLITUDE

- That your place is on the threshold between two worlds.
- That the worlds conflict, and you must hold that conflict in your mind and gaze upon it.
- That you will have no close confidants.
- That the light of God will dim.
- That your own light will dim and that you will have difficulty remembering your name. You will wonder how to find your way back home.
- That you and your mama share this threshold but not the words that could bring comfort and understanding.

A LETTER FROM MAMA
The Wild Electric Typing Machine
Time: 11:00 A.M., October 10, 1963
Place: Office of Mr. Sherwood

Mama now owned The Store of Lore which once had been Grandma's souvenir shop on Main Street in Baudette, Minnesota. She sold gifts and souvenirs to tourists vacationing on Lake of the Woods. When autumn weather blew in from the north, the tourists went back to Iowa, Illinois and Texas, and business slacked off until local Christmas shopping revved it up again. Between times she worked two hours each morning at the office of Baudette's attorney.

On this day he had no work for her to do and suggested she practice on his new "wild electric typing machine," a more touchy contraption than her Smith Corona. Her entire letter laughs with a repeated "k" produced by her middle right hand finger resting on the key while she pondered her next word. She practiced by writing to me at college, now in my senior year and student teaching at St. Wenceslas School in LaCrosse.

You are probabkly kk aklot smarter than most of the tekeachers you had here when you were in seventh and eighth grade, so you realky k shouldn*t be frightened.

I can hear her laughter. She goes on and on with family news and town gossip, all jiggling with those wild "k"s. Some people actually laugh that way, I think as I read, their bellies popping up and down, the "k-k-k-k-k-k-k-k" sound in the back of their throats.

Now I look at the laughing letter and suddenly realize that she was teasing me out of my fears. In a flash of vision I see the two of us connected by the words, across hundreds of miles, across boundaries of generations, across the years, beyond even death. She's in the law office, I am here, both of us with our fingers on the keys.

Mama had written to me at least once a week the entire time I was in the convent, but this is the first of the letters I saved after the one she wrote in pencil about Dad's crash of the 180 Cessna. Two whole years had passed, and all her letters from those years are lost. But this laughing letter has survived. Its crazy-k's invite me into paradox of time and space, and into wonder at how moments in life and the experiences that shape our souls might connect.

Where was I that October day, though, and why was I afraid?

I take myself back to the small bedroom on the fifth floor of Viterbo College. Maybe I'd just put down the book of poems by ee cummings. Maybe I'd just finished reading the one that pays attention to the syntax of things, when I opened her letter and began to laugh over her crazy-k's. Outside the window, bright yellow maple leaves detached and floated to the ground. I'd been walking in those leaves the day before with Sister Innocent. Her talk was crazy-talk. I was spending much of my study time that autumn listening to her and growing increasingly afraid.

All these years later I realize that Sister Innocent was experiencing a falling away of something in her that was essential to her happiness. What did I know then of the way hearts can shatter and minds can follow? What did I know of Sister Innocent? Very little more than nothing. Did I connect the darkness that seemed to gather around and within her to the icon of Christ she'd once given and taken away? Those haunted eyes? She excelled at every art: music, poetry, painting, prayer. But what is concealed behind a sister's linen-framed face? All of us were taught to walk alike, to speak in modulated tones, to keep our eyes downcast. Our souls we kept secret, and the soul's shadow we hid most securely of all. But a harsh light can cast a shadow so deep it cannot be concealed.

That October when she looked into my eyes it was to explain to me how she would gouge them out. "I've been planning it for a long time," she said. I was sitting at that desk in my tiny room where I'd been maybe reading cummings and looking at the yellow leaves. "I know what you are doing," she said. "You are seeing into me."

On the bluffs above LaCrosse the thorn trees grew. We'd hiked there on Sundays earlier that autumn. The thorns grew long, three inches, and each of them had three points. When broken off the tree the thorn was a perfect cross. "I'm going to use a thorn cross to get rid of your eyes." She said all this in her perfectly modulated convent-voice.

One night I awoke to see her standing beside my bed looking down at me. My body went cold. My scalp tingled. "Come with me," she said. She took my hand and pulled me out of bed. Usually we would

108

have worn white night veils if we left our cells, but she hadn't bothered with that. Our long nightgowns swished around our bare feet as we walked together through the dim light to her destination. Her short hair lay flat against her head.

She drew me into the large closet where the Sisters kept their trunks. We sat down facing each other. I saw that one of my favorite of her paintings had been hidden under a hastily applied coat of flat white. "I've destroyed my paintings. You'll never know when I will destroy you too."

I'm not seeing into you, I wanted to say. I can't. I don't want to. But my fear that night was too great.

It was into this terror that Mama's laughing letter came. I hadn't told her about Sister Innocent, but I must have packed all my fear into stories of student teaching. I must have transposed my fear of being killed into fear of facing thirty eighth graders required to read and discuss *Great Expectations.* After the night Sister Innocent took me to the trunk closet, I finally wrote to Sister Marie about my fears and that I didn't know how to deal with the situation which until then I'd kept completely secret. Would she believe me? Had any of the other sisters studying with us that year noticed? Even Mama, months later, would confide, "And all along I thought SHE was the strong one."

It was traditional for superiors to make "visitation" coming to each community in order to share news and prayer and to assess the climate or spirit of the house. After receiving my letter, Sister Marie notified us she would be making such a visitation. In just a few days she arrived by train. I don't know what I thought she might do— maybe wave a magic wand and fix it, fix us, fix whatever was going wrong with Sister Innocent. She arranged to meet with each of us, maybe eight in all. At lunch Sister Innocent whispered to me that she knew what I was up to, and then she shot angry looks in my direction throughout the meal. Afterwards she disappeared.

Acid filled my stomach. What if she killed herself? I'd been so worried she might kill me, but what if it really was herself she wanted gone? Sister Marie sent all the other young sisters to look for her. They were to be nonchalant if they ran across her and not try to bring her back. She shouldn't know that she was being sought. It might scare her further away. I would stay in my room in case she came back while everyone else was gone.

One of the sisters found her kneeling behind a pillar in the Adoration Chapel.

Even to this day I can't begin to imagine how terrified she must have been, and how angry. She must have felt profoundly betrayed. Sister Marie took her away from college to a hospital in Minneapolis for evaluation and subsequent treatment. How was I supposed to love her, I wondered. How had she changed from the sewing box tease she'd been back in the times of Mother Celine, to become the tortured woman who left college on that day? I wrote "Poem for a Lost Sister."

Sky fell orange behind the hills
Brown again and barren.
The bird flew without song, and a hush
Fell through stripped branches.
She is gone.
But her colors
On the stretched canvas
Of my days
Remain.

Sister Marie wrote from Minneapolis:

...Believe me, there is no doubt that this was the right move. I was so relieved that the doctor realized so much, so quickly. . . Thank you again for your efforts, I know that God directed each word. Whatever happens now we must give God the gift of our total trust. Sister Innocent has been faithful too, and who knows? Perhaps outside of religious life she might never have received the help she has and is now receiving. And it is she as a person whom we love—and will always love.

And now—as your "little mother" and sister: Be sure to catch up on your rest. . . keep up your appetite and keep our little family happy!

Truly, we can best support our "lamb" now in the sacrifice through a calm, grateful and joyful abandonment in, and acceptance of his Love in each moment. Thank you.

Love,
Sister Marie

I haven't seen Sister Innocent for many years. Her superiors intervened, and after therapy she was told that there were "other ways to serve."

Today our lives intersect once again through Mama's laughing letter. Mama signs off:

It is time to go home now. (That last paragraph was really rough.) I*ll master this machine yet, if I cankjust rememberkwhere the apostrophe is located.

I laugh out loud. What was that poem? The ee cummings poem that I might or might not have been reading when her letter first arrived on my convent-college desk in 1963? The one about the syntax of things? I push back from my computer table and go to the bookcase. I'm thinking of Sister Innocent, how she wanted to be a Sister of St. Joseph, but was told to return to her home. I'm thinking of Mama, how much she wanted to be a writer, but ended up owning a gift shop, working part time for a lawyer, helping Dad at the airport, and mothering two girls. I'm thinking of Sister Innocent and wondering where she might be today. I'm thinking of life, and how it doesn't necessarily, in fact almost never can, work out the way we think or hope it will. We stumble sometimes and get trapped in a paradox. We struggle and life becomes wild in us. And yet, wild as it is, it does work out in some kind of perfect syntax. Here's the book. Here also is the poem. It begins:

Don't cry

A LETTER FROM MAMA
I don't suppose I will get to see you...
October 30, 1963

Even while the heart-splitting events with Sister Innocent were taking place, the letters between Mama and me continued. Just before Halloween that year, Mama wrote with an undercurrent of loneliness I might not have detected at the time. She often was alone. Dad had built a new hangar at his airport on the edge of town. *He practically lives out there—doesn't quit any night until after ten P.M.* Betsy was a high school freshman, a boarder at St. Joseph's Academy in Crookston. On the day she wrote this letter, sitting at her typewriter in her Store of Lore, she was thinking of her older daughter, also absent from her life for over five years. *Business at the store is very poor,* she typed, letting me know that no one had come in, maybe not all day.

Now I read this letter, wishing I could walk into her store that moment in the past and call out "Mama!" How we'd laugh! How we'd hug each other! How we'd jabber about our memories. We'd keep it up while climbing into her green Oldsmobile and hightailing it to the airport where I'd hug my dad and ooh and ahh over his new hangar with the long desired maintenance shop. And as long as I am wishing, I wish up Betsy also, and there she'd be, fresh from school and eager for Halloween. Dad would take us out to Al's Steak House. He'd buy us each a sixteen ounce New York steak and give the chef five dollars to cook it up just right.

I'm enclosing the pictures which Doretha took when you were here and we visited you at the hospital. I read the sentence several times. I was there? Home? My mind wanders backwards to a summer day I'd forgotten until this moment. For some reason now lost to me, I was at Trinity Hospital, run by our sisters in Baudette, kneeling in the strawberry patch behind the building. I was in Baudette but had no permission to visit with my family. Home visits happened once a year and lasted a day. Even Sister Marie was unable to dispense me from that rule. I'd gone to Baudette for some other reason, and I don't remember what it might have been. What I do remember is the heat of the garden, the buzzing of mosquitoes at the folds of my black veil, and the odd sensation of being three blocks away from my house but unable to put down my bucket of strawberries, take off my apron and

112

walk or run those three blocks up to the front door, fling it open and cry out, "I'm home!"

The very culture and rules that had kept Mama from calling me two years before when Dad's airplane crashed, kept me that day from calling her. These rules, we had been told, had the power to create in us a perfect image of Christ. Looking back in memory at that young veiled sister kneeling in the strawberry patch, I can see how much effort she was putting into the attempt to believe such an irony. She could quote the scriptures that supported the rule: "Those who love mother or father...more than Me are not worthy..." I remember that she felt the emptiness and stinging behind the eyes that comes just before tears. But she would not cry.

How strange that what is perceived as fault from one perspective in our lives is seen as virtue from another. At that moment in the history of Catholicism we barely realized our predicament. We straddled what would become a chasm between the church we'd known all our lives and the church as it would be envisioned by the Second Vatican Council already taking place in Rome. For me the past and future of the church still felt completely personal and bore the names of Mother Celine, and Sister Marie.

Mother Geneva, the superior at the hospital, came out the back door and walked up to me. "Your mother is inside," she said. "I have decided to give her two hours with you. I have no authority to allow you to go home. But your mother is very kind to our sisters, and I've decided to grant her request to visit with you here."

Here. In "her" convent. She was captain of "this" ship and could do "here" what had been forbidden elsewhere.

I remember nothing of the visit itself, nor of my Aunt Doretha, only of the exquisite contradiction of discovering that Mama waited for me just inside the convent door. In memory I open the door and feel the rush of having and not having, of receiving and giving up, of promise and surrender: the paradox of all loneliness.

She must have felt it too; she must have been feeling it again that day before Halloween in her empty store, alone, her fingers clicking on the keys. She juxtaposes references to the two-hour summer visit with talk of the Thanksgiving holiday coming up, that my cousin Sally would be there, and Mama would have picked Betsy up in Crookston. *Having her and Betsy at home will be next best to having you and Betsy. Sal is really a lot like you and we will have fun. I wish that you could be here too. I don't suppose I will get to see you in Crookston either because we will pick up Betsy on Wednesday afternoon and you probably will arrive in Crookston Wednesday night—and leave again before we arrive there on Sunday.*

"I don't suppose I'll get to see you..." she took the rules of loneliness for granted by then. She and I no longer had charge of our relationship. The working out of the mother/daughter bond now took place within a structure of convent rules and authorities. She submitted. We both did. The more heartfelt world of Sister Marie still existed only within that rule-sustaining capsule. My cousin Sally would substitute for me on Thanksgiving, and for Mama her presence would be both sacrifice and gift. I'd be in Crookston on Thanksgiving break from college. Sister Marie would substitute in my life for my dear mama.

I read the whole letter yet again. Despite all obstacles to the physical presence in one another's lives, it was the love that mattered. That obstacles highlighted that love is the paradox. In that love all of us were not merely substituted for but superimposed upon each other and each person loved became a link to the presence of every other. Maybe that's best, I think now as I write. In the deepness of our being where individual intersects with and is transformed by divine Being, it must be most true. Maybe what caused me such suffering at the time of my father's plane crash, with its implications that any one of the other sisters could substitute for my presence and my love at my family's side, was my superficial response to a reality more profound than I yet could bear.

She looked up from her typing when the bell announced a customer, a child. *Just while I was writing this, a little boy came in— wanted a tiny bottle and nipple like they sell for dolls—he said they have four little kittens at home, and the mother cat has no milk, and the kittens are starving.*

I sit back in my chair and take my fingers from the keys. We made it work, though, didn't we? We made it work by looking up and seeing someone there, someone calling out for nourishment. I imagine how she might have taken that little boy in tow, because she would have had no doll-sized milk bottles in her shop, and led him down the block to the Ben Franklin store. I imagine how they searched together for this solution to the kittens' plight. Probably she bought it for him with coins from her own purse. And then she waved goodbye as he ran home to save some lives. By the time she got to the post office her loneliness had evaporated. She smiled as she dropped this letter through the slot for outgoing mail.

A LETTER FROM MAMA
Currency of Love
November 6, 1963

It was my twenty-third birthday. Mama commemorated it by writing a letter in which her thoughts are connected to a central concern that acts like the drawstring through the gathers of a coin purse. Reading her letter, I can't tell if she knew as she began to write just how worried she was. Later I wondered if she intended to reveal how overwhelmed she felt.

I imagine how this letter looked, placed diagonally in the little mailbox at the college. I imagine how I must have slit it open on my way back up the stairs to my room. It would have arrived a few days past my birthday, and beginning to read I still would have been feeling the love and attention bestowed on me that day by both the sisters and by Mama.

The sisters left holy cards by my plate in the refectory. They were our currency. Having no money to buy gifts for one another, we exchanged little cards decorated with pictures, prayers, or inspirational sayings. Each sister had a box—often a shoebox—in which the holy cards were organized. And to make sure we always had enough, the convent superior gave each of us a large stack of brand new ones each year at Christmas. Some of the older sisters became wealthy with the cards. Some sisters hoarded them. Some were lavish, five or more cards at a time tucked into a handmade envelope on which was written a personal message to cherish.

Mama's currency was of the larger world, and in 1963 she'd run short. The first clue that she didn't intend to trouble her sister-daughter with the family's financial difficulties is that she had ordered me a birthday cake. The cake was huge, enough for a whole dining room full of other sisters. The convent rules and culture forbade families to single out their daughters for gifts that didn't include everyone, but Mama determined that a birthday cake would be all inclusive. She did it every single year, not even listening to my superiors' discouragements. She refused to take into consideration what was obvious to all the sisters—that the cake did single me out, even when it was eaten by everyone. It arrived every year of my fourteen-year tenure, no matter where I lived or how many sisters

116

lived with me. Each year my superior called me aside to impress upon me yet again how unacceptable my mother's behavior was, and how I needed to convince her of this fact, after which I took up the unhappy task of pointing all this out to her. But birthday cakes kept right on arriving at the convent door the morning of November sixth. *I have had you on my mind frequently this day. I hope and pray you are enjoying it with your family of sisters. I am sure the cake arrived in plenty of time as yesterday I had a nice acknowledgment from the lady at the Bake Shop, and she assured me she would take care of it. I hope the lemon filling was to your liking.*

I can't help smiling as I copy down her words. How clear it was to her that she knew best, and that a mother's love along with the responsibilities accruing to it, trumped any convent rule or any religious superior's authority.

She also bought me a New Testament, a private and personal gift, and something each sister was permitted to keep among the things she used. We owned nothing. Technically, the book was given to the religious community for my use, and after receiving permission to use it, I could do that until it fell apart or I died. The point here, though, is that the money it cost her she made up by not purchasing a winter coat for herself. I don't remember putting all of that together at the time, even though the story of the coat occupies the paragraph following the one about the bible.

She and her friend, Evelyn had been to Crookston to return Betsy and Evelyn's daughter, Kath, to the academy after their Halloween weekend. They had dropped the girls off early in the morning and then gone off to Grand Forks to shop.

We got there when the stores opened, and we had fun shopping—but all I bought were a few things Betsy needed, and I got a pair of shoes for myself which I think I shall return. I had wanted a car coat but they were all $35 or $39, and I hated to part with the money, so I decided to get along until January and if I go down [to the Twin Cities] with George then, I will get one on sale for about $19. I am going to have that phony fur coat of mine cut off to make a car coat from it and it will do me here in Baudette.

Then, as if her fingers have been loosened by the talk of the coat she couldn't allow herself to buy, she flies off into talk about a bill she and my father have had introduced before the state legislature that

117

will result in reimbursement for losses they incurred two years before when Dad flew the coast guard rescue mission and lost the airplane that had provided them with much of their livelihood. She tells me she's been busy contacting local businessmen to write Senator Hubert Humphrey on Dad's behalf, to vote in favor of the bill. *Please pray that it will pass. It would be so wonderful to reduce our note at the bank by that amount. Just think—over a thousand dollars a year of our income goes just to pay interest on borrowed money. If we get that money to reduce our notes, we would have over half of the interest money to apply on principle, and soon we would be even with the world.*

A thousand dollars. It would have bought a fine new car in 1963. Mama confided later in her life that their largest annual income had been the year just before retirement that they grossed nine-thousand dollars.

Did I understand her financial concerns? Probably I did not. My convent vow of poverty had a paradoxical effect of removing me from the ordinary struggle to make ends meet. Certainly some of the sisters were saddled with money-matters. Sister Emma Joseph kept the books at the motherhouse. And every mission house assigned one sister to balance income with expense and send what remained to the motherhouse coffers. The rest of us never saw a paycheck, never paid a bill, never bought a meal, never paid a cent for our education, never wondered if we could afford our next meal, never questioned whether we would have a warm coat and shawl when winter came. We owned nothing and were given anything we really needed. Our commerce took the form of holy cards. Faith, not money, motivated our work. Mama and I lived in vastly different worlds.

She pulled the first sheet of paper from her Smith Corona and inserted another. Somewhere in the midst of that action, she began to think about death. Birthday/Deathday. I recognize her logic. Her mind collapsed the continuum. Her connections were vivid and often unexpected. She began to think of death partly because it was my birthday, and also because she was still working for the lawyer and people had been coming in to make their wills. These were people she'd known all her life, and she had been typing up directions for the dispersal of their property, recognizing their attempts at justice: their inclusions and exclusions of family members and friends. She began thinking of her own daughters, of Betsy and me. Betsy, still a child, and myself, the sister. She worried about Betsy.

As our will stands now, you know, it leaves what we have in equal shares to you and Betsy in the event of the loss of both your parents. You realize, I am sure, that she MUST receive a complete college education and be able to support herself adequately before there is any split made of the estate. To set this down in the will would involve legal entanglements – setting up a trust fund and guardian, etc. and the courts and guardian and attorney would each get a big slice. In the event that things happen now, we would like to think that the Order of St. Joseph would allow you to let your share stand until Betsy is educated and established, and then what is left over when she is of age and has a paying position, the balance of the estate would then be split—half for each of you. If, however, you, yourself, would have no control to arrange this, we will have to have it done legally with all the entanglements. Talk it over with someone when you get the chance—and let us know. At any rate, keep this letter for reference— we know you will respect our wishes in the matter.

A gloomy matter to write about—but better written than overlooked.

She dated it and signed her full name as one would a codicil. I kept it. Here it is, one of only three remaining letters from that year. At least I kept it. I don't know what else I did. I've an incomplete image of myself sitting in Mother Martha Mary's office talking about wills, but that might have been from the time just before my first vows when all of us were required to make our own wills, leaving every bit of our inheritance or other property to the religious community. It was a requirement of our membership.

I kept her letter. I like to think, that if the two of them had died while Betsy still was dependent upon them, I would have left the convent to take care of her myself. It would have been the best solution. I wonder now if I thought of that solution the year of my twenty-third birthday. I wonder if by then I had let go sufficiently of my youthful self-centeredness to make a choice for love. I wonder if I could even see, at that time, in which direction the greatest love might lie. But they didn't die, and the choice didn't need, then, to be made.

119

We live by various forms of currency, symbolic of our love. Some of those convent holy cards have survived the forty-five years since this birthday on which my mother wrote her letter. They are tucked here and there in books and among pictures—and as markers on the pages of my journals. When I find one, I lift it out, remembering the love of the sister who signed her name on the back. And Mama's letters, too, are a form of the currency of love. This codicil? Her love for her daughters saw beyond her death.

I take a breath. She seems to be standing right beside me as I write. "Loosen the strings of your purse always," she seems to say. I turn back to the day her letter arrived. If I could have loosened my purse strings then what would I have done? If they had died, I now wonder, would I have spent all my currency on my little sister? Would I have chosen Betsy? Would I have gone back home to her?

A LETTER FROM MAMA
It is like living a nightmare.
November 22, 1963

Mama was picking up the dishes after lunch. Dad had already gone out to the car to return to the airport. The TV was on; voices of her soap opera characters filled the empty spaces of her house when they were interrupted by breaking news: the shooting in Dallas. *It is like living a nightmare—Lincoln's assassination reenacted in our modern day.* Like many in America, Mama sat in front of the television set and barely moved all day. She sat at the breakfast bar where she could type and watch simultaneously. *Isn't it sad? I am here alone— watching T.V. and listening to every word, and it is now almost 9 P.M. He was a great man— a great president—(even though my party was not his party) and I am truly grieved like everyone else—to see the reactions of people on TV—the people on the streets—no person's death ever shocked and stunned so many, many people. What will happen now? Maybe it will bring people to their knees.*

On the fifth floor of Viterbo College we had no television or radio. At first, when I was new to convent life, I missed hearing music on the radio, but I'd gotten over that. Television was unavailable in my small town during the years I was growing up. I could count on the fingers of one hand how many television programs I'd watched in the past five years. The Kennedy inauguration. The John Glenn space flight. A performance of *Amahl and the Night Visitors.* The Cuban Missile Crisis. This would be the day that I discovered that my brain had not even developed the necessary synapses to watch television news and make sense of it.

The day began like any other school day. I gathered up my books for class and left my bedroom, walked down the hallway to the stairs that led to the second floor classrooms. I remember students milling around. Confusion. Cancelled classes. "The President's been shot." Sister Seraphina, our literature professor, wouldn't show up for class again until all of it was over. She sat in the assembly hall watching the only television in the college. She sat there through prayers and probably through meals, her veiled head bowed most of the time, her body broken against the seat in front of her.

121

I followed the other sisters and many students to that assembly room and sat close to the front, near the tiny television screen. I learned the names, Cronkite, Huntley, Brinkley. My brain worked to follow that cut and paste technique, the gestalt so normal to television, but so abnormal to my linear-book-reading eyes. I tried to absorb the references to current events. I knew nothing. As a sister in training I'd not been permitted to follow current events. For five years the only newspapers I'd read were those in which we wrapped the potato peelings. I was a foreigner. I was a stranger in my own land. With Sister Seraphina I skipped all classes; maybe they didn't have classes anyway—I don't remember. She sat half-way up the hall. I came in every morning after Mass and breakfast and sat as close to the front as I could get, hoping to make some sense of it. I leaned towards the screen; I learned the cadences of David Brinkley's voice. I saw Jack Ruby murder Lee Harvey Oswald. Every security I'd taken for granted, what remained of my sense of where I fit into the world shattered in that terrible series of gunshots, real, right before my eyes.

Night came, the first day, and Mama wrote: *I actually was in the process of wrapping a pound cake for mailing to send to Betsy when word came through that he was dead (the first reports were that he was wounded—and I put a note in with the cake to Betsy because I had to talk with someone—or rather, communicate with someone. I wish I could call you up tonight, but by now you are in bed. I feel so alone— I wish George would come home soon. He will—in time—and then we will pray our rosary—tonight for President Kennedy. He had a tremendous job to handle—but he always seemed so happy in spite of it. He really was dedicated. Some people are.*

The nation's tragedy brings her to the thought of dedication. Kennedy's dedication. Then she wonders about her own and whether in her life she's managed to accomplish something good. She believes I am dedicated because of my convent vows. She believes I will bring out the good in my students someday. She believes that young Betsy will also dedicate herself, probably to family, *when she gets over wanting to raise horses. She could become a wise mother sometime in the future. Betsy is definitely not an 'on the fence' kind of person—she decides, and that is it.*

Her predictions about Betsy proved true, but I left the convent. Aspects of Kennedy's dedication have, in recent years, undergone intense scrutiny. And what is dedication, anyway? I think such things now as I reflect on Mama's letter. Dedication isn't static; it unfolds and evolves as we evolve. Now, all these years after Mama's death, I see her own dedication in ways she apparently could not during the years she lived according to it. I see it as a perfect weave of compassionate commitment to her family, her community, her church, her nation, the world. Her heart transcended political affiliation—*(even though my party is not his party,* she writes.) She didn't have it in her to condemn; she would not assume she had the wisdom necessary for such judgment. She had an open heart, and maybe it was this quality that left her quite alone so much of the time. It's an intuition I'm having as I write, and certainly not anything rational—that a heart open to compassion could at the same time feel so alone.

After the Kennedy funeral I left the isolation of my convent-mind, making my way as often as possible to the assembly hall in the afternoon to watch the news. I must have had to shift my prayer time to do this. It's strange to me I don't remember that. What I do remember is that my dedication to the enclosed world governed by convent rules underwent a profound shift the day John Kennedy was shot, and my heart began to open, as my mother's already had, to a larger, more troubled and uncertain world beyond my convent enclosure.

I'll say goodnight…I hope you are well. There has been so much sickness here, and most people seem tired and overworked. Please keep yourself well.

The world is fragile, she seems to say. The world is my child and there is sickness, and we are tired and the work of the day has been hard. Be well.

I am her elder now, many years older than she was on that day, and I think I can understand something of her meaning.

Eternal Rest grant unto him, O Lord, and may perpetual light shine upon him. May his soul, and the souls of all the Faithful Departed, though the mercy of God rest in peace. Amen.

Love through Jesus Christ,

Mama

And to you, dear Mama. Stay Well. Eternal Rest, and all my love.

A LETTER FROM MAMA
Sing the Banish Song
February 4, 1964

The stationery is from the Hotel Dyckman on Sixth Street in Minneapolis. *Dearest Mary Jane...* Mama began, writing by hand with blue ballpoint pen. Already with that salutation I know her thoughts and feelings towards me were intimate. Sister Mary Christopher was nowhere near that room, and Mama had traveled back in memory to spend a while with her little girl.

She and Daddy were in the Twin Cities to attend the annual Aviation Trades Association Convention, the event that had become their only "vacation" together each year. They were staying at the convention hotel, hobnobbing with other pilots and their spouses, and dressing up for dinner in a banquet hall. *Daddy is happy here with his odd breed of men, airplane pilots. They speak and understand a language all their own—and I am relaxing now—but today I tried to shop for bargains. I'm in the room all alone. Daddy is still trading experiences and ideas with the other pilots.*

The banquet was over. She would have liked to call, but again it was too late to interrupt a sister who not only would be sleeping but also observing what we called sacred silence. Did she struggle more by then, as I did, with those rules? Beside her on the desk was a letter from me. It had arrived in her room before the banquet, but it wasn't until afterwards, when she stopped at the front desk to inquire, that she found that out. At that point Daddy said, "Didn't you see the letter from Mary Jane?" It had been in the room most of the day.

I'm trying to remember this incident, but I don't remember. She'd hoped to drive from Minneapolis to LaCrosse to visit with me, but it turned out to be too far. She'd hoped to call, but the letter from me must tell her I can receive calls only on Tuesday or Thursday, and the next day is Wednesday.

I am sorry—really sorry—I hope you weren't sitting with one hand on the phone (I'm quite certain that you weren't—but anyway I was trying to shop today while Daddy was at a meeting and when I returned to the hotel at six— No Mail—so I proceeded to dress and be *ready to attend the dinner gathering with Daddy. He came—said, "Hurry up, Mama, we're late"—so <u>I hurried.</u>*

How far is LaCrosse, Wisconsin, from Minneapolis? People typically drove the winding highway along the river, taking as long as four, maybe five hours. To be so close and yet so far away must have prompted both of us to nostalgia. I must have reminisced in my letter to her about my childhood and memories of other conventions. I remembered best a blue dress she wore. It flattered her, and when I was old enough I put it on, hoping to look as lovely, just by wearing it, as she did. She writes:

You really have quite a memory for your life with us at home. I'm glad you haven't forgotten. I still have the navy blue dress at home—I didn't bring it this time—saving it tho' for when the hemlines drop down again—I don't want to cut it off.

It was getting late, almost midnight, and still reminiscing as she closed, she wrote, *Goodnight Sweetheart—Sleep will* banish *sorrow. (Sing the Banish song, Mama! Remember that? You really thought* **I** *could sing!)*

She sang every night, all through my childhood. "Sing Banish, Mama!" I would call from the darkened bedroom to my mother in the kitchen. The closet door already had been closed. I'd already knelt and looked under the bed. The hall light cast a rectangular beam through my open door onto the bedroom floor and I could hear the click of our multi-colored Fiesta dishes in the enameled sink as she finished washing them. Despite all my preparations for the night, fear spun a tornado in my mind, a dark wind that could suck safety up into itself and carry it away. It could suck my mother up and she would be gone. "MOMMEEEEE!" I yelled, frantic by then because she hadn't answered the first time.

"What is it, Mary Jane?" Her voice lit the space between us.

"Please sing the Banish song." I called, not yelling now.

"Then you go to sleep, okay?"

"Okay." I pulled the covers up to my chin and waited for her voice.

"Goodnight, Sweetheart," she began to sing the love song my dad sang when courting her, 'til we meet tomorrow..." She possessed a lullaby voice, not always securely on pitch but with the reedy quality of a cello. I snuggled into its sound. "Goodnight, Sweetheart, sleep will banish sorrow." I began to breathe deeply and closed my eyes. I drifted down into her voice. I was asleep.

Were my sorrows deepening? I was nearing graduation. Sister Innocent was receiving treatment in another city. Daily sorrows must have been transitory, not even sorrows but simple annoyances. I consult my heart. All our lives Mama and I had felt the pull of a distance created when serious illness took her from me in infancy. All our lives we tried to close that distance. I clung to her in my childhood, wrapping my arms around her legs. When I did venture out, she worried. I was a tendril from her heart. I must not grow too far away. This caused confusing emotions in me. Sometimes I think I went to the convent to learn boundaries, to become a separate self. Ironically I enlisted the voice of an even larger Mother. Mother Church set the boundary I sought and then rejected as too rigid, too brittle, too like glass that when shattered, cuts. Was even Sister Marie too brittle then?

I sing the Banish Song to Mama often now, across the vast distance at the point of intersection between eternity and time. In my voice I hear hers. "Though I'm not beside you; still my love will guide you." I take comfort in that promise. She is present to me not just in memory, but in the gentle rhythms and tones of a love song, in the vibrations of sound that extend out like ripples through the universe, even to the Heart of God.

I read her words. I rest once more inside her song. 'Till we meet tomorrow..."

With God's Love – and His guidance.
Mama
xxxxxxxxxxxxx ooooooooo

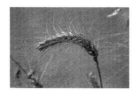

REMEMBER THE HIDING

- Remember the academy. It will be your walls. You will travel its hallways in dreams all your life. You will find rooms you never knew existed at the tops of narrow stairways and over thresholds that go but one way.
- Remember the task of locking away all the secrets you must never tell, and the person you can never be. Touch her shadow. Learn the art of canvas, of brushes, of oils to coax her appearance before you. Realize she is static, stuck on the canvas, cajoling you with just her eyes.
- Remember the attic in the quiet of a Sunday afternoon, sunlight through dust on a small window, dust particles riding stale air. Opening your trunk, lift into the dim light something wholly yours—a shell picked up on the beach of Lake of the Woods the night you left your childhood home.
- Remember the costumes of your soul in boxes hidden behind locked attic doors. You will take refuge there.
- Remember that you and this place sing counterpoint. Listen underneath the eaves for the music most secret, but in the classroom summon a more public song. Know that the counterpoint will narrow to a dissonance.
- Remember that these walls will shelter your dividing heart, designating chambers for your loves and locking them away with secret keys. Observe that you begin to divide your life into the different rooms.

A LETTER FROM MAMA
What sort of place?
1964-1967

The last time Mama drove Betsy to St. Joseph's Academy, my sister confided that she hated it there and didn't want to go back. She wondered how she could finish the school year.

    I was most disturbed about leaving her there. Mama wrote. *No one else will know – she only tells me – but she will be tired and withdrawn instead of trying to make new friends... She isn't as affectionate as you were, but she feels things more deeply. By that I mean, she isn't demonstrative so she creates a shell of indifference to the outside world – and I fear she builds up resentments within.*

    She wrote while preparing a Valentine's Day cake for her. *I fixed a couple of hearts on the top with powdered sugar and colored sugar – and I put it in a shoe box and mailed it.* She hoped to lift her younger daughter's spirits.

    I remember sitting at my desk on the fifth floor of the college, reading this letter and then staring out the window at the bare trees and the snow. She must have had a hard time writing to me about this since she knew I would be teaching at that very school the next year. How would I interpret Betsy's hatred of the place? Somebody, somehow, seemed to have failed my sister, but it wasn't clear who or how. If she sided with Betsy who had told her that the academy brought out the worst in her, changing her, taking something young and sweet and essential from her personality, then Mama somehow would be questioning me and the community of sisters to which I belonged. But if she sided with the sisters and the school, then she would be calling into question the very real experience of her younger daughter. Much to her credit, Mama leaned towards Betsy and her strongly expressed needs. *I had a talk with Mother Martha Mary – she wanted to know if Betsy would be back next year. I had to tell her that I really didn't know...Sometimes I think she misses and wants the security of her home—because she will discuss things with me, but there she keeps them bottled up. However, it is helping her to mature, and she is bright enough that with your prayers and mine, she should have the grace to emerge a better and wiser and kinder person. We won't worry*

128

about next year, as she may change her mind two or three times before then.

But I believe Mama knew already that Betsy wouldn't be going back, and she would not only support that choice, but she would welcome it. By the end of writing the letter to me, she knew what her own stand on this would be.

Was another seed of doubt planted in me that day? Though many of the young sisters had graduated from that academy, I had not. I'd attended public school through all twelve grades before entering the convent. What might this academy be that had so negatively affected my little sister? And what sort of place might it end up being for me?

A subtle but discernible change was beginning to happen in the minds of people. Ideas and practices and institutions never before questioned by my mother's generation or that of her own parents now were being subjected to scrutiny. What we'd inculcated through both church and culture seemed to be eroding, starting with the slow crumbling of certainties upon which we'd depended and taken for granted.

The letters stop. Mama didn't stop writing, though, and I know this from the box on the floor beside my chair. It's her box—made of heavy particle-board, veneered on the sides, carved along the edges to give it a rustic look, and finished with decorative bolts and a lock. It's large, the size of a small suitcase, and in it she kept my letters in response to hers, along with photos, poems, homemade cards, news clippings, programs from plays I directed at St. Joseph's Academy during my four years there. From the contents of her box I probably could reconstruct a facsimile of my academy years, but it would bear scant resemblance to the truth, because I didn't tell the whole truth. I gave her and Daddy my dreams, my old hopes formed in beautiful words. I didn't want to worry them. I wanted them, when they thought of me, to see me shine and to be comforted by my happiness. But I had fears. I had doubts. The convent life of which I'd dreamed and desired with all my heart was beginning, almost imperceptibly, to slip through my fingers and from my soul.

The academy was my first professional assignment. The building itself represented self-containment. It became the limit of my world. That first year, when I was twenty-four years old, I left the academy grounds seldom, and most often to travel the short distance to the motherhouse. I did none of the ordinary tasks common to other women my age. I held no bank account. I never went to a supermarket, nor clothing store, nor library, court house, gas station, public school, swimming pool, pharmacy. The trivial facts remind me how concentrated my life was. The world existed in my imagination, mediated by the few television programs I was permitted to watch and the literary works I now devoured with an insatiable appetite. My only real doors to the world outside were the lives of the girls I taught.

My image of this place is that of a gothic mansion, wood paneled hallways polished daily by one hundred girls in navy blue uniforms. Its stairways narrow as they ascend to the attic room where memories are stored.

The attic holds special meaning for me. Old Sister Anna Mary once took my hand into her trembling one and solemnly led me up the narrow stairs. Light, as if from dimmed spotlights, filtered through years' accumulation of dust on window panes and fell on the assortment of trunks kept there. Sister Anna Mary's, one of the oldest, bore the scars of an ocean voyage over sixty years before when she left her home for the motherhouse, then in Europe. One of its leather straps lay torn and useless on the floor. The other, securely fastened, protected the few precious things Sister cared for as her own: perhaps letters from her long deceased parents, some photographs, a tattered prayer book. She seldom opened the trunk anymore because her eyes, blind for many years, could not discern words upon a page. Her trunk was thick with dust. No one needed to fix the useless strap because this attic would be the trunk's final resting place.

She turned me away from the trunks and towards a locked off area of the attic where for forty years she had stored every costume from every play presented at the school. Although she was a history and civics teacher, costuming provided her with a way to unite her historical knowledge with her creative talents. Jealously she guarded her domain from Sister Augusta, the home economics teacher whose skill at tailoring and needlework made her a natural successor, and also from Sister Sophie Noelle, the long-time theater and English teacher. For years this sister had chaffed under Sister Anna Mary's absolute autonomy in costuming every play that Sophie Noelle directed. In her long career at the academy, Sister Sophie Noelle had never been permitted into the locked sanctuary of theatrical illusion over which Sister Anna Mary held sway.

She reached beneath the folds of the wide full skirt of her habit and produced a long cord from which hung a ring of keys. Fingering them carefully, she found the one for the padlock and inserted it, then paused.

"Sister," she turned towards me and spoke in a voice shaky from Parkinson's disease. Then she said something like, "I'm old. You're young. You'll be directing the plays from now on, not Sister Sophie Noelle. And my old eyes—I just can't manage. You'll need to know everything I've stored up here. But you must promise me; under no circumstances allow Sister Sophie Noelle into this place. Agreed?"

She told me I'd need a light, and flicked a switch. A naked bulb glared on boxes of all shapes and sizes, old, some disintegrating, stacked against every wall up to the ceiling. A makeshift table ran the length of the room down the center, underneath and on top of which were stacked even more boxes. Here and there wisps of material escaped, and faded bits of red, violet and gold hinted at the treasures inside. Hanging from walls and ceiling, hand props provided accents: a crutch, a pair of high-buttoned shoes, a brocaded footstool, two photograph albums from the late nineteenth century, and jewelry boxes overflowing with cheap beads and earrings. A feather boa cascaded down from a nail over a Knights of Columbus sword she was saving just in case Sister Sophie Noelle would ever have agreed to direct *Joan of Arc.*

Sister led me around the room, pointing her trembling finger at boxes and props her blind eyes could no longer see. "In the boxes with the black circles in crayon you will find robes for a Greek chorus. Farther back is a box with blue silk for Joan of Arc's tunic. I do hope you will do that play. Sister Sophie Noelle said it was too hard for high school girls. Of course I never agreed."

When she was satisfied that I knew what I needed of the stories, and that my eyes could serve me to discover less necessary details, we turned out the light and left the room. She then removed the key from her key ring and placed it in my hand. It was her last trip to the attic. She died that winter. In the spring we presented *JOAN OF ARC* in her honor.

The life of my time at the academy was my relationship with the girls who were students and boarders there. I must have a thousand stories of the ways in which their lives entwined with mine and required honesty of me. I lived with them. Each night I walked among the narrow, white-curtained beds in the dorm I supervised, sat a moment with each girl, smoothed her covers, listened to her secret hopes or fears, sometimes wiped away her tears, always traced a small cross of blessing upon her forehead. My own white-curtained bed stood only slightly separated from theirs at the end of the large room. At night I drifted to sleep on the light sound of thirty girls breathing, and I sometimes awoke to the sounds of sickness or loneliness. When I comforted a crying fourteen-year-old girl in the middle of a winter night, I had no doubts about whom I loved or where my loyalties lay. I gave them love out of both my public and my private self, and they gave me the power to influence them.

Sister Constance, whose bed was at the other end of the dormitory from mine, and whose reputation was that of a strict disciplinarian, tried to warn me of the dangerous situation she found me eager to embrace. She met me one night in the small office behind the school's assembly room, intending to call my attention to what she thought of as my irresponsible behavior.

It was snowing. We sat in dim light and I watched large flakes drift past the beam of a street light across the street. Her words felt harsh and even surreal. I kept my eyes on the snow in order to keep touch with the tender self within me, one that wanted to weave human love together with divine commitment.

"What do you mean when you say dangerous?" I asked her.

She told me she felt concern over my relationship with the girls. She thought I didn't understand that the good of each individual needed to be subjected to the good of the group. She said I made too many exceptions. Didn't I realize that girls the age of these were clever manipulators who only want their own way, and that they were making a fool of me? And even more essential, she said, was my vow of chastity. It wasn't just about sex! I was not permitted to feel closeness to people outside the religious community. She read a passage to me from our holy rule: "With jealous care they will safeguard their heart's liberty, without which there would no longer be for them any interior peace, since a divided heart is open to all the temptations of the devil."

132

I ventured the opinion that the girls were far from their homes and needed love and an understanding heart.

"That, Sister, is not yours to give." She told me that if I really were to fulfill my vow of chastity I must forego the luxury of even companionship. Then she referred to the snowfall. "Before I entered the convent I loved a man. I remember a time that we simply stood by the window watching the snow fall, and as it fell I knew my love for him was growing and filling me up. Never in my life have I been so close to anyone. I believe that even were I to have the experience of making love with a man, it would not be so intimate an experience as that was. So, I now know that it is not permitted me even to stand before a window with another person and watch the snow fall. It would divide my heart. You must distance yourself from the girls, Sister, or your vocation will be lost."

I thanked her for her concern, told her I couldn't believe that we, as sisters, were meant to be so restricted, and then, feeling fear, anger, and not a little uncertainty, I left her in the dim room and returned to the quiet dorm where I sat on my hardwood chair behind my white curtain listening to the breathing of the girls.

About one thing she was right. My heart was dividing right through the center.

I needed to love. I wanted some kind of mystic union with a holy presence I experienced as God. But I experienced that presence most in the prairie, in the night sky, in the gentle caress of moonlight, in the surging of waves and especially in the people I loved: my family, the sisters, the girls I taught. But whatever god it might be that existed *apart* from all I loved seemed to divide me from myself. I gave that god the benefit of the doubt.

In the language of the rule I argued against myself. Nature is selfish, my mind insisted against my heart. It will take to itself what belongs to God alone. Nature is passionate; it will forget God in the experience of its passion. Its loving will turn to lust. Its pleasure will become gluttonous. Its soothing, slothful. Its enthusiasm, avaricious. I must guard against the beauty to avoid the sin. I must guard against loving in order to avoid being consumed by the love of anything less than God.

133

Thus I divided myself. That god, it turned out, was a father of lies. "They will jealously guard their heart's liberty..." ordered the rule. But the heart will not be guarded jealously against the creation of which it partakes. The heart will love creation in all its manifestations, or it will wither. The heart will be free, or go mad.

Sometime during those years I had a dream that I still do not forget. I am wandering the hallways of that academy, climbing from the basement to the top floor on the narrow sisters' stairs in the cloistered section. I'm searching for a way out. I search in every room—kitchen, dining rooms, laundry, gym, the basement, sisters' community room, offices, elementary classrooms on the first floor, library, assembly room, high school classrooms, my office on the second floor, dormitories and the chapel on the third and top floor. The building had no door. I could see out, though, over a medieval city of crowded and crumbling huts surrounding gothic spires, all under a heavy threatening sky. Finally, after what seems years of searching, I discover a mouse hole leading to the outside. I lie on my belly, my long skirts and veil covering me like a shroud, and I look through. I will never get out of here, I think, and then the further thought rises that, even if I could make myself small enough to get through the mouse's hole, my whole world outside would be no different than where I lived right now.

Without realizing what I was up to, I began during those four years to maneuver my way out of that confined world. I would do whatever it took, but I didn't understand that the world I sought to escape, its huts and towers, its labyrinthine paths and dead ends, existed in my own mind. The brittle shell containing the convent, the church, the rules and everything else against which I struggled was a mental prison in which I confined myself of my own free will.

In the meantime Mama kept writing. Betsy had gone home to finish high school in Baudette, and she brought back into the house all the verve, excitement, intrigue, frustration, contradiction, rebellion and promise characteristic of adolescent years. Mama kept writing, every week, and sending birthday cakes and gifts for Christmas. After reading them, I threw all her letters away.

I must have since they no longer exist. To be merciful to myself, I really didn't know how important those letters would become to me later. I didn't know they would have an end. I didn't consider that eventually Mama would become incapable of writing them. They seemed a flow of words that would go on and on. I took them for granted. I know I didn't throw them away immediately. I collected them in a large envelope inside my desk drawer. I answered them when I could. When the envelope became filled to overflowing, then I threw them away to prepare for more. When letters survived it was because they escaped my attempts at detachment or common orderliness and found their way into a book or to the bottom of my black steamer trunk. A sister had use of a locker for her clothes, a desk, a sewing basket, a dresser drawer, and a trunk stowed in the attic. Very little of anything survived those years.

At first, my way out of confinement seemed to be through teaching. I drifted from the community of sisters, spending only as much time with them as required by the rule, and then hurrying away to the Newman Room to prepare my classes, to read the novels, poetry and plays I'd missed during my early college years in the novitiate, to write poetry and essays, to keep a journal. I took up painting.

I entered into the lives of my students. I learned the stories of their lives, I listened to their music—the Beatles, Simon and Garfunkel, the Supremes. I played a Gibson guitar that Daddy bought for me, and sang for them. I marveled at their talents, their freedom. I encouraged them to do all that I could not. Go forth. Be your dreams.

Hard as I tried, the fear of entrapment persisted. I shrunk into that fear. Although fear made me small enough to fit through the metaphorical mouse's hole, it also kept me from traversing there. By the time I emerged I'd very nearly disappeared.

Sometime during these years Mama wrote a letter that survived. It is a timeless letter, though it must have been written in 1967 just after Betsy's high school graduation. She dates it only *Thursday – June 13th – 10:10 A.M. – At Home – alone.* But for me it fits the time—that entire time.

I feel her in my fingers as I copy her letter here. I feel her love and her concern and it moves my heart. I wonder how I received this letter the first time I read it, knowing how close she came to the condition of my soul. I suspect her words hit me in the belly of my fear.

Dearest –

This is unusual—I am home—alone—this time of the day. I had to shampoo my hair (whether I wanted to or not) so I took the time off and now I am under the dryer and decided it was a good time to write to you.

I'm sorry I haven't done so sooner. I go glibly through the days— outwardly, that is—but inside of me, I worry—all the time—I worry. When my girls seem troubled. I want to take it from them and carry the burden myself. I have lived and I can carry the burden—but no one lets me.

That all is silly, isn't it? Who can transfer an emotion or mental burden to someone else? However, sometimes sharing it helps. When I see you silent and different, I want to put my arms around you like I once could when you would have a terrifying dream, and I want to make you forget whatever troubles you. I suppose I can't realize—seeing you only a few times each year—that you are maturing all the time and are not still the 17 year old who left here in 1958. I guess I want you to always have that love of life (forget the split infinitive—or maybe it is acceptable English now ... is it?)

You told me that God answered your every desire—you had such strong faith. Now that He has given you some burdens, I have the feeling that you think you are being punished and that you have to punish yourself further. I don't think He asks for self-punishment. Don't withdraw too completely from the world. You have a job to do—otherwise He would not have called you. I think it is your job to let your love shine through— for everyone. The young girls need a sparkling, loving teacher who recalls with pleasure and love her own teen years. I may be on the wrong track, but I don't think so. I have a feeling that you are trying to offer God a different you—a person who should become silent and morose.

You find pleasure in your music and guitar. Play it often, but as you become adept, play happy music. Be cheerful. God gave you a warm beautiful smile—USE it. As Father Fenlon of Rainy River told us—God created men and women. He did not intend women to hide themselves completely behind yards of material and huge head coverings, etc. He feels that the women in religion can do most by being very human and staying as attractive as God created them. (He was talking about an order of sisters he knew in Eastern Canada before he came here.) I think he is right, and I think the Sisters of St. Joseph feel that way too since they changed their garb and are constantly making more contacts with the world we live in.

Maybe I am becoming too prying or have arrived at conclusions which are not there, but I love you so very much, and I want you to be completely happy—as Our Lord wants you also. Is there any place in the Bible where he says we have to withdraw or where we have to go through the motions of living without demonstrating our love? You said in your letter you are often silent now.

If I have been conjuring up a wrong picture—just laugh it off as another of your silly mother's hallucinations—only please, please, Mary Jane— relax, be happy—be beautiful and lovely—and offer that to Our Lord— and gather all your young girls around you and laugh with them and play for them and sing for them and give them a great, great love of life. How better would you help fulfill your destiny?

I know you are about finished teaching Catechism and will be moving to the motherhouse for the summer. I hope you can get rested— physically—and will have time for your music.

Sunday is Father's Day. We will miss you—but will have you with us spiritually.

May Jesus guide you—always—

I love you,
Mama
xxxx's   ooo's

A LETTER FROM MAMA
Ponderings
August – 1966
the seventh day ...

I read this letter from Mama the evening after I made my final or perpetual vows. I'd been in the convent eight years. It was quiet in the chapel at the academy and I was alone. She'd written it the night before and placed it in my hands that afternoon following the ceremony. *At this almost final minute I am getting butterflies.* She wrote from home in Baudette, preparing for the trip to Crookston, preparing to give her elder daughter up for good, along with every dream she ever had of loving the grandchildren I couldn't give her now, surrendering holidays together—surrendering all the normal things that families do.

Earlier that year, during the winter as I approached the deadline for deciding whether or not to request from my superiors the actual permission to make these vows, I was not so certain it was a good idea. Uncertainty fluttered in my mind and belly then. I couldn't eat. My skin broke out in flaming patches of acne. I asked an older sister if she'd ever had doubts. She said that when she was my age, before her own final vows, she'd fallen in love with a priest. (Is this a common affliction, I wondered?) She still could remember the priest's eyes gazing at her over the chalice in the sacristy when they finally had declared their love for one another and said goodbye. She requested an assignment in a different mission and never saw the man again. "I'll meet him in heaven," she told me. "I never stopped loving him, but I've been a good sister all these years, and I'm grateful that both of us fulfilled our calling."

The movie, *The Sound of Music,* was released right around that time, and the theater in Crookston had a preview showing for the several hundred sisters and priests in that city which was the diocesan center. The story of Maria von Trapp confused me even more. I experienced an adolescent thrill when Maria married Werner von Trapp in the convent chapel. Now, looking back, I realize it was the paradox that thrilled me. Something in me wanted both lives simultaneously. But that was beyond thought. Impossible.

A few nights later I was taking a bath, something we were required to accomplish quickly and with as little awareness of our bodies as possible, when the thought rose up like a bubble. "Who else but Jesus would want me?" Now, as I write, I shake my head and smile sadly. That poor, silly, deluded young woman! She couldn't see that by the very asking of the question, she was revealing the hope for someone else to want her—a Werner von Trapp, a Prince Charming; she was expressing in that question her preference to leave convent life. She couldn't see that for her to make those vows while harboring that question really was like picking up the crumbs of her failure to become something, someone else. I thought then that the question meant I was destined to remain. The next day I wrote my letter asking for permission to pronounce my final vows. That summer, living at the motherhouse, preparing for these vows that I believed would bind me forever, beyond death, I recovered the ideal I thought I had lost, the dream that I hoped would become my reality.

Mama writes: *Why do I always procrastinate? Why didn't I arrange all sorts of beautiful and lovely things for my daughter for this coming greatest day in her life? What could I have done that would measure up?—Let's see now? What do I have for her? A few material gifts, but they never endure. What should I have done that I didn't do? Perhaps I should have arranged for a multiple of Masses to be offered this day—but I procrastinated and time ran out. What can I yet do?*

I think the greatest we have to offer has actually been taken care of (through HER own prayers I think now)...without prodding from "pushy" me, her father and her sister both went to Confession yesterday and received Holy Communion this morning...for HER, I am certain. ... Yesterday her sister came home with smiling face and shining eyes, proudly displaying a new Miraculous Medal suspended from a chain around her neck and announced that she was "very happy and from now on going to be very, very good."

I prodded her father just a wee bit—suggesting a letter or written message she could keep to remember the day—but he reminded me that he can't express himself on paper, assuring me SHE knows how proud he is of her and how often he thinks of her. (I am sure she does because his love is immeasurable.)

...for myself, I must confess—first a great pride in what she is doing and when I think quietly by myself of the magnitude of this step, I almost burst from emotion. On occasion I have wondered, when I have seen her classmates prepare for marriage to a man of their choice, I am tempted with fear that perhaps she has moments when she would prefer this also. This past week during her retreat, I have tried to join her in thought during the quiet moments. I have offered my Masses each day, and in Holy Communion have asked Our Lord to cherish her. Today I know and I feel that she knows wholeheartedly that this life is right. Endurance is what matters and this life will endure.

That evening after making my vows, sitting in the academy chapel, I must have breathed deeply, believing she was right. I'd made the best choice, and this life would endure. The entire summer of preparation had led me to the same conclusion. All doubt had fled. I read the mystical works of Pierre Teilhard de Chardin. I walked with my beloved mentor, Sister Marie, along the path through the woods behind the motherhouse. We discussed the implications of the documents of the Second Vatican Council for the three vows of poverty, chastity and obedience. We were evolving, just as Teilhard said. I wrote a paper on those implications and she arranged to have me present it to the entire community of our sisters during the retreat before vows. I felt buoyed up on their love and acceptance. I took out my oil paints and created a portrait of the child in me, holding a lit candle in the dark. I dreamed of grace spilling as rain from the sky. I picked raspberries in the convent garden and sang "Today," as I'd been singing it for my students at the academy all that year. I sang aloud, paying no attention to the restrictions about silence, and I had no guilt. On August eighth, in a clear strong voice I made my final vows.

Both sides of the paradox were real. I loved being a sister; I hated it. It created and destroyed me. I was both true and false to my vision. I'd been called to this, and not called, and called further than my vision could reach. And Mama, too, was caught up in a paradox. She wanted me to be a sister. She wanted me home. She felt proud of me. She felt separated from me. She felt honored to be the mother of a "chosen one." She felt bereft and inadequate.

Now I can glimpse a rift between vision and reality into which "falls the shadow." I can see the effects on my life of teaching

140

adolescent girls and being surrounded by them twenty-four hours of every day. I listened to their whispers, giggles, sobs, and snores. Their adolescent energies swirled around me. Their delightful, irritating noise made ripples in my convent silences. The heavy quicksand of their emotions pulled at my heart. Their music repeated itself over and over in my mind. To hold my vision I should have been a hermit in a mountain cave. I should have been an anchorite attached to a medieval church. I should have been a poet in a hut on desert sands. Alone. To hold my vision. To be one-sided. To have escaped the complexity that had only just begun to shake my life.

I am still unable to find the right way of expression. I am humble and proud. Proud of her in her courage and her great love for Our Lord, and the fact that she will be His for eternity and humble when I realize that I have no place for pride in myself where this is concerned because of past failures to understand. She did it not because of any encouragement I have given, but because He chose her and she listened and abided by it.

Tomorrow, AUGUST, 1966, the eighth day, is to be her greatest – the gift of herself—not to a mere man—but to God, the Supreme Ruler of all, of everything, everywhere.

My Lord has done great things to me! (Now is the time I can tell her—with tears of remembrance in my eyes—she was conceived in a great love on Valentine's Day, and little did I know then that it was really God's love and for this purpose I was made to live—with her father who loves and cherishes all four of us. On that day which glorifies LOVE, God created his child of love to be His Very Own and on this day, August 8th, 1966, I (we) give her back to him with all our heart and love.

I read the ending of Mama's letter over and over in the chapel on that day. It felt like a holy sign, a confirmation of my choice, a hint of destiny. I rededicated myself that evening, not only to my vows, but to divine love. Valentine's Day! Conceived in love. Tears came to my eyes. Those months, even years of uncertainty now seemed a temptation which I'd overcome. I'd done the right thing. I was safe.

How ironic. Dear, dear Mama, I was anything but safe.

Cherish her, Dear Lord, and show her the way—without doubts at any time, but with a constantly growing love for You—but please share her on occasion with her

Mother & Father

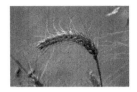

REMEMBER THE PRIEST

- That you would call him Father and he would call you Sister.
- That poetry and metaphor would be your language.
- That your work together would be prayer, and your goal the renewal of the church.
- That you would share his priesthood as companions share bread.
- That you would not touch one another except with eyes, and after eyes with hands brushing lightly, after which would come the fear and the distances.

IMMORTAL DIAMOND

The young priest kept his distance. Chaplain and teacher of religion at the academy, associate pastor of the neighboring parish, he seemed always in a hurry, distracted, whipping in and out of our lives. Father Kelly was the only man in an enclosed world of one hundred girls and twenty-two sisters. I really didn't care for him much. Threatened by his ready Irish wit, I backed away. I resented his relegating to me the twenty sophomores, juniors and seniors who were failing his religion classes, expecting me to teach them successfully. My entire first year of teaching, I competed with him. The second year I avoided him.

Avoidance began with a question posed by one of the students about his ability to love. The girl wondered if he might be afraid of love since, though he talked about Christian love in class, he refused to let any of them get close to him. I responded that I was sure that whatever special affection he might feel certainly was not appropriate to the classroom. None of us were in a position to judge his ability or willingness to love. But her question and her interpretation haunted me. I began to watch him closely. At Mass I riveted my eyes upon his eyes, upon his hands, and noticed for the first time the intensity of his reverence. I saw evidence of tenderness as he performed the sacred actions and pronounced the sacred words.

About this time Sister Sophie Noelle and I had occasion to walk downtown together. Sister, whose place I had taken as teacher of English, speech and drama, had remained part of the local religious community and spent the beginning of her retirement tutoring individual girls. She was a little more than seventy years of age at the time and thought of as a somewhat eccentric and beloved poet and mystic. To me she seemed the most beautiful and mysterious of women, and I sensed that she had adopted me as a protégé.

As we walked in sunlight through newly fallen autumn leaves I told her about the girl's question and my changing perception of the young priest. I wondered aloud what my new feelings meant for me, for him, and for my religious life. I told her I wanted to pray for Father Kelly. I wanted it to be a prayer of love: "Take my love and use it to take away his fear of love." I asked her what she thought.

We walked in silence for a long while. Her silence did not communicate trouble, but rather blessed me with calm. Finally she spoke with gentle prophesy.

"This young Father Kelly is a very holy man, a diamond within. The Spirit flows in him with such intensity that he doesn't yet quite know how to live that powerful love openly. You, Little Sister, are his feminine counterpart. I have seen it. You are the mystic bride of that priest. Your love joined with his could be immortal diamond. So pray. God alone knows where those prayers will lead."

He represented for me not the image of the husband, but rather of the priest. The one who enters the Holy of Holies, his hands filled with the fire of divinity. He was the man beloved of God. He was the image of my own priesthood. He was the masculine counterpart of my religious commitment. We would never call one another husband and wife, but companion—two who share bread on the journey. He called me "Chris" so that he could address me in letters as "U-Chris." I came to be, he said, his thanksgiving, his Eucharist, the feminine image of his priesthood. But there was no model for our kind of relationship, no way to live either together or apart.

I thought I'd begun to love him so I ran away. If he came down the hallway towards me, I slipped into a classroom and involved myself in a discussion with one of the girls while he walked past. It seemed that my soul followed him to where he disappeared into the library office. I made excuses to the girls and ran farther. "I need to check the attic for some costume material," I explained, and climbed the narrow stairs to unlock the door of my sanctuary and hide among the costumes of virgins and clowns. He was stealing my soul. Yet still, I prayed: "Take my love and use it to relieve him of his fear."

One night even before I made my final vows he came to me in a dream: he is there walking towards me through the rain. I stand in darkness, waiting through an eternity of rain. I dare not even reach my hand to him, nor make a sound. My long veil becomes the rain and I am hidden in it. But he *is* the rain and he covers me with his words.

"I will bring you more of grace than you could ever dream. Do you want to know your life's secret? You will find it because of me."

The dream faded into wakefulness and the rain turned to tears. On my convent bed at the core of night I abandoned myself to weeping.

145

I faced myself once again. Who was he to me? I desired him: this young priest. But I desired him *as* priest. Perhaps I desired to *be* the priest, but there could be only one way to priesthood for me, a woman—to be the soul of his priesthood. Already I'd bonded with him through the love-prayer. I couldn't escape it. I didn't want to.

Soon I would be making my final vows. I would come to those vows bearing this strange bonding with this priest. The vows I would make forever to Christ, the source of all priesthood, I began to believe would confirm a secret marriage between us. Better that he remained unaware of what I felt, of what I was about to do. It would be enough for me to share my soul's power with him in the privacy of prayer and to receive the grace of his priesthood in the prophecy of Sister Sophie Noelle, in the promises of dreams, and in the celebration of Eucharist. Where this strange marriage would lead, I didn't know. But that it was of God, I was more certain than of anything.

At summer's end I pronounced the vows that committed me for life to a radical dependence upon the Holy God, to a spiritual life, to this community of women, and to my love of Pat Kelly into whose priesthood of Christ I entered irrevocably and forever.

DECONSTRUCTION
1966-1968

First there was the murder. It was the nephew of one of our older sisters, the laundress at the academy. He killed his wife and then turned the gun on himself. Both of them died. Father Kelly, described it. He'd been driving by the salon behind which they lived. It was her salon. So why not stop? They were parishioners at his parish. "If only I'd come even one minute sooner," he said. His face looked as though it had been taken apart and reassembled with the torn parts not quite matching up. A few women sat in the salon, hair wet, hair half cut, set hair under dryers, all of them resembling manikins, eyes wide, stun on their faces. "I could smell the gun smoke," Father Kelly said. He told them to call the police, and he went into the apartment in back. The air was heavy with smoke and blood. Both their heads were blown to smithereens. The priest told us this in broken tones. "It was as though I'd seen life as a painting by Monet, all in muted greens and blues, and suddenly, right down the center, a gash of orange."

My heart went out to him.

Then the school faculty chose to join the humanities courses into thematic units of study: literature, religion, social studies, music. Another sister, Paulette, and I had lesson-planning sessions with Father Kelly every Saturday.

I met his mind.

The Vatican Council in Rome was at the height of its revolutionary work of restructuring, and the young priests of our diocese decided to meet regularly to discuss the pastoral and theological implications for the local church. Why not have a few sisters in on it? Father Kelly asked Sister Miriam, one of the elementary teachers, and me to join them. He picked us up at the door of the academy one afternoon each week, and we went off with him first to one parish and then another and another in little towns close to Crookston. We discussed a different religious topic at each meeting. We celebrated Mass together, Sister Miriam and I standing around the altar with the priests. Never before had I been so close to the mystery of priesthood, to the act of transubstantiation, as though Christ were acting through me as well as the men. My emotions soared with an awareness of what might be possible now that the Church was renewing itself, letting go of the strictures based on mistaken judgments, insufficient knowledge, and cultural accretions.

The first documents coming forth from Rome had been translated from Latin and made accessible. Our discussions centered on the implications of three core principles of church restructuring: collegiality, subsidiarity, and accountability. My intuitive mind concocted images of concentric circles of responsibility with Christ's light at the center flaming out through rings of ministerial functions. This was my image of collegiality—a completely different sense of hierarchy, not a stairway but a circular rainbow of love and service. The principle of subsidiarity gave new understanding to my concept of authority. No longer did I envision authority as coming "down" from the top of a pyramid. Authority in the social sphere of life came from God and was planted in the human heart of a community. If a need could be addressed in the local sphere, the authority was there to do that. If it could not be addressed because wisdom or means were lacking, the authority to address it would need to come from a wider more inclusive sphere with each sphere accountable to the others. Together, collegiality, subsidiarity and mutual accountability made up the community of love and compassion that was church.

These discussions gave me a taste of freedom, and I yearned to share it in my teaching and through my work in convent renewal.

Then Father Kelly brought a book of poetry to one of our Saturday class preparations. Listen, he said. He walked up and down, reading, rhapsodizing really. Why wasn't Sister Paulette there that day? Why were Father Kelly and I alone? "Now listen to this one." And I listened, feeling the cadence of each line. For my birthday he gave me a book of the poems of Dr. Zhivago, the Lara poems. "You are my Lara," he said and read the poem about the heroic life, the root of beauty, that drew us to one another. It would require heroism, I thought, to combine love for a man with my convent vows and church renewal. Could I do that, I wondered? Probably it would produce a lot of tension, but it might be exquisite tension. Heroic tension.

The drift of a life is slow, slow enough that only years later can we see how little crosscurrents affected the entire flow. Father Kelly's effect on that flow in the beginning was minimal. Meetings with him happened seldom and caused only minor disturbance, like a water bug that lands on the river, rippling it, setting off widening concentric circles of almost imperceptible crosscurrents.

The school year ended and I didn't see him the entire summer. I didn't miss him or his renewal meetings. I was teaching two classes that summer at the motherhouse and reading more works by Pierre Teilhard de Chardin. My own personal renewal was evolving within me as I read and assimilated the vision of this Priest/Scientist/Mystic whose life-work in the first half of the twentieth century had led him to integrate science and theology. He'd become convinced through direct contact with the history of earth as a geologist and paleontologist that the whole universe was in the process of evolution towards "the Omega Point." The result would be personal. The universe was evolving into a person whom he called "the Cosmic Christ." He wrote: "This is what I have learned from my contact with the earth—the diaphany of the divine at the heart of a glowing universe, the divine radiating from the depths of matter aflame."

Every moment of free time I could be found with one of his books open in my hands—in a clearing in the woods behind the convent, on a lawn chair in the cloister yard, in the little cubicle late at night with just a dim slant of light on the page, under a tree in a side yard with Sister Mary Kathryn.

Mary Kathryn also filled my mind and heart that summer. She seemed a demonstration of that fire at the heart of things. She was several years older than I, both in age and years as a sister, so we were only acquaintances until that summer. We'd sit under the tree and talk—my topic almost always turned towards the new vision, Teilhard's vision, of reality. This is different from what we've been taught, I'd say. The core of reality is completely different. It isn't the holy rule anymore. It just can't be. And she'd shake her head. A dangerous notion, she thought.

In the field behind the motherhouse wheat shot up and turned from green to gold. We watched it change from day to day. We watched it undulate in the wind.

We are the cauldron in which evolution takes place. The Spirit of God is the fire. Each incident of our lives is taken into the divine fire and transformed. It's not obedience to any holy rule that perfects us as individuals or as the world. It is how much we are willing to experience, to take in, to submit to this transformation. It is the work we do to transform each experience, each love—bringing it closer and closer to the perfect form of the Christ Person. This is what Jesus Christ is all about. This is what our friendship can be, I told her. I believed it. I was fervent over it. Opening the book to page 139, I read to her from Teilhard's *The Divine Milieu:* "This is the moment to abandon all conception of static adherence; it can only be inadequate...God does not offer himself to our finite beings as a thing all complete and ready to be embraced. For us he is eternal discovery and eternal growth...Like a huge fire that is fed by what should normally extinguish it...so the tension engendered by the encounter between man and God...volatilizes created things and makes them all, equally, serve the cause of union."

Our friendship could be the fuel for divine transformation! I could feel her fascination with this study of mine grow. When I finished *The Divine Milieu,* and went on to read *The Hymn of the Universe,* I loaned her the first book. But in two days she returned it to me.

"I can't read this," she said. "It's dangerous to my religious commitment." She told me that this direction in which I was heading was wrong. It went against the holy rule which was central to our lives as sisters. Probably it would be better if the two of us no longer met this way or discussed these things.

I argued with her. I think I even cried. But she was adamant. Already she'd begun to change, she said, and become dissatisfied. She simply couldn't do that.

Actually I have only impressions of what we said to one another that day—not any memory of the exact words we spoke. But this is closest to what remains. The day she told me all of this and after which she no longer sat with me beneath the tree in the side yard, the combines roared into the wheat field. As we severed ourselves from one another we could hear the noise of the harvest and could feel the chaff that blew towards us on the late summer breeze. Her veil lifted a bit on the wind, or maybe it didn't, maybe she just got up and walked towards the motherhouse leaving me alone to look out on the devastated fields.

Father Kelly, however, didn't fear Chardin's vision. He welcomed it as an undergirding for integral renewal of the individual, of the church, and of the world itself. I knew this from the discussions with him and the other priests. By the end of that summer I had begun to feel a greater connection with him than with most of the sisters in my community.

It may have been the end of August when he took Sister Mary Andrea, Sister Paulette and me with him to St. John's University in Collegeville for a film conference. Our plan was to integrate short films into our thematic units of study, and this would be an opportunity to view the best of them, art films like *The Red Balloon*, and *The Parable*.

I'd heard about St. John's but had never been there. The abbey church, completed only a few years before, was famous for its innovative design by the architect, Marcel Breuer. Experimentation with new liturgy that would result from the deliberations of the Second Vatican Council had barely begun, but St. John's would be center for that kind of renewal in just a few years. That summer, though, the monks still used a catacomb of small chapels built into the underground sections of the church. Each monk had his own altar, decorated with art to his liking, where he celebrated Mass each day alone. This would stop with liturgical renewal when all the monks began to concelebrate in one communal Mass in the enormous chapel upstairs where sunlight burst through multicolored stained glass set in a gigantic honey comb of windows.

Father Anthony, a friend of Father Kelly's, gave us a tour through the monk's individual chapels, describing the art in each one, naming the monk who'd chosen it. As he drew the other two sisters along to one chapel after another, Father Kelly held me back, offering more comments, providing interpretation. Before I knew it the other three people had moved several chapels beyond us. I felt singled out and special. Even to myself I could not admit what was really going on: that the priest had gone beyond the boundaries of our commitments and our goals and had begun flirting with me, and I was succumbing to his attention. But even had I admitted it, might I not also have seen the experience as an opportunity for evolution? As fuel for that divine fire of the spirit?

We watched films and discussed them. Evenings we walked along the monastery paths and sat by the lake. One of those evenings all four of us sat on the dock where the monks tied their boat. Someone was out on the water, and we could hear the paddles dip and the creak of wood as the boat moved forward. No moon lit the sky, and the stars hung in layers through the black space. All four of us talked and laughed, mostly about the films we'd seen that day. Father Kelly sat at the end of the dock to my right, and Sister Mary Andrea sat to my left. We grew quiet, listening to the lap of water—stargazing. Suddenly I felt the warmth of Father Kelly's hand next to mine where I had rested it on the rough wood. I didn't move. I barely breathed. Then his hand covered mine and stayed there.

For Christmas he gave me a charm—a little silver drum. "We march to a different drummer," he said. My superior, Mother Margaret, ordered me to relinquish it because it violated my vow of poverty. I told her I would not, and I clasped it by its thin silver ring onto my wristwatch where that superior could have witnessed my rebellion every day if she so chose. In the grip of all my other speculations regarding vast changes coming in the future of the church and convent life, I considered that little drum a symbol of an "heroic" stance from which, surely, beauty would result. It would signify a call to new life, transformed in the evolutionary and divine fire.

I prayed and then I spent some time with Sister Marie. We sat in the convent parlor and I told her about Father Kelly, the little drum, the poetry, and the dream of rain. At the time, knowing nothing about how dreams work, I took this as a literal message. Sister Marie was not so facile. She began to discourage me from having any relationship with him at all. For the first time I felt she must be wrong. Her judgment of what I was sharing simply didn't fit the trajectory of her former guidance. So it seemed at the time. She herself had a close friendship with a priest with whom she gave retreats. She had always represented the progressive side of convent life. I didn't say those things, however. Instead, I closed myself off. An icy stream began to run up my spine. My thoughts and words froze. Later that evening, kneeling by my bed, I tried to pray, to reconnect the link that had joined Marie and me for years. But God was silent on that matter. I felt I'd lost her—either that, or I had lost myself.

152

Thus I began to deconstruct, breath by breath and stone by stone, the life that had taken me eight years to build from my lifelong dream and desire. I thought God wasn't answering my prayer, but the work of God in the human heart is careful as it is often slow. The way it appears to me now from a distance of almost fifty years is that my creative energies, detached from the possibility of expression in the religious community of my sisters, began to focus themselves through the priesthood of this one man. Narrowed to a fine point, the desire and love which I had brought to the convent, I now directed at life through this priest. It is probably fortunate for both of us that we did not leave ministry for marriage, as marriage at that time could have faltered under the onslaught of such energy. I did love him, it is true, but not with the ordinary love of a woman for a man. This love was imbued with the sacred. I'd filled this love for the priest with my longing for God. A Jungian might have told me I was in love with an archetype that I'd projected onto this very human individual. Not understanding this and therefore having no idea how to communicate my experience, finding myself distrusted by my sisters, fearing any attempt to explain myself to the priest himself lest he, too, would distrust me, I lived in deep loneliness.

I wrote to Mama about that exquisite tension, the evolutionary fire, and the heroism it required. I put it into my Valentine's Day card to both my parents. Daddy intercepted my letter and called me, saying he couldn't give it to her because it would break her heart. "You can't tell your mother these things." He said. I listened and then started to cry.

"When you are hurting, Daddy, who do you tell?" I was begging him.

"You get used to it." He said.

"Please!" I was grasping.

As it ended up he did give Mama the letter and called me back. "You were right," he apologized. "If you can't tell your mother, who can you tell?"

She drove to Crookston and demanded to see me. "We're leaving here for the day," she said. And I said, "But how?" You couldn't just leave for the day. Even if the holy rule were no longer uppermost among your motivational priorities, you couldn't simply walk out without permission.

"I'm your mother," she said as if that explained it. She was a lion, a bear. I loved her so much that day.

She took me to the rectory where Father Kelly lived. "What do you have to say for yourself?" She confronted him like the ordinary human being he actually was, and a man who only happened to be a priest, not at all the essence of priesthood, but a human male who might or might not be trustworthy. She didn't know. He took us to his office and seated both of us on the other side of the desk from him.

"I don't want to go to bed with your daughter, Mrs. Lore." He said to her. "I want to go to heaven with her."

She didn't like him, I could tell. She didn't like him that day and only barely tolerated him for all the years to come.

A rocky time followed. Mama came often. She came for every play I directed. She came between times. She stopped in at the academy every time she drove with her friend, Evelyn, to Grand Forks to shop. I'm sure she wrote to me and wrote to me. Where are the letters?

For months I'd been working on an essay for the renewal program in our congregation. Finally I finished it and took it to the motherhouse. But I received no comment on it. Nor was I asked to contribute further to this process. One evening Sister Mary Andrea stood waiting for me as I came down the stairs from the girls' dorm. "Sister," she spoke quietly and with obvious concern, "Sister, you must give up your friendship with Father Kelly."

"What do you mean?" I felt my body chill and take a protective stance.

"I've just come from a private meeting of sisters who are part of the renewal program. I was surprised that you weren't there because of all the work you've done, and asked where you were. It turns out they don't want you working on the renewal as long as you and Father Kelly are friends. They don't trust you anymore." She stopped, possibly assessing whether or not she should continue. Then, "Sister, I'm afraid that if you keep up this relationship you will end up being *no one* in the congregation. And frankly, I don't understand what you are up to either. If you just stop this foolishness immediately

154

maybe the sisters will reconsider, but if you don't—well—just don't expect to ever have any influence. They won't permit it."

"Was Marie there?" Certainly she, my mentor, still wanted me to participate. She also disagreed with Pat's and my friendship, but deep down she knew my heart.
"Yes."

"Didn't she speak out for me?"

"No, she didn't. She was in agreement with the others."

Mary Andrea proved to be right. The renewal continued without me. No more studies and papers were requested from me. Another sister replaced me in the rectory meetings. No one but Mary Andrea ever explained. If she had not shared this privileged information, I never would have understood the coolness with which the sisters began to hold me at a distance. More distant that all the others, Marie seemed too busy with her new group of young sisters to notice that I no longer was involved. She was the renewal coordinator with the power to include me, and she chose not to.

The creativity in a sister was assumed to proceed through her religious community commitment. My connection to Father Kelly and the intensity of energy that flowed through it, must have been felt by the sisters as a threat of gigantic proportions to my commitment. I could not turn towards their coolness, and since I was forced to choose, I turned towards the warm enthusiasm of the priest, and also towards the teenage devotion of the girls who were my students. The sisters became keepers of my public life, and Pat Kelly kept my private life more and more until most of what was private in me resided in him. In this turning I now see that I'd begun my departure from religious community life, but would not recognize it for five more years.

Outside my office at the academy was the door to the fire escape. It was at the dead end of a long hallway, and the sisters and students would stand on its metal grate to shake our dust mops after having pushed them up and down the waxed hardwood floors. You had to take care not to let the door close. It would lock and you'd be stranded there two and a half stories above the ground. I fantasized about the fire escape, about letting myself out that way and hearing the door click shut behind me. I wondered if the stairs would work correctly, if the last section really would drop to the ground like it was supposed to. What stopped me was the question: where will I go after I'm on the ground? And the only place I knew was the rectory where Father Kelly lived, just a couple of blocks away. But once I got there, what then?

I should have done it! Sometimes just the feeling of flight is enough—you don't really need to go anywhere. I could have simply walked around the building and rung the front doorbell. What a catharsis! What wonder in the eyes of the sister who would have been summoned by the bell to find Sister Mary Christopher on the outside!

The Jewish Seder has a song called "*Dayenu*"—meaning, "It would have been enough." The people go through each freedom God bestowed upon them throughout history and sing "*Dayenu*"—So it goes, "Even if you had brought us out of Egypt and not parted the Red Sea—It would have been enough. *Da, da-yenu, Da, da-yenu; Da, da-yenu, Dayenu, Dayenu!* Even if you had parted the Red Sea, but not brought us into the land of Canaan, it would have been enough." On and on until everyone is in a mesmerized uproar of gratitude.

Even if I'd only climbed down the fire escape, and never found a place to go beyond those stairs, it would have been enough.

One weekend I did go home to Mama. Just up and going home was not done, it simply could not be done, but I did it anyway. If the tension between what I wanted and what I had, or how I saw myself and how I really was became too taut, I called Mama, collect, from the phone in the little work room behind the assembly hall. "Daddy will come to get you," she said that year in October. But how was that possible? It was possible. My superior said I couldn't go, but I went anyway. The choice turned my stomach with fear as though I were about to dash from a U-boat onto Omaha Beach. Daddy flew south to Crookston in his plane. My superior told me no one would give me a ride to the airport. A friend of my father's picked me up in his little GW sports car, and I pushed open the heavy front door of the academy and ran down the long cement stairs. Three hours from the moment I called Mama she was taking me into her arms. "Sweetheart," I seem now to hear her croon, "It will turn out well in the end. You'll see. Rest now, my darling girl, sleep will banish sorrow."

A LETTER FROM MAMA
My strongest impulse is to say, "I'm sorry."
September 7, 1968

I found a brown envelope of papers that Mama never sent. They resemble journal entries more than letters, but she hadn't kept a journal since 1932 when for half a year she recorded daily events in a brown leather diary. These papers are fragments, typed on her Smith Corona, never more than a page or two at a time, often ending in the middle of a thought, the sentence trailing off and dangling. Some of these are remnants of the family story she always meant to write, her "manuscript," in which she tries to formalize her style to make it worthy of that almost sacred, definitely confessional piece of work.

Inasmuch as I actually, in a moment of despair, she begins in a way that distances her words from her feeling: despair.

...despair when I needed something to do to vent my feelings, commenced with my tale of events relative to relatives, etc., this morning I must take time out and endeavor to come forth with another page...If it ultimately reaches such proportions as to be called a 'manuscript,' it seems important here and now to set the stage for this day. I, Alyce Rose Kathryn (Klimek) Lore, am at home in our small unpretentious house on Henderson Avenue in Baudette, Minnesota. We have a small house, three bedrooms with a basement and a story room upstairs which we call the attic. George Raymond Christopher Lore, husband and father of our two girls, Mary Jane and Elizabeth Anne, has been operator...

Here the page ends with a handwritten note at the bottom (*Must finish this sometime*)

She is struggling with words. She is in a moment of despair. It has something to do with Daddy. The moment she begins to write of him, she stops, mid-sentence. Presumably she rises from her typewriter and for at least that moment, she walks away.

I didn't read her words until after she had died and I found the envelope in a box of her things. Her actual letters of this time tend to be newsy, carbon copied to both of her daughters. She alternated the original copy. Both Betsy and I lived in the Twin Cities. On September 7th, I'd just arrived at my new assignment, a parish and school where I taught seventh and eighth grade English, and was the director of religious education for adults and high school youth. The convent there was considered one of the most progressive in our congregation under the guidance of a vivacious, trusting, joyous woman appropriately named Sister Vivienne. We called her Viv.

If Mama had sent her darker thoughts to me then, I probably would have been unable to take them in, or I would not have wanted to take them in because I needed her and Daddy to be a fixed constellation in an otherwise changing sky. The academy high school had closed that spring, but even had it not closed, my superiors would have moved me somewhere else, far from Fr. Kelly. I rankled from the shame of it, but once I found myself with Viv and the other progressive sisters in West St. Paul, I began to sense a glimmer at the other end of that tunnel in which I'd been stuck. I might get through this without having to leave the convent altogether.

In the meantime, Mama was home alone. She sat down again and inserted a second sheet of typing paper. *Daddy and I just had our first, yes—I mean our FIRST contact with serious discord; in other words, a disagreement, a quarrel— a feeling which leaves me empty and exhausted. What do I do now?*

"Your daddy and I never fight," she insisted all the years that I was growing up. I bragged to my friends who considered me lucky to have parents who got along so well. What didn't fit this doctrine of family were the cries and tears and slamming doors, even that cast iron skillet thrown by my mother, sliding towards me across the tile floor, its handle broken. My dad walked out. The truth was, they never fought *together*. She fought. He walked out, leaving her to fight with shadows.

Nevertheless her perspective was of a peaceful family life with him, in direct contrast with her own family of origin in which disagreements resulted in loud and hurtful words, tears, headaches, and slammed doors. I still can hear them, my mama's family, tearing into each other in the room next to mine at Klimek's Lodge. "You stay right here," Mama warned before she closed my door. I curled in my bed like a fawn in a thicket as the arguments rose to fever pitch and I feared they would kill each other. Finally over the pandemonium I'd hear my daddy (who never walked out when Mama was threatened) command in his deep voice, "That's enough now." They always stopped at the sound of his voice. I heard their door open and close as the other members of the family left the room, and then I heard only the murmurs of my mama and daddy. She felt such gratitude to him for the peace he brought. Maybe she felt it even when he walked away from her those times when all the voices that argued were fighting their endless battle inside her own head.

Mama had doe-eyes that registered the vast extremes of her temperament. When she fell back into it, the yelling, and he wouldn't stand for it, walking out as he did, what happened to her emotions in that very moment, I wonder, as she stood bereft of his response and of his presence? She often needed to leave Betsy and me to retire to her bedroom with a headache. Sometimes she slammed out of the house after he drove away, climbed into her own car, leaving rubber as she squealed down Henderson Avenue who knew where? By the time they both came back they were calm, as though nothing had happened. We lived daily with that way they never fought.

On the day she wrote, Daddy must have stayed. He didn't walk out; he engaged her. They'd met in 1925 and married nine years later. Forty-three years, and for the first time he hadn't walked away from a fight with her.

My strongest impulse is to say "I'm sorry. I don't like you to be angry with me!" (However, it isn't too long ago he caught me up short for always saying, "I'm sorry") I guess I say it too readily, but then, I generally am sorry and feel that everything I do is really the wrong thing. Actually, I have little confidence in my behavior—but I guess people don't like hearing someone always say "I'm sorry."

Tonight, I shall not say those apologetic words, but I'll feel like dying if we both go off to bed without resolving this—Good Heavens! What was it that started it all?

Like everyone, my father had many sides to his personality, and the key to our family, to Mama, Betsy and me, was the fundamental characteristic of my father as a whole. He was inaccessible. What most likely attracted Mama to him in the first place was the adventure of finding the mystery at the center of his personality. What began to enrage her as they grew older was her failure to gain access to that core of him. Maybe he had no access to it himself. My mother did everything she could to get him to open himself to her, but he seemed not to notice her efforts. He preferred to disappear rather than tolerate her anger.

The three of us yearned for him as people yearn for the Unknown God. I developed an idealized image of him and imagined that I knew how he felt. But he disappeared into the sky. He flew his airplane into the wilderness where he could be alone. Over and over he deserted us.

That time he fought first; then he walked away.

She never got over that—saying "I'm sorry." Sometimes she even made a parody of herself, singing it. I'd pick up the phone and there she'd be, singing her sorry song. Maybe I can understand what it was that angered my father in hearing her say it. What angered me was the strong sense I had that she felt sorry about being herself—maybe, even, about simply being at all. And what would we all have done without her?

Where was I on that sorry day? I was in West St. Paul, harboring a sorrow of my own, trying to revise the words of my own story to make them fit the original vision of my chosen life. Did I also stop in midsentence? Daily. I might as well have let the story go and simply lived, but even with the hope instilled by Viv, I feared I would be stuck forever between vision and reality. I couldn't admit that I was sorry more than Mama's song could say for being on a trajectory towards a life I thought I hadn't chosen, with a story that I didn't want to write. I ignored my losses and told myself life was beginning right here, at this moment, in this place.

Why haven't I started the manuscript? She questions herself, the story of the fight that day and the larger story of her family reflecting back and forth as if in mirrors set just so, to capture something in the two stories that extends into infinity. She seems to sense she is on the verge of an awakening. But she can't quite get her eyes to open far enough to focus. *I am a procrastinator. I think I must have hours and hours of time—uninterrupted time, that is,—before I can attempt to begin the story of my life and the lives of my parents and grandparents before me. Recently I read a story by former president Dwight D. Eisenhower entitled, "At Ease," and found that he put down facts about his life in a more or less disjointed fashion, and as the chapters developed, the events fell into their proper places even though he did considerable skipping around. This all makes me realize that I do not have to use a chronological beginning for my story. Therefore, let us now consider that it has begun.*

And that was the final sentence of that story Mama wrote.

A LETTER FROM MAMA
You and your clothing
September 23, 1968

Hi Chris, Mama wrote. The atmosphere had changed and I'd become something of a hybrid of her Mary Jane and that Sister Mary Christopher from the motherhouse and college and the academy. The sisters, with encouragement from Rome, were about to change their names. The point was to doff all masculine names; we were women, after all. No more Matthew; no more Stephen or Michael or Jerome or Christopher. You could keep a feminine name if you'd been given one, or feminize a masculine name, or return to the name given you at Baptism. I decided to change Christopher to Christin. I wonder what Mama thought of that? Not be Mary Jane? Not take back the name she'd given me with such love? Mary, to honor the mother of Jesus, who brought her through a dangerous pregnancy. How often had I heard the story? And Jane, to thank the physician who delivered me by giving me his daughter's name. I could have become Mary Jane once again, and I chose not to do it. It must have felt incomprehensible to her, but she never questioned me about it—not once. Now, I can barely grasp it myself—how I could have been so insensitive—but I just breezed through it as though switching from one identity to another were the most normal thing in the world.

We also were about to venture out into the world in secular clothing. I wasn't clear yet just how that would work, and as a consequence, neither was Mama. I must have written her about it, because she responded, *I have just now had time to think about you and your clothing. I don't quite understand it all—you said you will wear your habit and veil to school—will you always wear a veil or will you go without it when your habit is worn out?* The reasons behind the change were clearer than the practicalities involved in making it. The Sisters of St. Joseph had never intended to wear a habit such as monastic nuns did. Our sisters originally came together to be able to live without husbands and to do the works of mercy. But it was dangerous for unmarried women in France in the seventeenth century, so they needed to dress in a safe manner. The widow's garb of the times would be the safest. Women so dressed could go into the streets, two by two, and be given respect and access to the homes of the sick or those needing education.

When Mama's letter arrived I still was wearing the transitional habit (a black dress, mid-calf length, with a white collar, and on my head a black veil similar to that worn by Red Cross nurses during World War I.) I remember the first time I ever went without the veil, and it must have been before this letter. Father Kelly had come to town. I called him Pat by then, as did most of the sisters at the West St. Paul convent. There were no restrictions on his visits. I don't think I ever knew why he made the trips south, but once there, he showed up on the convent doorstep, regaled the sisters with his Irish wit and stayed for dinner. Afterwards he visited with me in the parlor and then, often, took me for a ride in his 1966 black and white Mustang. One afternoon he took me to Minnehaha Falls, and before we got out of the car, he told me to take off my veil. Why? Well, because people might wonder—seeing a sister and priest together. He removed his Roman collar. It was silly. Deep down I knew it was silly. Useless. Who wouldn't know, both of us dressed all in black as we were? And anyway, even knowing, who would care? I felt strange, taking off my veil in front of him, as though it were an immodest gesture. I told myself that uncovering my head was not immodest, but I knew I was lying to myself. Modesty wasn't even the issue. I'd been veiled since my first day in the convent. The act of removing it under those circumstances held profound symbolism. As I took off that veil I felt a definite surge of fear.

The falls glistened in the lights. We stood on the metal stairway looking at them, and I shivered in the cold spray.

Later that year the parish rummage sale facilitated our sisters' transition from the transitional habit to ordinary secular clothing. The organizers of the sale invited us to the parish hall to rummage for free before the sale began. Sister Diana, Sister Joanne, Sister Phyllis, Sister Vivienne, and several others showed up. Maybe like I, they were flirting with the image of themselves in regular clothes. Maybe we'd all just hang our frumpy transitional habits in our closets and never put them on again. Some parish women helped. It had been years since any of us had considered style. None of us had worn anything but a

THE EDGE OF TENDERNESS

religious habit since we were teenagers, and we were not teens anymore.

"This will look great on you, Sister." One of the parishioners held up a blue dress then draped it over my arm. "Take it back to the convent and try it on. Take anything you find, and if it doesn't fit or you don't like it, bring it back in the morning." Many of the dresses were almost new because hemlines had gone up, and these dresses, a fine length for sisters, no longer made a fashion statement. I kept the blue dress and another one of aqua-green. There was a soft grey suit. Several skirts. Sweaters. Blouses. Color, color, color. A golden brown wool coat, full, with a belted back.

Sister Vivienne invited a friend of hers over to the convent to teach us how to style our hair, how to back-comb it, give it height. I never even thought about how the bunch of us might look, Sundays, parading into the parish church all decked out in the clothes that had so recently belonged to the women sitting in the pews. "There's Sister Christin in my dress! Imagine that! She looks okay; not like a sister anymore at all." But for every one who might have been pleased or at least noncommittal about this change in sisters' mores that had existed for eons, it seemed there were two more who thought it a scandal.

"How will God recognize you?" one woman mourned. "We've had all of you kneeling in front of the church all these years, praying for us. Now it could be any one of us kneeling there. How will God know?"

Mama, for her part, had been hard put to think about clothes those days, as she and Daddy were being sued by a pilot-friend, who as it turned out, lied about the circumstances. They'd been locked out of their bank account and she was worried about paying bills. *Just a quickie to tell you that your intercession is already paying off.* Mama believed firmly in the power of prayer. *Some real nice men flew in from St. Joseph, Missouri, and were waiting to be picked up [by a resort shuttle], and I was quite disturbed and got to visiting with them, and I finally decided to tell them the tale. The man, who is a big industrialist, found some loophole and also reminded us that George's liability insurance and also his airport liability would handle it.* By the time she wrote the letter, her call to the insurance agent had been made and the big industrialist, whom I'm sure she considered an angel in human form, had been correct.

All in all, I think I'm getting too old to take confusion, she finished up after listing another whole paragraph of worries and concerns. They all were very real, and reading it now I see that she was not complaining but rather simply stating facts of ordinary life as most people experienced it. A relative who might have been going blind. Daddy's blood pressure that suddenly had shot high, although it had been low for all his life. A used car they'd given Betsy who would need to be reminded to transfer ownership. *Please call Bets. Remind her.*

I will get your ring from the safety deposit box and either send it to you by insured mail or bring it down to you when we come sometime...

She was referring to the heirloom ring that once belonged to my grandmother. It had occurred to me to wear it as a way of showing that I was a woman bound by vows. If we sisters planned to wear ordinary clothes, we'd need to find another way to signal our vowed status. Our profession crosses, the symbol of our vows up to that time, were large and heavy, unsuited to modern dress. We discussed whether small crosses or rings that we would wear on our "wedding" finger would be more appropriate. The older sisters often opted for the cross, the younger sisters for the ring.

Mama and I lived separate lives. Hers was real. Mine was symbolic. I resisted admitting such a thing back then. I would have argued that my life was of a sort of ultimate reality, and although I would have agreed that a sister's life bore the mark of symbolism, I would have raised that one notch to say it was a sacramental life—a symbol that effected what it symbolized. (When actually, it was marriage that did that—marriage, not religious vows, was the sacrament). It was a question, really, of where God might be found. Was God in the stuff of everyday, the often chaotic jumble of family cares and struggles, or was God a center of love and peace we could not fully experience until the trials of this life were over? A sister was a woman set apart by the church as a symbol of total commitment to a spiritual life, in the world but not of the world. To some, that meant we were not struggling with the world's cares, but could stand apart as islands of refuge where people could retreat for prayer and assurance.

Reading Teilhard made me call that idea into question. The religious community as a whole was questioning it. The religious habit, which had transformed itself over the centuries to become a mark of our quite separate, virtually iconic life, we were about to hang in our closets never to be worn again. We were about to enter the chaos of the real world where people like Mama struggled every day. And for the first years of this immersion, the real and the symbolic would clash in ways we didn't predict. I was still so young. Twenty-seven years old. To the young, change can mean a release from tension built up during those first years of responsibility. I went waltzing into all the changes like Tarot's Fool.

The ring came in the mail, in a four-by-four square box, plastered with insurance tabs and stamps warning of fragility. This ring was the one I took off my finger on the day I entered the convent in 1958 and placed in my father's open hand. "Keep this for me," I'd said. My mother's mother wore this ring most of her life. It held three half-caret, perfect, diamonds. When she died the ring had become mine, and my parents had its diamonds reset in a more contemporary design of yellow and white gold.

I slipped my grandmother's diamonds on my ring finger. Three diamonds, three vows. The fire of the diamonds—symbolic of the fire of spiritual transformation.

"You can't wear diamonds!" Even Sister Vivienne knew symbolism didn't reach that far, was not subject to that extent of manipulation. "You are a sister!"

I removed the ring.

The next time Pat Kelly came to town he brought a plain gold band. "You could wear this," he said. And that arrangement, it seemed, the sisters found more acceptable.

We love you, Mama closes her confusion letter—*wish you could come home again—keep us posted on events when you have the time.*

Much much love –
Mama

IMPOSSIBLE DREAMERS
Summer, 1969

I no longer felt like a sister; I felt like a pioneer. During meditation I seemed always to be planning some new-fangled prayer ritual for an adult discussion group or an adolescent retreat. I preferred folk songs to hymns. I engaged in theological speculation rather than in prayer. My rosary got lost someplace in my desk or dresser drawer.

I didn't look like a sister. Viv, Diana, Joanne and I accepted invitations to the homes of parishioners where we discussed movies like *They Shoot Horses Don't They* while we drank our first Black Russians. The houses were new and large and suburban, and the wives kept an eye on all of us as we parried ideas with their husbands. I'm sure we seemed like any other single women only possibly more exciting and exotic because we represented some strange forbidden fruit. The young doctor's wife took Joanne and me outside one winter evening. She was a tall woman, and I remember how she looked down on us. "Leave my husband alone," she ordered in a voice as cold as the night. Good Lord! Joanne and I exclaimed afterwards. Our interest was in ideas, not men, though when it came to ideas it was the men towards whom we moved. Who wanted to talk about babies? Who wanted to talk about recipes and decorating houses? I'm sure these women felt our arrogance even born of ignorance and insecurity as it was.

From time to time Pat Kelly took me out to dinner. He owned a tweed suit jacket by then, so we went incognito to the Afton Restaurant where I drank my first glass of French wine, a 1967 Beaujolais, and watched an older man and woman sitting at a table in the corner of the room negotiate their entire meal in silence. "I never want to experience that," I told Pat who promised me, as though he had the power or the right, that I never would.

By springtime he was gone from my life. "We can't continue this," both of us admitted, and I said goodbye to him with a confusing combination of sadness and relief. What was the "this"? I now ask myself. Was it that exquisite tension, that Teilhardian fire of transformation about which I'd been so romantically entranced the previous summer? Now I suspect the thing we couldn't continue consisted more in our ignorance about how to actually live such a paradox. It was the frustration of having no pattern, no model for such a life. Celibate love and union—how in the world could two people make that work?

That summer I went back to school. So much in the church's theology had changed since the end of the Second Vatican Council, and I was ill-prepared to continue directing the parish religious education program. I suggested that my superiors send me to St. John's University in Collegeville, where I'd attended the film festival a few years before, to study towards my master's degree in theology. They agreed. I applied, was accepted, and off I went.

Sister Diana drove me from the Twin Cities into the lush countryside of central Minnesota just north of St. Cloud, the area made famous throughout the country by Garrison Keillor's fictional Lake Wobegon. In the Catholic world the area was already famous for the Benedictine monastery and university established there more than one hundred years before. By the time I began the Master of Arts in Theology program this center had become a masterful example of both classic and modern church architecture with their new abbey church internationally renowned. The monks were known worldwide for their scholarship, and the school offered programs in Vatican II theology and experimental liturgy at a time when everything theological and liturgical continued to be in flux. Our religion felt the seismic shifts of a world made smaller by technology, more complex by easy access to worldwide differences in beliefs, and challenged by scientific principles of relativity and uncertainty. We were in the throes of a new kind of war in Viet Nam and a politics of dissent. We mostly young sisters and priests set down that summer in the Minnesota countryside were well aware of all these things and most of us were determined to integrate these shifts into our professional lives, our religious commitments, and our personal identities.

"I'm scared." I confessed to Diana as she dropped me off in front of the modernistic grey concrete dorm building.

"You'll be just fine. You'll have fun." She laughed. "You'll be free."

She drove away. For the first time in my life no one was watching me. No Mama. No superiors or sisters. No parishioners. I lugged my suitcase up to the top floor and into the room that would be mine for six weeks. The large window looked out on the lakes and rolling countryside. I hung my clothes in the small closet, new summer dresses I had sewn. A white sundress with a flared skirt. A bright yellow one with dropped waist and longer sleeves. Several other summer things I'd found at Goodwill.

The large bells rang for Vespers. I walked down to the abbey church where the deep voices of the monks rolled and echoed off the banner of stained glass honeycombed by white concrete. I looked around me at groups of sisters and priests, some dressed like I was dressed, but most still in some version of transitional garb. A shell began to slough off my personality, a shell I didn't know was there until it had crumbled, and I felt like wind. I felt like sunshine. I felt like singing right out loud. Nobody knew me or had any expectations. I could be Mary Jane again. I could be anyone. I could be myself.

That summer became a jewel of memory the like of which I wouldn't see again for almost twenty years. How can I say what I was? New. I was new. I was wet and newly born. If only I could have, would have, gone on directly from there, ridden the momentum of those days, been too fast moving for encumbrance. What a dream that would have been. Impossible, I guess, just like the song.

A lot of us were dreamers at that time. I met them, one by one, women and men, glorious people, brilliant, ecstatic, holy dreamers, looking wide-eyed into the distance toward a future we all thought we would see, tomorrow, next year, surely by graduation time six years distant from those golden afternoons when we canoed on the lake towards the little stone chapel in the woods, read poetry there, sat on the stone floor, told secrets probably none of us remembers, we held them that sacred to our souls.

One of the first people I met was a little package of Irish energy named Sister Bridget. She was a Dominican, I think, still wearing the mostly white habit in its transitional form. It didn't take her long – it didn't take any of the Dominican sisters long—to hitch a ride with one of the priests over to the mall where the spring fashions already were on sale. She then wore her habit only on formal occasions such as Sunday Mass. We played with looking different from who we'd been less than a week before. She cut my hair, a pixie cut, easy and free.

On one of those trips to the stone chapel, Bridget climbed a tree that stood on the lake's edge. She was like Mary Martin playing Peter Pan, laughing, scrambling, not very sister-like one might say—or else, more sister-like that we ever yet had dreamed. Don't go so high, I called. She laughed that she was fine, that she climbed trees all her life until her convent years. Two men were with us, one a priest, I don't remember his name nor that of the other, a Jesuit deacon. Bridget laughed, and at the apex of her laugh, ripping through it, came the splintering sound of wood and the crashing of the branch from which she tumbled to the ground.

"I'm fine!" she tried to reassure us once she caught her breath. Somebody said she needed to go to the clinic. But no. She was fine. She emphasized it. She insisted that we continue on, push off in the canoe, paddle, climb the bank and follow the path to the stone chapel.

She held her arms clasped around her ribs. She looked pale. As the afternoon wore on and we read poetry and lighted candles, she began to look clammy, and finally admitted (after repeated denials) that she really was in pain. One of the men carried her to the canoe. We paddled back to the other shore; he laid her in the back seat of his car and drove her to the hospital in St. Cloud. She'd broken several ribs.

That evening she showed up at the Ecumenical Center where several theologians from different religious traditions were discussing interdenominational ideas with a select number of students and professors. I don't remember how Bridget and I came to be invited to this gathering, new as we both were to the university. But there we were, hobnobbing with some "Greats" in the theological world. I do remember feeling shy. Bridget's ribs were wrapped, and she was high on pain pills. Her Irish came out—as they say—and her descriptions of her "attempts to fly" vied with theologians' flights of mind. They would tumble too; we just didn't know it yet.

The courses I took that summer excited my mind and opened my notions of Christianity to possibilities heretofore unimagined. I studied sacramental theology with a Dutch theologian, and read Rudolf Bultmann in a class on the letters of Paul. I de-mythologized. I was amazed. I wrote a paper on Paul's letter to the Galatians. Its essence: "I cannot bring myself to give up God's Gift. If the Law can save us, what is the point to the death of Christ?" My spiritual understandings that summer moved out of the sphere of doctrine and law and into the sphere of promise, of Spirit: what was called the "Death-Resurrection Mystery." A few years earlier, in my study of Teilhard, I'd sloughed off a kind of Christianity that had as its base a belief in a code of behavior, and had embraced a Christianity at the core of which was experience—the Christ-experience of an ever evolving death and resurrection not only of my individual self, but of the whole creation towards the "omega point," the coming of the "Cosmic Christ." Now these insights were being supported by the scriptural writings of St. Paul. You are the children of the Promise, Paul had written, and I came to believe that and depend on it as truth.

But what I learned in class wasn't all there was. I agreed to do some things so crazy and so wonderful and free that I barely could believe, even while it happened, that it really could be me there doing such things as that. After exams one weekend I joined that same Sister Bridget and two priests from Duluth on a car trip to Lake Superior. We had dinner by the lake and then went out on a small yacht belonging to the local priest's friend. The lights of the city gleamed and flickered. The water lay mysterious and black. Above us layer upon layer of stars seemed to hang like ornaments in the sky. I climbed to the roof of the boat and lay there looking up and singing Judy Collins songs—"Michael from Mountains," and "That's No Way To Say Goodbye." Most young women by their late twenties would have done many such things, but for me it was a first and an only. I still can feel the emotion of it as though I'd been created that moment and placed there, new, somewhere between the water and the sky.

The young priests organized dances in the dorm lounge, every Friday night. I missed the first few of them, but with Bridget's encouragement began to attend after that. We danced to recorded music under the one light that had not been unscrewed. Candles cast shadows on the small groups that sat around the edges discussing such things as the suspension of a whole coterie of priests for their liberal position on the Vatican's ban on birth control. A list of those priests hung on the bulletin board. Everyone had crowded around. One of our group was among them. A suspended priest was as good as gone. All his rights and privileges were taken away. He was as good as fired. Everyone was shaken, running their fingers down the list, looking for names they knew. On Friday nights we put our heads together on this issue and others over which the church seemed at odds with itself. The professors of theology sat among us. We figured we could work this out simply by finding the right words, the combination of logic that would make it obvious—the 'thing' that needed to be done to convince Rome of its error. No thought at all that we might be the erroneous ones. One or another of the priests left the discussion and brought back a highball from the stash of liquor available on a table in the corner. There was a lot of pain accompanying their dreams. Every now and then two young seminarians gathered everyone into a circle to dance to Herb Alpert's "Zorba." We danced ourselves wild.

One Friday night I danced to waltz music with a Franciscan friar. I was wearing that white dress with the perfect circle of a skirt. Until that moment I didn't remember that I knew how to dance like that, but he was a professional dancer. I don't know how that could have been, but it certainly was so. I'd seen him dancing in the sanctuary. He danced before he entered religious life, I think. He was a swan. He was Nureyev reborn. My body bent and floated. He lifted me, swirled me like a banner in the air. I could do anything, it seemed to me that night; I could, if I wanted to, lift up on the music's power alone and fly.

After that dance I became a dancer in the eyes of the others who were there that summer. An African-American Dominican sister and I teamed up for a liturgical dance at the Eucharistic celebration on the Fourth of July. We danced to poetry performed by a Jesuit deacon. We costumed ourselves in the flags of the United States and of North Viet Nam. "I am the enemy you killed, my friend..." the poem ended with both of us lying dead upon the ground.

These events characterized the summer. The mirror of those eyes in which I saw myself then reflected someone different than I'd ever expected I could see. Alive, spontaneous, I said what I thought and laughed and sang out loud.

And to top it off, a missionary priest, a Maryknoll working in Guatemala, fell in love with me and wanted to take me back there with him. "It's okay. Lots of priests are married there. Nobody says a thing. They think we're strange when we DON'T have a woman!" He was a handsome fellow—sort of a youngish Van Johnson whom I loved as a kid. He loaded me down with gifts made by native women--two ponchos, a purse and jacket, a winter scarf, a set of placemats and napkins, a long swath of hand woven material which I later made into a dress. He came up behind me in the mail room one day as I was getting my mail, bent down, pulled my head around to his and kissed me full on the lips!

Another sister whose name I don't remember—I knew her only slightly—saw the attention this priest paid me. Maybe I was being a flirt, but if so, I wasn't aware of it. I was happy and lively and feeling free. His attentions made me want to laugh. Anyway, I was walking past her dorm room when she called me in. She had a face that always looked about to break into tears. She turned from her typewriter and said something like this to me: "You are young. You have lots of chances ahead of you. He liked me first; let me have him."

"What?" Really, I must have been so naïve. I had no idea what she meant.

"I'll never have another chance, and I love him." The missionary, of course. Who knew? Take him! Who was I? Did I own the man? In fact, after that kiss I really felt I needed to keep my distance.

I told her that I had no attachment to the fellow. It all felt surreal. He kept following me around, though, like a puppy. Finally I told him I was sorry if I'd caused him to misinterpret my feelings, but I really couldn't ever go to Guatemala with him. He was disappointed. After all, he'd given me all that stuff. I guess you'd have to call me shameless. I didn't give it back.

Then one morning, early, one of my new friends knocked at my door. "There's a Father Kelly asking around for you," she said. Two worlds collided. His visit was unanticipated, unexpected, and now I realize—unwelcome. He came, bearing in his mind, the image of someone that I didn't want to be. Someone I hadn't been all summer. Someone foreign to me by then. But I invited him into that new way of being, overcoming whatever reluctance I felt. His experiences that summer hadn't been all that different from mine. He'd travelled to San Francisco for a conference, and still felt possessed by a spirit of play which inspired him to contact me. Away from his diocese and I from my community, we must have fancied ourselves more free than we actually were. We talked long hours, walked in the woods, partied with the others, prayed, sang Sousa marches while dancing down the

173

country road under midnight stars. But just because we did not feel the restrictions, did not mean they were not as real as always.

He called Crookston to say he would be late arriving home, and ended up talking to the sister who had been my superior back at the academy. She was appalled that he had stopped to visit with me, but he seemed not to have noticed that, and when he left he said these days had been a time out of time. Now he would be going back to our agreement to separate and be in one another's lives only through the Spirit of Christ.

I believed this relationship was possible—that I was called both to religious community life and to union with Pat Kelly in Christ's priesthood. It didn't feel to me that I had chosen either of these lives, but that I had been chosen by them. I had to believe the two could fit into one another, otherwise life, or God, or whatever had placed me in this position would be found either cruel or insane.

Nothing supported my experience. As time passed, Pat and I seemed to love one another more, but also felt more questions and fears surfacing. Would our love outbalance our commitment to priesthood and religious community life? If that were to happen, then the core of our own relationship would disintegrate and we would be left with nothing. When these questions became too strong, we would once more separate, believing that our love, rooted in God, could not be harmed by discontinuing our communication. I can no longer remember how many times we did this. Sometimes we would be apart for weeks, sometimes for months. Each time some event outside our control would bring us into one another's presence again. We would find that our love had grown during the time apart, but that our ministries had suffered from our lack of communication. We would then begin once more to believe our closer communication must be our destiny, and the cycle would begin again.

No letters from Mama survived the summer of '69, though I remember the image of her envelopes diagonal in the little mail box assigned to me. I don't know if I wrote to her. Looking through the box she kept of my letters to her, I see that the last ones are from 1968. Perhaps I didn't write to her that summer when I wasn't trying to appear as something I was not.

I began to believe that summer that anything was possible. Opposites could be combined. I ceased feeling like the sister I'd trained to be, and I became instead an adventurer in some new world where divine and human combined, dance was prayer, and I could sing into the stars. Vatican II made this possible, I thought, and the rule-structured life that had gone before appeared that summer to be partial and simplistic, one-sided. and because of that, untrue and even wrong. I risked everything that summer, I embraced an edgy life. To break free became for me an exercise of virtue.

After Pat left for Crookston I had no expectation that he would communicate with me, and he didn't. What I didn't know until later was that my former superior, Margaret, concerned about whatever she assumed his relationship with me to be, had called his family. Three of his brothers came to confront him at the rectory, assuming he was having an affair with one of the sisters. "You can go to hell for all I care," said his brother, "but you damned well won't take the Kelly name with you!"

It broke him. Over the years I patched his story together, picking up pieces as he shared them with me. After his brothers' visit, after one of them had condemned him to hell, he packed the trunk of his Ford Mustang with what it would hold of his few possessions. He sold his coin collection for survival cash and gave his radio to a sister at the academy who was his close friend. Then he drove north, towards the lake retreat belonging to one of his brother-priests—the place his friends went on their days off to relax. He didn't ask the bishop for a leave of absence; he simply left. For all he knew he was losing everything on which he'd ever set his hopes. Without the bishop's permission, he could not serve as a priest. He left with neither goal nor vision.

Something happened along the way. Something struck him—maybe it struck him dead. Afterwards he wasn't sure. Maybe it was a panic attack that knocked him cold. He felt it coming on—the nausea, a blinding light, the racing of his heart, his sense of needing to stop the car, no more sound, blackness. "I either died or had a psychotic collapse," he told me years later. And finally, finally when he actually *was* dying, he confided that his death had begun on that day sixteen years before. "The seed of death was planted in me..."

He woke, still in his car by the side of the highway and, shaking, continued to the cabin on the lake. There he stayed for the remainder of the summer. His priest friends came at least once a week, keeping the secret of his whereabouts. He prayed and meditated. By the end of August he'd formed a plan.

Again he packed his car and drove south to Collegeville and the Benedictine monastery there. The abbot of a monastery has all the ecclesial powers of a bishop, and within his jurisdiction a priest could be given the necessary faculties (permissions) to serve. Pat's plan was to meet with the abbot and ask him for those faculties. Politically speaking, the Crookston bishop was indebted to the abbot at Collegeville because the abbot sent priests to fill vacancies in diocesan parishes. If the abbot accepted Pat, the Crookston bishop could not—and would not—try to block that move, because he couldn't risk losing the abbot's good favor.

He drove to St. Cloud, to the Newman Center at the State College, where he stayed during his negotiations. While there, the Newman chaplain told him of an opening for chaplain at the College of St. Benedict in St. Joseph, Minnesota—right next door. It is the sister-school to St. John's. By the end of September he had an apartment on campus and what turned out to be a creative and vital ministry to the young women and faculty of that college. I never saw him happier than he was during his first two years there.

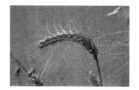

REMEMBER A TIME OF MANY NAMES

- Remember the voices within and listen to the high pitches and the low; do not ignore the shrill, the keen, the argumentative, the resulting suffusion of tears.
- Remember the yearning: a scent of lilacs, the spray of waves, a rainbow above the island close to home.
- Remember the eyes of those who looked at you, whether they drew you in or turned you away.
- Remember how night fell and how dawn poured onto the horizon, suffusing clouds.
- Remember the taste of God's name upon your tongue and let that be enough.

A LETTER FROM MAMA
The Voices Inside You
September – December 1969

The annual retreat at the motherhouse followed directly on summer school, and I attended with all the enthusiasm I'd stored up during the six weeks at St. John's. Several of the other younger sisters and I gathered to read poetry, play guitars and sing. We designed prayer rituals that often included long poetic passages from the works of Teilhard de Chardin. We walked to the clearing in the woods close to the river behind the barley fields, had a picnic, and built a bonfire which after dark shot its sparks into the starry sky. At one of our chapel sessions, I delivered the paper I'd written on *Galatians.*

I returned to the Twin Cities to find that the Archbishop had assigned a new pastor. He was a tall, John Wayne sort of man. Or maybe a Vince Lombardy sort, as it was Lombardy's words he'd framed and placed above the rectory mantel. He came to the convent to meet the community, then each program director. With my six weeks of theological education under my new hairdo I felt confident. I set out the religious education program for the year and invited him to attend my first teacher-training program just after Labor Day. The evening arrived and so did he, along with his assistant. They stayed ten minutes and then left.

A week later our three major superiors from Crookston, among whom now was Sister Marie, showed up at the convent and summoned me to a meeting. The pastor wanted them to move me to a different mission. "He wanted us to fire you," they said, "but we told him he'd have to do that himself if that's what he wanted. However, we want you to know that we stand behind you. He's waiting for you right now in the rectory."

I knew what this meant. The parish contracted for our sisters as a group, not as individuals. The pastor had to take what he got or nothing. After my little tantrum some years before in Crookston when Sister Mary Andrea said these very women didn't trust me anymore, their support in this situation overwhelmed me with gratitude. I felt strong as I walked across the street to the rectory, and it's a good thing, because what was about to come was something for which I was completely unprepared.

At first he was gracious, almost ingratiating. He invited me into his living room and showed me his Vince Lombardi quote. I have only a vague memory of learning why he thought Lombardi was a good model for pastors. Then he motioned for me to sit down in a chair by the window. He sat opposite me and crossed his legs the way a woman does. He said I'd need to leave the parish. I asked why. He said I advocated free love and draft dodging and he wouldn't stand for either. Maybe I laughed. I was nervous. I felt like laughing. I asked him who ever told him such a thing; certainly it wasn't included in the ten minutes he'd listened to my little teacher-training introduction. Lots of parishioners had mentioned it to him, he said. I didn't know how that could be. He told me that of course no one would tell me to my face. That was for him to do. I denied that I advocated either of those things. I challenged him to find one time that I'd actually said anything even remotely connected to either issue.

His face got red. And to be fair, I was acting like an upstart, like someone without an ounce of diplomacy. I knew I was in the right, though, and at that age I mistakenly thought that the mere fact of my innocence in these matters would be enough. That was when he scared me.

"Look at you!" He leered.

"What?" Really. I didn't know where this was going.

"Look at your body!" He gestured at me. "Your legs!" He grimaced. "Your breasts!"

I just stared at him. This meeting wasn't about something I'd said or taught. It was about me, about me as a woman. It was about sisters no longer wearing those garbs that hid our bodies under layers and folds of black wool. I began to get sick to my stomach.

"I don't need to *hear* you say that you promote free love, I can *see it* just by looking at you." He was leaning forward. He could have touched my knee if he'd reached out. He said more. Maybe fifteen minutes more of similarly insulting remarks before he told me to leave his presence. "I want you gone from this parish," he said.

Was it my sense of justice that rose up, or was it just the stubbornness, the anger I'd learned from its flare-up between Mama and Daddy that ended with his silent exit and her skillet thrown through the air. "I'm staying," I replied as I walked past him out of the rectory.

By the time I got back across the street and into the convent, I was trembling so hard my legs gave out and I collapsed in the back hallway. One of the sisters helped me up the stairs to my room and I lay on the bed shaking uncontrollably. That priest had terrified me, and I could have been free of him, but I'd refused to leave. There would be a battle, it couldn't be averted, and I couldn't imagine that I'd be able to get through it with even a veneer of sanity.

When I could stand I stared out the window. What should I do first? I wanted to run away—not forever, just for a while, overnight. I needed to break my connections with the parish at least that much, to get ideas that weren't church ideas. I knew by instinct I couldn't talk to the sisters or the neighboring priest who was a good friend and colleague. Who, though?

I called my cousin, Sandra. It didn't take more than an hour before she pulled up in front of the convent, hustled me into her car, and drove me to her home in a north Minneapolis suburb to spend the night with her and her husband, Woody, and their two little boys, Robbie and John.

Mama writes: *I'm sorry I didn't get another chance to talk with you—Bets hinted that you were having some worries—but now I know that you received encouragement and advice which I couldn't put into words nearly as well. I'm grateful to Sandy and Wood for being accessible when you needed a place to go, and she was most happy that you called her. She is quite a terrific person, you know, and a lot of things she says make very good sense. She told me much about the evening before, and I know how you must have felt—quite all alone and confused about the whole thing—until you had a chance to talk it out in a relaxed atmosphere.*

Woody made daiquiris, which I'd never before tasted, and both he and Sandy sat with me in their contemporary living room, listening to my story of what, by that time, was feeling so personally abusive that I couldn't imagine walking back into the situation. I couldn't imagine being in the same room with that priest. Wood, who was a manager at a major corporation, encouraged me to make contacts with other church professionals who had standing in the Archdiocese to ascertain how much broader support I actually had.

180

Wood and I progressed from management systems talk to church-talk and questions about the changes being wrought by Vatican II. He'd distanced himself from Catholicism in recent years, but had been raised in a strict French-Canadian Catholic culture—family and extended family all around. He couldn't bring himself even to imagine that anything about the teachings of the church could change. Looking back now I realize that Wood and the parish priest stood in similar positions vis-a-vis church doctrine and practice, and neither of them accepted my revisionist notions. But Woody listened, and he respected me.

Wood's suggestions that evening led me to make phone calls later in the week which garnered support from the archdiocesan organization of religious educators—the closest we had to a union. Later, at a parish council meeting, the president of that organization would present teachings from the *Documents of Vatican II* to argue that the pastor had no right to fire me. Only the parish council could do that, and this was an action that council refused to take.

I haven't dwelt much on your problems, Mama wrote later, *but what can I say? Time and hard work with your projects which you know you must carry out to the best of your ability will help you through, but my motherly advice has to be now for your physical condition. The feel of your boney body when I squeezed you makes me unhappy at the thought of you not eating. You CANNOT cope with things if you don't have proper nourishment to give you the stamina you need. PLEASE remember that. Eat—three meals a day!*

She had arrived in the Twin Cities to check on me. I remember her arms around me and her murmurs, "You're so thin!"

I look now at pictures of me from those days and I am skeletal. I couldn't stomach food. Mostly, fear had nauseated me so that the mere appearance of food would turn my stomach. But even when I didn't feel afraid and did have an appetite, the food could turn on me, making me ill. Viv sent me to the internist who didn't find an ulcer and determined that I was simply (simply?) anxious, and prescribed Valium—as needed. I took so few, fearing them as well, that I never refilled the prescription.

181

Every religious education event became an occasion for fear, in case the pastor might show up. This was something he seldom did, however, and I realize now that he didn't like being in my presence any more than I liked being in his. The sisters had refused to remove me which must have been a blow to his sense of power. He seemed to be expanding his complaints to include all of us who directed parish programs. From me he went to Sister Diana, the school principal who reacted with calm professionalism. From her he went to Sister Vivienne. Viv just laughed. She had at least twenty years on Diana and me, and saw the priest's antics for what they were. Her amusement must have irritated him more than my resistance or Diana's professionalism, because he took the matter to the archbishop. The parish split over who would support the sisters and who would support the pastor. Viv and the major superiors from Crookston met with the archbishop. The whole war continued for years until, finally, the pastor won. The sisters vacated the convent and he had it rebuilt for his own use. Then he hired a principal and teachers for the school among the laity. He advertised the educational system there as progressive, the first of its kind in the diocese, the wave of the future when such radical sisters as we represented to his mind would be a mere remnant of a rogue wave in the ocean of church history.

In the meantime, though, I struggled and Mama worried. A committee of conservative church women had taken me to task and I'd called her for insight. She listened, but only later, when she'd thought about the situation, did she respond.

I have been working around the house by myself since I talked with you this morning, and I have been mentally composing a letter or carrying on a conversation with the ladies of that committee, telling them of you as a child. Who are they to sit in judgment? They don't know you or any of the sisters for that matter. They should have been around and watched you grow and develop in God's image and realize your motivation. Why would anyone who wanted so dearly to serve Christ ever do anything against His Will knowingly except to try to carry on thru the message of the Holy Spirit? (I surely would like to be able to write it out—my fingers put down the words better than my tongue can say them.) I can recall so many little incidents in your childhood which at the time I tried to ignore, but surely it was each time a message from the Holy Spirit, and I still have the written notes and thoughts which you left in so many places—the Bible and in your books. You see, they only see the outside You—and I'm sure it is the same with the rest of the Sisters. I feel sorry for these people and I can't believe it is the Holy Spirit prompting them unless Our Lord is testing you. Forgive them. Try to understand them, and do what you feel in your own thoughts is right. I have often wondered just what Role you were supposed to play in this religious life, and now it is beginning to transpire. He is using you in a very important role...and He expects you to play it to the best of your ability.

Bear in mind—you must WIN these people and if you plan your strategy and remember your timing and forget about your own self-pity (I actually don't think you wallow in it, but it is only human that you should experience it), and be able to build to a climax and bear down on the punch lines as the Holy Spirit dictates them to you, the show will be for His great honor and glory in the end. Just remember that as long as the Holy Spirit prompts you, YOU ARE RIGHT.

I can't help but think how Joan of Arc was propelled to follow her VOICES in spite of all criticism and bribery not to do it. That takes more than just strength and courage—it takes God's Will. Listen to your voices inside you—and when you come home we can talk and talk and you can relax and see the vision of a dream. I wish I had your courage and your knowledge. Except for you and Betsy, I guess our lives, George's and mine, have been rather pointless ... but that is as it should be, I suppose.

Love and our prayers for you always,
Mama

This must have been the letter that inspired me to call the woman who had been most vocal and fiery in her opposition to me and the educational programs I'd initiated in the parish. She sounded like the pastor's mouthpiece, and when she spoke my stomach churned.

I ended up in her living room, looking at her wedding album, listening to her dreams, her own fears, her hopes for her several children. We met often. I joined her family for winter sports, sliding down hills on those round plastic snowboards, whirling, kicking up that dry snow—that powder. We became good friends, and though we never did agree on where exactly the changes in the church should lead, we loved one another, and ended by supporting one another in those meetings where the pastor advanced his war. From her I began to respect and finally even to cherish the often very different paths upon which God sets individual people.

At the time she came into my life, I'd taken on the responsibility of implementing the changes wrought by the Second Vatican Council, and I knew only one way to do that—the way I'd learned during the summer during my very brief stay at St. John's with professors and students of theology who were experimenting with forms and structures of implementation. We were the dreamers, but no one yet knew how the vision set out by Vatican II could be implemented. The theologians didn't know. The bishops didn't know. The priests didn't know. The parishioners didn't know. Everyone wanted guidance, and there wasn't any. I was twenty-eight years old and eager to do the work of the church, so I forged ahead, pretty much plowing under every ancient tradition and structure that didn't fit the new vision. But this woman loved the pre-Vatican II traditions. If I'd been more honest with myself I would have recognized that my activism was in large part a result of grieving the loss of them. Both she and I had expressed our faith through those traditions. The whole idea of exchanging them for something new, well, she just couldn't see how that would work. And she was right. It's not something an individual or an institution can do in a summer, or a few years. It can take a lifetime – sometimes generations of lifetimes. She really didn't want to lose what she once had. And while I came to respect that and to cherish her, I still felt determined to do all that I could to bring about the changes as I believed the church intended.

A LETTER FROM MAMA
Don't get lost
Thanksgiving to Christmas 1969

The next parish down the road hired a lively, iconoclastic, guitar playing, folk singing sister on a leave of absence from her religious community, and we teamed up to do teacher training and youth retreats. Her name was Stephanie (Steph), and she boarded at the parish convent. Almost as soon as we met she was concocting schemes for the two of us to move out of our convents into an apartment. She'd drive up in her little second-hand car and honk the horn or breeze into my convent or the religious education center. She'd catch me up in her energy, and we'd take the afternoon off to explore the classic brick apartment buildings found in almost any section of St. Paul. We didn't have a red cent to spend on lodging—though she did receive a small salary. What money my work earned bypassed me entirely and went into the convent coffers. The money wasn't mine. This was the first time and probably the last in my whole convent experience that I wished it weren't set up that way. What a relief it would have been to have a refuge away from the parish where I worked.

Even if my superior had given me the money, though, it would never have been enough. I believe it came to seventy-five, or maybe only forty-five dollars a month. The organization for religious educators had begun to work on negotiating better salaries. A small minority of us were not members of religious communities. They had families to support. They earned more, as Steph did, but it was a pittance compared to what might be considered a fair wage. And the very idea that sisters ought to receive a fair wage seemed beyond comprehension. Even years later, after I'd left the convent and was making nine thousand dollars a year at a different parish, I was let go because the pastor said he could get five sisters for the price of me.

Steph also had spent the previous summer at a university, in a theological program where she met a handsome young professor/priest from Holland who'd written a scholarly paper on "the third way." I'd never heard of it. It was a kind of marriage, she explained, between celibates. It was like St. Francis and St. Clare—except that the women were not cloistered, but were active in the world. It was a union between a celibate man and woman that bore

185

witness to such strong love and spiritual commitment that they could be together, even live together, working for the fullness of Christ in the world. She'd fallen in love with this priest theologian and they were committed to live the third way together. He was back in Holland at the moment, setting things up. Many men and women (priests and sisters) were responding to his vision. There would be a community of them that he would gather together. Steph's eyes danced with that shine you see at the edges of fanaticism, when a person feels suddenly awakened to a sense that she now sees realities to which the rest of the world is blind. "We will lie together chastely." She smiled. "We'll sleep together, sharing breath, listening to one another's heart beating."

I wish I could say I listened to her rhapsody with skepticism, but in my post-Vatican II world so many things I'd never dreamed possible had taken on the aura of possibility. Who could say we would not evolve to this third way? Might this not be the very way the Holy Spirit was leading us? In fact, I ran into the idea many times in the years to come, often among the most creative priests and sisters I knew. And it was cropping up as well in newly organized religious communities combining men and women. Maybe it was part of the new world coming, as Mama Cass was singing on Steph's car radio.

I wonder what ever happened to that girl? I want to ask now as I'm remembering her. She was so young, I want to add—so wild.

Around Thanksgiving the Catholic Religious Educators' Conference was being held at the Palmer House Hotel in Chicago. Steph wanted to attend. She knew the city—I'd never been there. She'd drive her car. We wouldn't need to pay for a room at the Palmer House because we could stay with sisters who were her friends. She presented all this to me with that kind of flair some women possess that catches you up in the intoxication of having been specially chosen. It has tremendous ego-appeal. It's what makes the plain girl follow and serve the pretty one in adolescence. And Steph and I weren't emotionally far beyond that age. I obtained the necessary permissions from Sister Vivienne, and I went.

Got your card. I hope you girls enjoy Chicago and don't get lost. I'm sending you ten dollars, just in case you should get in a bind and need a little extra cash. It isn't much—for Chicago—but you might need it.

They couldn't afford even that much, as once again Dad was being sued by an unscrupulous man who claimed he used old parts to fix his airplane. Mama hastened to explain that Dad had not done this, had the receipts for the new parts, and an employee to vouch for him. *George wants to do what is right, but doesn't want to pay if it is someone else's fault—you know your father—honest, but tough too.* Litigation, now so commonplace, had been rare up to then. And Dad was a small businessman who knew most of his customers personally. If something went wrong with a job he'd done, he would make it right. But he was starting to see more and more deceit. This man didn't want his airplane repaired because of a botched job, he simply wanted all his money back for the job already done. Deceit my father would not tolerate.

I took the money though, and there must have been a little more for meals and gas provided by either the convent or the religious education budget, or most probably, both. Steph picked me up and then we went together to pick up a third sister from a different parish. We were loners among the Catholic School educators in the archdiocese. Ours was a new profession, its description, qualifications, responsibilities still were in flux. We created our job as we went along. Typically the women and men were thought to be mavericks even before they slipped into the newly created, free-flowing position in the parish. We were a motley crew of mostly sisters and former seminarians, radicalized by Vatican II thought, eager for change and creative in developing methods and programs for bringing change about. We were not always wise.

The trip is hazy in my mind. We were in the parking lot, putting suitcases in the trunk, and then we were pulling up in front of the Palmer House on a street gleaming with holiday lights. We let the other sister, who remains faceless in memory, out of the car underneath the marquee. She walked in through the ornate doors.

The scene switches to the convent. I was holding a cocktail glass with a Maraschino cherry in the bottom. Candlelight gleamed through a Manhattan. I hadn't known what a Manhattan was, but the sisters said I'd like it, so I had two. Steph laughed with her sisters. Their memories bounced against the old wood paneling and lots of doors to smaller rooms. I would sleep in one of them on a narrow bed.

My suitcase was already in the room. My stomach felt queasy and a sister handed me 7-UP. She laughed.

In the middle of night I woke with my heart out of control, pounding, fluttering, terrifying me. I must get help or die. My stomach turned. Maybe I had food poisoning. I had to wake someone, but I didn't want to cause a disturbance. I tried to get up and the room whirled. I stumbled into Steph's room and shook her from sleep. "I'm sick," I moaned.

"You're drunk. Be quiet or you'll wake the house."

Torn bits of Chicago remain, stitched together like a crazy-quilt. The Palmer House—elegant gold and embarrassingly rich--dwarfed us under its magnificent ceilings. Our meetings, though, were held in typical hotel conference halls and rooms. The first day, after registration, we met in focus groups. I'd just introduced myself when Steph pulled me aside to say these meetings were a waste of time and we should be Christmas shopping.

"We can't just leave," I whispered. And anyway—Christmas shopping? I hadn't come to Chicago for that. I'd anticipated recovering some of the freedom and intellectual excitement of my summer at St. John's.

"Sure we can!" She grinned. "These small group things are useless. Besides I need to get a Christmas present for Pierre" or Andre or Philippe or Marcel or whatever his name was. "Get your coat."

I obeyed.

Snow was falling outside. It was the very scene I now see each winter on national news weather reports--holiday shoppers bundled in coats and scarves, snowflakes in their hair. "You'll love Marshall-Fields," Steph started off across the street. I became her puppy. She negotiated the various levels and departments of the store like she'd grown up in it. Up and down the unbelievably long escalators I felt simultaneously dragged along by her will and completely forgotten. If she'd turned around, looked startled, and said, "Oh, are you still here?" it would not have surprised me. By that time I'd gone beyond chagrin to annoyance to anger, but said nothing. I barely dared think through to what the feelings meant, because another feeling had inserted itself right into the pit of my belly. Fear. I was afraid of being lost. What a crazy feeling. It didn't make sense to me because I certainly was smart enough to find my way back to the hotel if I chose to. I clenched my teeth and tried to keep up with her.

Jessie Jackson gave the keynote address, and I had no idea who he was. "He's really famous in Chicago," Steph tried to educate me. What a strange group we were that crowded into the conference hall. Priests in Roman collars, priests in colorful dashikis, sisters in full flowing black or white or brown habits, sisters in transitional garb, sisters in dowdy skirts and blouses, sisters in mini-skirts and boots. Several hundred of us in all. And Jessie Jackson in his Afro, lean and acrobatic, prancing on the stage. He didn't always talk in rhyme back then. He did talk of compensatory justice, and this was the first I'd heard of or considered the notion. Jessie lifted his fist and cried out "I AM somebody!" And this motley crowd of Catholic educators echoed him. "I AM somebody!" Jesse cried out again, "I am SOMEbody!" And we all echoed him again. It went on like that, a litany of self affirmation, for what seemed several minutes. We were accustomed to litanies, the call and response in which we'd prayed all our lives— "Holy Mother of God—Pray for us. Holy Virgin of Virgins—Pray for us." But nothing quite like this. I confess to trying it with the teenagers back at the parish after I got home. What a drama it was. It was play— a way of trying on for size something at least I could not quite believe.

After that I barely saw Steph. She must have driven me back to the convent each evening, and to the conference again in the morning, though I don't remember that at all. Maybe that happened only once— conferences never lasted long. Starting Friday night they usually were finished late Sunday afternoon. So probably it was mid-morning on Sunday that she came up to me with the news that she'd gone back to the convent to retrieve our luggage, and mine was in safe-keeping behind the hotel reservation desk. We weren't going back there that night. I wanted to know where we were staying. She told me that she didn't know where I'd be staying, but she'd met up with a priest she'd known back when she'd been assigned in Chicago, and that she would be staying with him. "You can probably get a room here," she said. "Then I can pick you up in the morning and we can get on the road."

"We're completely full," the man at the reservation desk told me. "We have this conference going on."

189

"I know, I'm part of it." I said. I hadn't stayed in a hotel since I was a child and went to Minneapolis with my mother. Certainly I'd never attempted what I was attempting now. I think I explained that I'd been staying somewhere else and suddenly that option was closed to me.

Finally he said there was a closet with a cot. It was a storage or supply closet. Sometimes an employee would stay there. Did I think that would be adequate? I must have had a check book from the parish religious education program—otherwise how did I pay for this closet? Mama's ten dollars, given in case I was in a bind, wouldn't have been enough even for the little roll-away cot I found in the storage room, and the folded sheets I found on top.

I probably used Mama's money for supper at a café I found down the block. Afterwards I stood in the snow under thousands of holiday lights on probably the most famous of Chicago streets, alone, afraid of being lost if I ventured further. If someone had asked me then who I was and what I was about and why I'd come to this place, I would have had a stock answer, but deep down I wouldn't have known. I was already lost. I'd been lost for quite a while, and I didn't know it. But I felt it that night. How would I ever sort it all out? The life I'd chosen was also a life I chose to change into something different— something that would fit me, perhaps, so I could remain alive in it—so my life as it really was and the dreams I'd had in the past would fit each other. My fear of being lost in Chicago was really the fear of being lost in the chasm that was, even at that moment, widening in my mind. And I would go on for years gathering words to make it right, words like stones, piled one on the other to shore up the walls of my desire to be a sister, because those walls were crumbling. They were crumbling not just in me, but in the life itself. I couldn't fit the stones together fast enough or securely enough to save it.

I lay awake all night in the tiny storage room too frightened by newness to go to sleep. The next morning Steph was in the lobby, and I got into her car and we drove through a snow storm back to the Twin Cities. I don't think I said a word to her about everything I felt. I don't know if I dared to recognize deceit when I saw it. What would my father have done? *George wants to do what is right, but doesn't want to pay if it is someone else's fault—you know your father—honest, but tough too.* That's what Mama wrote. "I AM somebody," I had called out

190

with the others as Jesse Jackson strode up and down the stage. But was I? And where was the deceit, anyway? In Steph? In me? In the whole mess of us, taking ourselves apart, taking our church apart, putting ourselves back together in new ways? Steph stopped the car at a café just outside of Eau Claire. We couldn't go any further until the snow let up. We couldn't plow our way through, and the windshield had accumulated so much ice we could no longer see our way.

A LETTER FROM MAMA
"Just too too perfect"
January 13, 1970

One of the sisters brought this letter from Mama into my bedroom, and I read it for the first time propped up on pillows so I could breathe and keep from coughing. I had the debilitating strain of flu, rampant that year. Mama called when she hadn't heard from me and Sister Jean Ann told her how awful my cough was and that they'd taken me to the doctor because of it. Coughs brought Mama to attention, catapulting her mind back to her year in the tuberculosis sanatorium. *She said your chest is very painful . . . I cried when I hung up the phone. I SHOULD HAVE KNOWN SOMETHING WAS WRONG! I feel so helpless here when I should be there looking after you...I'm sending $2 and I want you to have someone get you some oranges—good big navel oranges with thick skin so there is lots of white along with lots of juicy fruit. Eat just as many as you can hold.*

I see her fingers clicking on the keys. She decided to distract me from my flu miseries by becoming the home town gazetteer. She wrote about Evelyn and her daughter, about Eddie who was Dad's mechanic at the airport, about Donna whom she'd taken in as a roomer and ersatz daughter, about the diet she and Dad were on so they could fit into their clothes for the upcoming Aviation Trades Association Convention, about Betsy's new job. She reminded me: *We really had a wonderful Christmas season here, didn't we? It was just too too perfect— (you know something? You already had a start of the illness, didn't you? You had a sore throat, remember?)*

I'd been home for Christmas!

Now I sit back in my chair and gaze outside at the bare branches of these Oregon oaks. The sky this morning was rosy with sunrise the week before Christmas. Christmas is a box of memories, stored, mixed together. That Christmas of 1969—where are the memories and what was the "too too perfect"? Maybe it simply was having the family together after she had surrendered that togetherness, thinking that I never would spend Christmas with her and Dad again. I hadn't thought so either. Some things just don't occur to you when you set off on a path through life. Common things. Things you can't imagine doing without, and so they don't come to mind. That first convent Christmas back in 1958 a pottery lamb was one of those things I hadn't considered.

Mama sold Frankoma pottery in her Store of Lore. For years she'd displayed an expensive life-sized lamb, exquisite to my eyes so that as an adolescent I'd beg her before each Christmas to let us take it home. But it was too fine for us. She needed to sell it to someone who could afford it. Year after year it remained in the store.

The Christmas of 1958 I'd been in the convent only four months. Each day required the loss of something I'd taken for granted about life, and its replacement with some new way of doing things, or looking at myself, or understanding the world. I learned how deeply I'd thrust my roots into the traditions of my family at home. "<u>This</u> is your home now," Mother Celine instructed.

What happens to the mind and heart so turned around, so pulled inside-out? The process was different from the more normal, slow evolution every young person experiences upon leaving home for college or marriage. Military training might be analogous. I let my mind and heart be taken over by a deliberate intention outside of me, an authoritarian intention with the goal of separating me from the culture and traditions in which I'd grown up, and replacing them with convent culture and traditions. My first real awareness of how intimately this process would reach into me came that first convent Christmas Eve.

Central, even now, to all my Christmas images is that Frankoma lamb.

All the bustle of a family preparing for Christmas—shopping, making things, decorating—was absent from the novitiate. Advent prevailed with its violet and rose matching the prairie sky, and its yearning cries and prayers, "O Come Emmanuel." We practiced music for the Christmas Masses—three of them on that day—but to me Gregorian chant felt like the wrong music. At home we'd sung a Mass in four parts that I had loved. Christmas Eve day Sister Emma Joseph arranged the manger scene in the chapel. We all kept silence that entire day, ate a simple supper, and went to bed early so be awakened at eleven o'clock for Midnight Mass.

As the years went on I came to love convent Advent and Christmas so much that I never was able—even now—to adjust back into the materialistic, secularized Christmas of American culture. I couldn't even adjust back into a family Christmas with its games and presents and football and laughter and loudness. I'm caught somewhere between where I suspect I shall remain until my life is finished here.

That first convent Christmas I was also caught somewhere strange, between past and future in a present moment with not much joy or comfort. Sometime during the novices' nap on Christmas Eve, sisters began arriving from convents throughout northwestern Minnesota. The chapel was filled at midnight. We sang the ancient Gregorian chant Christmas Mass never attempted by our little Baudette church choir. Afterwards, the only night in the year, sacred silence was lifted, and all the sisters met in the hallway outside the dining room, to greet each other with hugs and that French way of touching faces, first one cheek then the next—"Praised be our Lord, Jesus Christ! Merry Christmas, Sister!" In the dining room the sister-cook had set a feast of pink grapefruit, homemade bread, sausages from the Benedictine sisters down the road, scrambled eggs. And beside each plate was a collection of holy cards—enough to last the entire year of feast days.

Where was my real family? Mama, Daddy, Betsy—what were they doing? How could there be Christmas for any of us, at least a Christmas without a gigantic hole, an absence in the heart? Mama would send me a picture, later, of that Christmas Eve. She's not in it— she's holding the camera. It's the dining room table with the remains of Christmas Eve dinner—always walleyed pike from Lake of the Woods. Betsy has her arms around Daddy's neck and her head is resting on his shoulder. No one is smiling. Both of them are looking into the distance, but not at the camera. The little phonograph sits on the table with the dishes. *We played the record you made before you left so we could hear your voice. So it would seem you were home with us—*

I could barely see or hear the loveliness of that first convent Christmas, I was so focused on the family I had lost. That night, after the postulants and novices picked up the remnants of our celebration and had washed the dishes, Mother Celine led us all into the community room to admire her Infant Jesus of Prague, dressed in white and gold satin. Like a tiny doll, this statue's clothes were changed for each season of the liturgical year, and the sisters spent many hours hand stitching his tiny garments. She'd lit the Christmas

194

tree, and we all stood in a group to admire her "Infant Jesus." I stood also, with the others, but I barely looked at the "Jesus," because under the tree was none other than Mama's white Frankoma lamb. My chest tightened. I couldn't breathe. I didn't want to breathe because if I did, I'd cry out.

"And look what Mr. and Mrs. Lore gave us," Mother Celine was saying. Her voice told me it meant nothing to her. My belly was a stone I held rigid.

It was a problem I had, that I still have. Tangible objects seem more than they are. They shimmer with a meaning beyond themselves. Mama's love was in that lamb. I imagined her love overwhelming her as she prepared the statue that she knew was much too fine for her own household, and brought it to the convent. I imagined how she anticipated everyone's joy in seeing such a marvelous thing, and especially my joy in finally having what I'd so long desired. I thought: "She thinks it will be a Christmas tradition to take this lamb out each year and place it under the tree, just as we would do at home. But this isn't home."

I could barely hear what Mother Celine said next, I'd made myself so impermeable—something about it not exactly fitting here, lovely as it was, and when this Christmas was over she would share the gift from the Lore's by giving it to one of our other houses, and maybe it could be used in the parish. I knew I would never see the lamb again.

Reading Mama's letter now, I remember that the sisters in the Twin Cities decided as a group that each individual sister could go either to the motherhouse or home to her family for Christmas. I chose home. Betsy, who was now Liz but we hadn't gotten used to that yet, would pick me up after work on the day before Christmas Eve. Since we would be driving right past Blackduck, she agreed to also bring the Bauer sisters, Sister Elsa and Sister Breta, who had also chosen to go home. When Betsy/Liz arrived at the convent in her little 1965 Mustang, her friend, Maralee, was sitting in one of the front seats. The three of us sisters stuffed ourselves into the back, one of us perched on the hard driveshaft each of us promising to shift off and on with every stop on the way.

It was already dark, I think, when we started out. But maybe it wasn't. Maybe I'm remembering the winter skies and the way they turned quickly dark once we left the city, got up past Little Falls and turned to drive through Grand Rapids and the big forest between there and Deer River. It was snowing.

Snow in the headlights streak in hypnotizing lines that seem to extend to infinity. Then Liz was saying, "Black ice." The forest highway was a skating rink. Her little car slid; she knew how to work the brake on ice, but there was no traction. We all became quiet, willing the car to stay on the road. It stayed. Liz crept along for miles. But oh, it was beautiful in the heart of danger, small as we were among the tall trees, with the snow falling everywhere around us. We missed the turn to Blackduck. One of the Bauer's remembered another way, a road the locals used. She pointed: *That one!* Liz turned. Snow accumulated. Where were we? The Bauer sisters weren't sure. If we got stuck in the deepening snow, we'd be there all night. I felt adrenaline.

Somehow we arrived in the Bauer yard and the sisters' parents came from the house calling their daughters' names, saying thank you and asking if we wanted coffee. We wanted to be home, still almost a hundred miles away, and the snow continued to fall.

Mama's Christmas tree glittered in the front window.

It was too too perfect, Mama writes. I think now, yes, it was perfect, wasn't it? I search for the perfection of it: Mama's smile. The bustle of her preparations. Dad's pleasure in her. The slickness of her sheets as I slipped into the bed at home, so familiar and now so strange. The cut of dry forty-below-zero cold. The little knotty pine church filled with recognizable faces grown older. Daddy's special Tom & Jerry drink. Mama's turkey dinner.

I missed the convent. Despite all this perfection of my parent's Christmas, I missed something that had happened at the motherhouse on Christmastide days. Where else would I ever find a group of women who would run out into the rosy dawn, into the drifted pink-lit snow, and cry out *"benedicite"* to God? Where else would I find music such as we had there? Where would I find friends I loved as much as my sisters who would sit together on the chapel floor in front of the Christmas crèche and sing "O Holy Night"? Where could I ever again experience the heightened sense of nature: skating on the river with

196

twenty veiled women, gliding on clear ice under frost-covered trees, Sister Diana performing pirouettes like a bodily prayer, her black wing of veil floating around her, a red-berry thorn bush along the path through the woods where I walked with Sister Marie who said, "You are my *Deo Gratias*."

Liz and I flung open the front door and Mama took us in her arms.

You come around again and again, I think now. Each moment lasts forever just as surely as it is fleeting. Mama takes me in her arms, right now, somehow, here in my Oregon home on Christmas Eve in the year 2014. Nothing lost is ever lost for good. I am all the Christmases that I contain in memory. She smiles as if she knew that all along. "My little lamb," she whispers across the vast reaches of eternity.

A LETTER FROM MAMA
I'm not all that busy
But it's fun to think I am
May 12, 1970

Somehow that spring I finagled a two-week visit home for June, and from March until I got there Mama and I kept the postman busy. Each letter moves rapidly, gallops almost, with her excitement, because in addition to being able to spend all that time together, we are collaborating in a project that will involve much of our little town.

Each summer the Sisters fanned out across the flatlands of northern Minnesota to spend two weeks teaching religion to children who had no opportunity to attend the few Catholic schools in that part of the state. I'd taught every year since I was a senior novice, but by the summer of 1970 I no longer felt satisfied with the traditional teaching methods or content. Vatican II had transformed my notions both of what I should teach and how I should teach it. All year I'd worked closely with the fledgling organization of religious educators in the Archdiocese of St. Paul—the ones who had supported me when the pastor tried and failed to fire me. We all met often for workshops and organizational meetings, and these people seemed to me the vanguard of a transformed Catholic Church. I had all the zeal of a reformer. How could I go back to teaching the pre-Vatican II catechism? But I knew from experience that most of the parishes up north were happily conservative, continuing with business as usual. No way would they accept a whippersnapper young sister coming in wearing fashionable clothes and spouting new fangled and maybe heretical ideas.

Already in June of 1966 I'd been assigned for two weeks to the parish in a different small town—Badger or Greenbush or Felton—I don't remember. But I do recall the pastor sitting the other sister and me down in his parlor and lecturing us about teaching the traditional doctrine. "I don't want any of that Vatican II confusion around here," he impressed upon us. "You're not planning to bring up heretics like that Chardin fellow, I hope." We shook our heads. No, Father. Of course not. But I had my copy of Pierre Teilhard de Chardin's *The Divine Milieu,* tucked away in my suitcase. In my reformist zeal, I dismissed his restrictions as uninformed and even a bit foolish. Certainly I would not mention the forbidden name, but the thought of this French

198

priest/paleontologist had so transformed my thinking by then that I could barely open my mouth without uttering a facsimile of something he'd written.

In 1970 the only place in northern Minnesota that might be receptive to my own brand of Catholic teaching would be my hometown parish, and the people there would receive me because of my mother.

My idea entranced her. I must have sent an audio-tape after describing what I had in mind because she wrote in April: *Please send the tape soon as we want to play it over and the four of us who are on the program committee want time to hear it and decide if there are places in it to shut it off for a minute and discuss the project, etc....but don't leave us without your taped explanation as no one can interest the ladies in it like you can yourself.*

She'd already negotiated with the Lutherans to use their Bible Camp facilities for a high school retreat. She'd talked to the leader of a local teenage combo band to add verve for that event. She'd organized volunteer teachers to work with the elementary children. It seemed that the whole town was on alert. *I'm not trying to run your project; just trying to help* she sort of apologizes, after which she gallops on to her next idea. By the time she wrote in May she'd even scheduled me to sing at the wedding of her dear friend's youngest daughter.

Mama's words literally dance, they whirl. She was celebrating her daughter who had been gone so long and now was coming home to shine with all the knowledge she believed I had acquired.

Between her letters and the reality of that June, memory blooms here and there like the lilac bushes in yards along Baudette's streets. I am walking there, from home to the church and back. I am breathing in the fragrance. A breeze ruffles my hair just as it did when I was a child and walked these same streets. I am home. I breathe more deeply because I can breathe deeply here, because here I am free. I am who I once was before the veil and the long wool dress and the rules and the vows. I've forgotten them for the moment. I begin to hum and then to sing the way I used to do.

How is it that we don't recognize the signs when they are so clear? How much simpler it would have been for everyone if, at that moment, I'd been able to accept how happy I felt to be Mary Jane again. Years later, Sister Diana who was visiting me in California, would tell me she had thought happiness must not be part of my destiny. "This is the first time I've seen you happy," she said. By then I was almost fifty years old.

That day in June, though, I was filled with contradictions, hidden from myself for the moment, but close to the surface of consciousness and ready to emerge. Yes, I was Mary Jane who wanted only to be free and good and loving, but I was also Sister Mary Christopher who had gone to the convent because she was seeking God, and I'd become Sister Christin with all that professional, theological, reformist zeal. These three parts of me would come into increasing conflict as the years went on.

It was Mary Jane in the choir loft, singing for the wedding, but Sister Christin who chose the songs from the Judy Collins collection rather than from the *St. Gregory Hymnal*. It was Sister Mary Christopher who felt shy about drinking wine at the wedding reception. But it was Sister Christin who chose to wear the cream colored sundress with the full, but too-short-for-a-sister skirt.

Snippets of the two week program survive in memory: Discussions with small groups of women who had known me all my life and were also loyal to my mother. Cancellation (much to my mother's dismay) of the Bible Camp retreat due to low registration. Meetings in the church basement with parish youth. All very ordinary things. But one thing I considered ordinary turned out not to be ordinary at all.

I believe it began the day after the wedding. Sister Carol Ann and I had practiced for a "guitar mass," emphasizing folk songs from popular culture, as the first event in the religious education program. Church musicians hadn't caught up yet with the Vatican II liturgy in English. Even at St. John's University masses we had sung Peter, Paul and Mary's "Hurry Sundown." In Baudette, among other songs, we sang Bob Dylan's "The Times They Are a Changing." We belted it out, two young sisters in colorful dresses, strumming our guitars. I was there to change them. I see that now. But why? They had created the very atmosphere where I'd just found freedom again after so long. You'd think I'd hope to keep them as they were, to be that pure air for me to breathe, to be that refuge from unhappiness. But Mary Jane didn't have the say here. Sister Christin did, and she also got a chance to speak to the congregation at that Sunday Mass. I introduced the program we had in mind and referenced—probably often—the song we just had sung. I'd become committed to change. I sought it actively. I interpreted it theologically. To me the new world that Mama Cass promised was no different from the divine fire of transformation, the omega point, the Christ of cosmic love towards which Teilhard de Chardin's vision evolved. I believed the church canonized this evolutionary change in the Vatican II documents. And how was Bob Dylan any different? All of them pointed the way towards freedom and a greater love. It never even crossed my mind that anyone would find my words odd much less threatening. "Your sons and your daughters are beyond your command." What was I thinking?

Mid-week the priest summoned me to an evening meeting at the rectory with the man who belonged to one of the most influential families in the town. Their company employed hundreds of the townspeople, and he had just become Vice-President. According to Father Archer, the two of them had some concerns they wanted to discuss with me.

I don't remember being worried. I'd known this man since childhood when he was a boy not more than six years older than I. The connection between our families began in my grandparents' time, and Mama was godmother to the man's daughter. At first I thought these people wanted simply to discuss theology, something I loved doing. Mama looked me in the eyes. "You be careful." She said that whole family had strong conservative leanings when it came to politics. But politics weren't my concern. I wasn't dealing with politics. She must have seen my naiveté, but didn't confront it directly. Instead, she talked about small towns. Baudette was a small town, after all, and I'd been gone for a long time. Maybe I'd forgotten that. People have certain expectations.

I had, in fact, forgotten; imagining I was free, feeling myself back home, assuming I still could get away with things a child can. Small towns have rules of behavior as strong as any convent's.

Those weren't conscious thoughts. I wish they had been subject to my analysis. I told her not to worry, and I went to the rectory without even a vague notion what I might have said or done that could cause my mother's friends to be concerned. The man and his wife were already there, sitting in Father Archer's threadbare chairs among the books he had piled on the floor, on the end tables and desk.

Probably it was Mary Jane who smiled and held out her hand to greet old friends. But it was Sister Christin who soon took over.

"How dare you sing the song of that communist in church?" He confronted me. He didn't want his children hearing such anti-American drivel. If I couldn't assure him that his children would be safe from such thoughts, he'd pull them out of the program, and with them would go a big portion of the other parishioners—not just children.

I don't remember what I said. Did I placate him? Did I pull out my Vatican II lexicon and embellish it with examples from my previous summer at St. John's? Maybe I even told him that Jesus was a communist—just look at his lifestyle with those disciples all living a common life. I hope I didn't tell him that, but it was the way I thought back then.

"No more Bob Dylan!" he probably insisted. I probably conceded that point while at the same time attempting to draw a parallel between church and culture and how we needed to meet young people in the language of the culture they knew. He probably said Bob Dylan didn't represent the culture of *his* children. Did he tell me he never expected such words as I'd spoken to fall from my lips? I think he did. I wonder: did that topple me? Did I remember at that moment how free I thought I'd been, singing down the sidewalk just a few days before?

He took his wife and left with a warning. No more of your left-wing politics and communist songs, or else.

Father Archer shrugged. Just be careful about the music you choose, he told me. The rest of it will blow over. It's the music has the power.

It seems strange that I don't remember how Mama greeted me when I came home that night. Did her eyes have that "oh dear" look? I wonder now how it worked out afterwards for Mama in her little town, whether or not she continued to feel comfortable with that man I had offended with the Bob Dylan song. I hadn't considered the very real possibility that my offense could double back on her.

I don't remember how it ended, those two weeks. I don't remember leaving her and Dad when it was finished. I don't remember all the homey things we must have done. I don't remember so much I really want to know about that time. And it must be because I was unraveling. It must be that I'd become like a three-ply strand of yarn, and it was beginning to come undone. That part of me, that Mary Jane, the part that walked free and singing and would have kept the memories—I must have pulled that strand out sometime during those two weeks, and maybe it happened that very night. And Sister Mary Christopher with all her dreams, she still whispered in the core of me. Over and over she recited the Langston Hughes poem about the dreams that die and the bird with broken wings. But Sister Christin? Her strand was strong and visible, and she was moving forward, thinking she was the one with dreams, thinking she was on the freedom-road, thinking she would find the love I sought in her version of the renewal of the church.

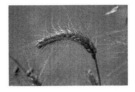

REMEMBER THE FORBIDDEN

- Remember the knot in the belly, the catch in the throat, the shortness of breath, the hand that won't move, the refusal of feet to descend the hill.
- Remember the edge on your laughter, the shrill on your song, the urge in eyes when they look on you.
- Remember how the spirit rose from your belly rather than your heart, how the reasons proceeded from voices in your mind, contradicting the voice in your soul.
- Remember the silence that muted the voice you thought belonged to God.

A LETTER FROM MAMA
Greet Pat
July 23, 1970

I imagine the sun shining while she typed, casting a bright wedge of light across the living room. She set the typewriter to double space. She hadn't much time but wanted a full page of words. Those summer days their business had slacked off—a real concern as it was the tourist season when they saved for the winter. *I hope it is not a foreboding of things to come. We need a little more good business, but if it is just a short time of rest, then it is most welcome.* I imagine her fingers clicking away on the Smith Corona. In a minute she'd rush out, letting the screen door slam shut, not bothering to lock anything—it wouldn't even have occurred to her. She wanted to get the letter in the mail and shop in preparation for Dad's birthday.

Daddy got your card today and opened it right away and he was very, very pleased. Wasn't sure just at first that he understood the message, but—then—he did and agreed with you wholeheartedly. I've no idea now what I might have written, but since I was back at St. John's University, I'll wager it was couched in esoteric theological language. She says nothing about my being at St. John's, although I know I was. She ends by writing, *suppose you will be leaving soon for West St. Paul.* And then—*Greet Pat.*

The words stick out, not only because she virtually never acknowledged his existence, but because he had to have been with me at school.

What goes on in memory? This time is such a blur. I once had a collection of letters from him with the St. Ben's logo on the top. I kept them in a metal file for ten years past his death. I'd stored the file on the top shelf of the closet in my writing room, thinking that someday I reconstruct the events of those years—try to sort out what I'd felt and how I came to the choices I eventually made. But I couldn't open the box. Every time I did, a wave of sadness passed right through me. Finally I took the box outside, fired up the Weber grill, and one by one I burned his words and with them the history of that time.

Greet Pat, Mama writes the summer of 1970, the year that fell right in the middle of all this.

205

One day during that second summer of my studies at St. John's and Pat's chaplaincy at St. Ben's he drove up before one of my classes and parked his car in the lot by the library where I stood with a group of other sisters and priests, talking, before going into the lecture hall for a class in Christology. He wore his Irish cap, the white summer one to protect his balding head from sunburn, his black clerical trousers, and a sports shirt open at the neck. The shirt was new. In the past it would also have been black with a clerical collar. You could almost conjure the theological leanings of a priest by the kind of shirt he wore when not "on the job," and Pat took pride in being in the vanguard of the Vatican II renewal. He walked towards us, a jaunty walk, teasing, a leprechaun sort of walk, his meerschaum pipe clenched between his teeth. He could talk that way, teeth tight around that pipe, blue eyes twinkling. He joined the group of us, engaging them immediately, laughing, telling some ecclesiastical joke, an inside joke he'd made up himself from events at the Vatican he'd picked up in the *National Catholic Reporter*. I virtually always fell into silence when he was around. I'd feel myself fading into the background.

Circumspect, he called it. We had to be circumspect. So many sisters and priests were leaving the ministry to get married, and we didn't want to be perceived as among them, did we? Also, we didn't intend to marry, did we now? Yet, we were good friends, right? We were more; we were soul-mates—didn't I believe that?

Circumspect—consider the circumstances. But what could possibly be acceptable circumstances for the two of us to be together? There simply were none, except for the church we envisioned, that future church, the church existing only in our imaginations. So the word took on a wholly new meaning for me of secret or clandestine, and it required the development of a fine art of role-playing.

Pat showed up on campus, and I immediately felt exhausted. My whole personality drained out of me. One night during that summer the university threw a cocktail party in honor of several eminent theologians who were visiting. Pat and I were there separately, by agreement, meeting just as anyone might. But not like anyone, not normal, because both the separation and the meeting were planned ahead of time so as 'not to give the wrong impression,' which actually would have been the 'right impression,' or why would we have needed to plan? I moved from group to group, as people do at such events, and Pat moved, crisscrossing, together, alone, back and forth. But I felt tethered by the plan we had made and sickened by the thought we had to make a plan at all. I remember standing with a glass of wine in my hand, talking with a group including John Gallen, the liturgist who was my professor that summer, and feeling a glimmer of my old self, when Pat sidled in beside me. He redirected the conversation in his erudite way, and I suddenly felt like an accessory.

I moved away. It wasn't long before I left the party altogether and walked alone in the darkness along the campus paths. My brain whirled. What was I doing? This man drew me and repelled me simultaneously. No world existed in which we could be together.

The trees made giant shadows across the stars. The space above and around me was infinite, but I felt claustrophobic. I breathed in the warm night air, trying to create space inside myself, a world at least that big. It seemed ironic that I'd once seen in Pat an open door, that he'd been a sign of freedom. Now his presence cramped me into a space so small I struggled to breathe.

I finally wandered to my dorm building, climbed the stars to the third floor, opened the door to my room and locked it from the inside.

Despite this suffocation, I went with him. Why did you do that, I want to ask that young woman I was back then. Will I ever know for sure? Are some things not given us to know? He already was a dead man, but I didn't know it yet. If I'd paid more attention to my body, to my instincts, to that suffocation I felt, would I then have escaped all that was to come?

Pat's car became a capsule. Afternoons of no classes the door of his car opened and I disappeared inside. The car whisked me away from St. John's to the homes of sympathetic strangers. One was a monk living way out on the edges of church renewal who was experimenting with communal living among young college students. Another, a sister, lived alone in a little house on the edge of a wooded area at the far end of town. We lit candles and listened to Janis Joplin sing "Bobby McGee," to Bob Dylan's raspy "I Shall Be Released." The folk song writers are the theologians now, Pat opined.

We all discussed theology the way people now discuss politics—as though it held the key to a new way of being, a new world of freedom and of love, a world in which all would be united in loving service to one another. In that world the tyranny of governments, both church and state, would be transformed into something more evolved, based on an awakened consciousness—something actually spiritual. All the dense theological texts we were reading seemed to say the same thing the folk music conveyed more simply. In our conversations, "freedom's just another word for nothing left to lose," became a kind of holy surrender, a divine hope, a sacred simplicity of life. These meetings among the sympathetic strangers with open souls became my breathing room. While Pat and I were with them, or with a chosen few of the priests and sisters on campus, I often recovered the sensation of hope that our vision of the new church was true, and that our attempts to bring it about by living it beforehand made sense. In those brief encounters I thought we could do this. Yes, of course we needed to be circumspect, but maybe there were indeed circumstances where the two of us could be together and at the same time be ourselves. We told each other we could be companions in the ministry of the Word. We, all of us together, could live that heroic life, the root of beauty.

Now, reading Mama's letters and remembering these things, I am aware of having always felt my life would not be an ordinary one. From childhood I'd imagined a reality beyond the limits of the ordinary that I would attempt to reach. As in the fairy tales Mama used to read to me, the path might well entail a dangerous crossing, but one I had to make if I were to find the place my life was meant to occupy. This impulse drew me to the convent. This same impulse drew me out to the edges of church renewal. This impulse drew me also to Pat Kelly, not so much because I felt attracted to him as a man who might become a partner in marriage, but because I was magnetized by his vision, his daring, his own impulse towards that larger-than-this-world reality, and especially by his priesthood. I believe now that I thought he could point the way, and that through a relationship with him, I might be absorbed into that priesthood, experience it as my own, and we would be empowered to make that dangerous crossing together.

But I romanticized the danger, and it wouldn't stand for that. In my naiveté, before I knew what I was doing, I walked too close to the edge and into actual dangers. I would learn the faith that issues from despair. But first, I would need to realize that I'd been searching in the wrong place. Over the chasm to where I was headed, there was no bridge.

Greet Pat. She must have known I couldn't do that, not really, not in the normal way she must have meant as she tried to come to terms with the incomprehensible changes that were taking place in her church, in her nation, in her daughter. Still there were birthdays to attend to. Something normal in the midst of a chaotic summer, a failing business, and not enough money. Greet Pat, as if all of it must make sense, somehow, after all.

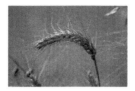

REMEMBER PARADOX

- Remember the difference between the lies you tell, the secrets you hide, and the opposites you must embrace.
- Remember the goodness of those who surround you and do not allow them to leave you without reward.
- Remember in each moment both God's call and God's warning. Observe how you recognize this, and do not avoid the truth.
- Remember that you are not alone.

A LETTER FROM MAMA
No place in my mind to put you
September and October, 1970

Mama was excited. She had been talking to a man who wanted to buy Dad's airport business, providing an opportunity for them to solve their financial problems, travel a bit, and still allow Dad to work part time but without the stress. She was sixty. He was sixty-two. She hoped to convince him of the wisdom of selling. *George is content to keep things as they are—but who knows what the future has in store for him and me?*

I read and lean back in my chair. Was it a premonition she had? Might he have avoided that massive heart attack three years down the road had he agreed?

Adding to her excitement, both Betsy (Liz) and I were hunting for new places to live. Liz had tired of her childhood name as well as her young adult apartment building and was ready to live on her own in the heart of Minneapolis. She eventually found an apartment at Cedar and Lake. *I'm not elated about the area,* Mama wrote, remembering her own youth in the city and the wild days of Lake Street in the 1930s.

And I was hunting for a new dwelling, not because I'd left the convent, but because a group of us sisters teaching at different schools in the Twin Cities wanted to experiment with a life style we called "creative community." We all were young. Five of us: Joanne was twenty-six; Emilie and Paulette were twenty-eight; I was almost thirty; and Diana was thirty-two. We'd been discussing the idea among ourselves and had drawn up a proposal to present to the three sisters elected to what was by then called the administrative team: Sister Ruth, Sister Marie, and Sister Margaret. Formerly they would have been called our mother superiors. But our interpretation of the documents of Vatican II had us throwing out hierarchical government in favor of decision making by consensus. Leaders were no longer superiors, but rather were facilitators among equals. There would be no more "mothers." We all would be sisters now.

I wish I still had the proposal document. Memory tells me we wanted to experiment with virtually everything that made up religious life. We wanted a different sort of prayer, a different sort of relationship to "the world," our families, the parishioners. We wanted greater intimacy with one another, a sharing of souls, of joys and heartaches that we'd been told in our training we must keep to ourselves. We would re-interpret our vows: obedience would become responsibility; chastity would become availability to humanity; poverty would become simplicity of life. We would live among the people, in a regular house without convent restrictions. I barely remember the meeting at which we presented our plan which was accepted with not a little skepticism on the part of the three. We took to calling them the triumvirate or the troika to reflect the feeling that we hadn't yet achieved the abolition of hierarchy, but had simply changed the words with which we spoke of governance.

By September 10th we had a house and were preparing to move in the last weekend of that month. Liz would be moving that weekend also, and Mama wrote: *I would like to drive the car down, and then we could use it to haul your things over and do errands. I really would LOVE to be there, and I'll even bring my own sheets and blankets if necessary.* But by the 20th she knew that she couldn't make the trip. *I had hoped to get down there and see where each of you lives. When I try to visualize you at any time, I have no place in my mind to put you. I see Bets in the old apartment—but she is no longer there. Until I see you both, I guess I will have to just have you floating around in a vacuum.*

As the month wore on, she became increasing frustrated and troubled. Not only did Dad not want to sell the business, he also couldn't seem to hear her concerns. *I guess your Dad and I are just not able to cope with things anymore—or also there are just too too many things even for us in the best of our prime. We seem to be getting swallowed up in all the reports and extra activity—and with me it's further pressure due to undone housework and the knowledge that I am not able to actually do Christ's work because I come home tired. I don't visit at the Pioneer home anymore—or even at the hospital. Days get shorter and shorter...* And she worried over the state of the world she witnessed on TV—the bombings in Beirut. *I pray they will be touched in their consciences and change their way of living.*

Did I register all of this at the time, or was I too focused on my smaller concerns and the excitement of living in an actual house rather than in the institutional convent building?

The house sat in rolling, wooded countryside. It belonged to the mother of a Christian Brother who taught at the same high school staffed by our sisters. She'd left it entirely furnished, right down to the sheets and blankets, and really hadn't intended on renting it, but her son convinced her it would be beneficial to have a group of sisters living there and caring for her property. Memory holds it as a fairytale house, alone on a hill amidst trees, a curving road up to the garage that was connected to the house by a breezeway. A bungalow style, the house resembled an English cottage with slanting roofs and a door with a rounded top. Inside, the rooms fit cozily next to one another. Gone were the institutional hallways and rooms like compartments separating each facet of our lives. All five of us were exactly the right age for this: we began to nest.

We flopped down on the easy chairs and overstuffed couch in the living room. Glorious! Even the furniture in convents had been designed to remind us how we were expected to behave. Straight-backed. Firm. Here at the house we called by the name of the street, Courthouse Road, we had comfortable chairs in a living room. In the convent we'd always had a community room and a parlor. The parlor was reserved for visits from guests. The community room ordinarily had a long table surrounded by wooden chairs. Comfort was to be found in the presence of God within us.

At Courthouse Road we had a small kitchen with a dining nook. Mama sent us a set of Frankoma pottery, an earthy slate color, quite unlike anything we'd ever seen in any convent. We took turns cooking meals, something we hadn't done since leaving home as adolescents. We wrote to our mothers for recipes—foods we hadn't tasted for years. I made wild rice with bacon, onions and celery, and Mama's special date bread. Eating our mothers' foods, made by our own hands, had an almost magical power. I can't say how the other sisters felt, but I now realize that something long neglected in me was, because of this food, beginning to revive. I think now that it was a linkage I'd broken by entering the convent. Generations of women in families create a living chain of homey repetitions. Recipes. Patterns of quilts and crochet and knitting. Holiday traditions. Everyday traditions. Ways of cutting grapefruit, making a bed. The very first year of convent life, Mother Celine ordered us to forget the ways of our families and to observe new traditions. "You are a Sister of St. Joseph now. You are the fulfillment of your family, the completion of its genetic line." So we worked hard to forget. At Courthouse Road Joanne baked her mother's pumpkin pies, but she'd forgotten too much and covered them over the top with a second crust. Only after they were baked did she remember, and she almost cried. She would try it again another day, getting it right, re-linking herself.

We opened the doors of the house to the people of the parish, and the week we moved in, they flooded through those doors with housewarming gifts. It became a party. They stocked our kitchen with food and other supplies like plastic wrap. One woman laughed at us for washing and drying it for re-use. "It's meant to be thrown away," she insisted as she balled it up and threw it in the garbage. They stayed late into the night, singing and drinking wine.

In October I wanted nothing more than to rake the yard. Out behind the house red maple and yellow poplar leaves drifted down onto the grass. A clothesline stretched across the expanse and one of the sisters was airing out a woolen jacket that flapped in the autumn breeze. Behind the yard, the woods. Over me the blue October sky. I leaned against the rake and took it all in, breathed it in. I could almost forget what I was. This could have been my own house, my own yard. It wasn't, but it might have been. I began to rake the leaves, remembering other times I raked leaves back home, remembering piles of leaves I'd jumped into when I was a little girl. It was all that existed for me at that moment, this raking of October leaves, just getting them into a pile before the wind lifted some of them again, scattering them across the grass. I didn't care. The swirl of leaves thrilled me. The gathering and the scattering—a movement without end.

We invited our parents for Thanksgiving. Such a thing had never happened before. Each of us would make our favorite holiday food from our own family tradition. We'd haul card tables from the school to set up in our living room, making a banquet table.

Mama's words dance across the page.

Got your letter when I arrived out here before lunch. I read it FIRST and then read it aloud to George (who had already read it himself before I arrived)—and then I said, "Oh, Daddy, COULD WE?"

At the moment, he said he didn't see how we could....but then, November 26 is a long way off yet, and we are a family of procrastinators (your father is too, you know – and that is probably the main reason for our general half-way failure in our business ventures—I don't mean HIS procrastinating but the combination of both of us being guilty of it).....anyway, we would love to be there and don't write us off as not coming....we will make every effort. It will hinge a great deal on whether or not our collections come in and besides that, he has an engine to sell which should bring us enough money to make it possible. Pray!

They didn't make it.   Mama sent a check in case we "needed something extra" for our Thanksgiving celebration. *May everything go well for you five young ladies in your very own house with the two tall pine trees and the lamp in the flower box which can all be seen from the heavily traveled highway 55 —(wish I could see it), and may you keep well and not have dishwater hands or plugged drains or rocks through the windows or trouble with the television set (if you have a television set), and may you all help to bring PEACE to our world.*

Luv,
Mama

Thanksgiving morning the first big snowstorm of the year blew in, filling the long driveway with snow thigh deep. We took turns shoveling a path down the road to the highway. Only a few family members managed to be with us, and the only ones I remember are Emilie's mom and dad who lived not far away and braved the storm.

Mama never saw the house at Courthouse Road. We lived there, now I see it, for a moment. October through December, and it was over—a time of dreams, a pause on a threshold. The man who might have bought Dad's airport disappeared with Dad's refusal, but he might have disappeared anyway. A few days before we left the house, we danced in the living room, each of us separately. (This is my memory) Perhaps we danced to Mama Cass. We paused, on tiptoe, there at the threshold. "The song I came to sing remains unsung." wrote Tagore. The dance. The leaves. The motion of life. "The time has not come true." We could observe the moment, and that was all.

A LETTER FROM MAMA
Dear hard-to-get-ahold-of Chris –
December, 1970

Mama's writing on the run. There's Christmas, of course, but there's also her Betsy's need for a new car. "New" because her second-hand Mustang is costing her up the kazoo for repairs, and Mama sympathizes. There's the Ladies' Aide Christmas Bazaar, "An Old Fashioned Christmas," coming up at church, and there's shopping from catalogs for family gifts because *it's tough trying to shop in a small town where this year they DO NOT have anything to select from.* She's not yet started writing Christmas cards—a long list—and she's busy with church meetings led by Father Krebs from Crookston. These are church renewal classes preliminary to the formation of a parish counsel, a recommendation of Vatican II. It's a lot more work, this renewed church, what with the laity making decisions and planning liturgies. The priest used to do it all. Now the parishioners are involved as never before. It's exciting, but it's time consuming also. She's on a youth liturgy committee. *By the way, if you have anything you can spare that will be helpful to our Liturgy committee, send it to me, will you?— especially for the young people who are going to plan their own Liturgies for their own group. Don't forget!...They are sort of floundering as to what is expected.*

She's tried to call me, but can't reach anyone at Courthouse Road. If the five of us Sisters were gone on Sunday afternoon, as Mama says, we probably were looking for a new place to live. The woman who owned Courthouse Road had become intrusive. She'd come into the house while we were gone and leave little notes. "Don't put your empty water glass on the window-sill. It will leave a mark." Little motherly recommendations. "Clean the oven before those drippings bake on." We began to imagine her peeking into our closets and dresser drawers. Diana called her and suggested that she let us know when she wanted to inspect things so that one of us could be there. She judged that arrangement unacceptable. We talked about all this among ourselves in the woman's cozy living room, and decided that there must be another house, maybe even a better house, one with benefits not available at Courthouse Road: separate bedrooms (here we needed to double up), nearness to the schools where we worked, closer

216

availability of services. Diana called the woman and told her we would be out by the first of the year.

And this is how we ended up on New Year's Day at the Bidwell House. We laughed: from a courthouse to a place that bid us well! The house was only a few blocks from the parish where Diana, Joanne and I worked, and it was less than a mile from the high school where Paulette taught music. Emilie was the only one of us who would need to travel any distance because she taught across the Mississippi in Minneapolis.

The Bidwell House was ranch style and large with five bedrooms and a finished basement. B. T., a member of the parish, owned it, but hadn't really lived in it since his daughter went to college the year before. He traveled for his work and thought that a small apartment would suit his life style better. But he didn't want to put the house on the market because what if his wife got well? She'd been placed in a mental hospital some years before with such severe mental illness that she no longer recognized her family. B.T. could barely tolerate being in the house without her. He'd walked out of it, leaving it exactly as it was, with all its furnishings and also all the buildup of living. We became Merry Maids, scraping, scrubbing, chipping away at sinks, toilets, the oven, the fridge, windows, everything.

It was nearing Christmas and all of us were hard to reach. Maybe I was planning an event at the church. Maybe I was scrubbing B.T.'s refrigerator or cleaning up the room Joanne and I shared at Courthouse Road. Maybe I was giving a youth retreat at one of the retreat houses in the country. Maybe I was trying to avoid the parish priest who continued his efforts to get rid of me.

Maybe I'd squirreled myself away somewhere to write.

I'd forgotten that I was writing and submitting little pieces back then. But Mama reminds me: *I have been wanting to tell you— and congratulate you—but each time I changed my mind thinking it would spoil your plan. I thought maybe you wanted it for a Christmas surprise, but now I am not able to hold it any longer.*

Congratulations on your article on Poverty and Conscience. (I don't have it here at the airport right now and the title slips my mind). It happened as such a surprise to both George and me. It was at Fr. Krebs' second meeting – he gave the magazine to your dad and when he opened it, there it said "By Sister Christin LORE"— popped right off the page at us. It was surely a thrill—and well written too and no doubt inspirational to all who read it. . . Just think, our daughter is a writer and has had articles and stories PUBLISHED!

If you only got one magazine, you would have sent it to us – and since we already have one, you should keep your own. We'll consider it your Christmas present to us anyway.

I couldn't be found those days because I spent so much time out and away. Was I trying to escape? The essay that had been published in one of the Catholic Monthlies (I no longer remember which one) could be evidence of escape, as could have been the "Creative Community," and the many projects for the archdiocese I took on outside the parish. I didn't think of it then as escape. I thought I was expanding my involvement. But maybe I was beginning to move into a different sort of life, and if I was, that might have been most evident to people, like the pastor, who wanted me to disappear anyway. The other people, my friends and colleagues, urged me on. They believed in the words I spoke and wrote, promoting the progressive theology that also supported my choices, visions, and involvements.

The article Mama loved so much came out of a relationship I developed with a family in Minneapolis, and especially with the woman/wife/mother of this family whose name I no longer remember. I will call her Lois. We met because of a project I started with the youth of the parish where I worked. They were enthusiastic children, but isolated in their suburban lives. In addition to learning religious teachings, perhaps they could begin to implement them in the larger community. Maybe we could be of benefit to people in the inner city who were not so well off. And so I met Lois. She and her husband, a university professor, had sold their house in suburbia and moved to a big rambling run-down house in the poorer district of Minneapolis. It was an open house. It was an open family. Anybody could go there, eat there, sleep there, and Lois and her husband would welcome them, helping much as they could. What money they had from the professor's salary went for the benefit of both family and guests, for both short and long-term goals.

The first day I visited, she'd just welcomed a pregnant teen from Texas into her home. The girl looked gaunt and sick and had hitched her way to Minneapolis because she'd heard that the state government would take care of her there. But she wasn't a resident, so funds were not available to her, and she became just another of the nameless, homeless ones. Then she found Lois. That first day I was at her home, Lois was busily negotiating appointments with doctors for which she and her husband would pay. Later they would pay for a surgery the young woman needed. They would care for her and her baby in their home until she had the skills to support and care for herself.

Lois inspired me. Dorothy Day inspired me. I knew I could never live as they lived, but I could write about them, and I did. I also knew I could introduce the youth from my parish to them, and I did that also. We developed an ongoing program for stocking a food shelf in that neighborhood. These were things that could be done, actions that immersed me in the "world." Wasn't this where the Gospel sent us? Wasn't this the intent of the Second Vatican Council—to develop a priesthood of the laity who would consecrate the world, just as the clerical priest consecrated the bread and wine? Weren't we all involved in transforming the face of humanity into the face of the living Christ?

I wrote the article. The magazine published it. Fr. Krebs read it and brought it to my parents. My mother felt really proud. It must be good, what I was doing. It must.

But I remained caught between worlds.

On Christmas morning our little "creative community" attended an early Mass and then went to the women's jail in Minneapolis to visit the inmates and sing Christmas carols. Maybe we brought gifts—I suspect we did. What I remember keenly, and will probably remember until I remember nothing at all, is the face of a woman who was locked away from the others. She was young, younger than any of us, and her face looked out at us, hard, brittle, from behind the stark bars. I think I tried to engage her in conversation, because in memory I am standing there, as instructed, far enough away so she can't reach me through the bars, and she is saying something inconceivable to me, something like, "Who do you think you are, whore? We don't need you. We don't want you. Go home to your church. Go back to your God. Shut your mouth. Leave me alone. Go to hell!"

219

Tears came to my eyes. She started banging on the bars. "Get these whores out of here!" She yelled. And I wanted to go. I wanted nothing more than to escape her eyes, her yells, her banging, banging, on the bars. Finally the guard came to tell is it was time we left.

"Christmas is a hard time to be in jail," the guard explained as we left lock-up.

If my still unconscious plan was to escape convent life, this jail encounter should have convinced me of my naiveté about the world I intended to enter. I'd better be careful where I went and which route I took.

While I was, maybe, attempting to escape—calling it by different names like renewal, transformation, development, expansion, evolution—I also continued to hold on. I grasped at the dream I came to the convent to find; I also grasped at a vague dream of the future. I insisted upon being safe, but also teetered at the edge of some yet to be defined "new world." I held so tightly that I could feel my fingernails digging into the sharp edges of my dreams. "Oh the mind, mind has mountains." Holding, clinging, grasping, say the Buddhists, is the source of suffering.

The dreams would crumble, and soon. When they did, it wouldn't be just my mother who would be unable to find me. I would have taken flight so far from anything I'd ever dreamed that I would be unable even to find myself.

A LETTER FROM MAMA
You hit a solid wall every once in a while
February 5, 1971

After I read Mama's letter, I sat by the big front window of the Bidwell House and stared out at the car across the street. For days I'd watched it disappear under the snow. Probably the owners were in Florida. The plow had gone around it so many times, it would be stuck there until spring. I looked down at my notebook, scribbled another pro or con. I wasn't getting at the real ones, the deep ones, the ones my body called to my awareness by its refusal to take in food, by its reluctance to budge from the house. The other sisters had gone to school. More and more I was staying away from there since I got sick to my stomach when I even approached the place. The pastor had taken his complaints about our sisters (and I'd started the whole mess) to the bishop, asking that we be removed. Our congregational leaders had entered into a little ecclesiastical war with him, also going to the bishop to ask that the pastor be removed. The people of the parish took sides. I'd hinted at this in my Christmas letter. Really it was the Vatican II Catholics vs. the Old Church Catholics. Nasty rumors spread. "That Sister Christin will have run off with her Mexican lover by the end of the year. Mark my words!"

"I'd like at least to meet the man first." I tried to laugh it off, but my stomach hurt all the time. If I ate anything substantial, it gave me diarrhea. The doctor told me I had gastritis from stress. He gave me a diet of bland food. He gave me potassium tablets, Lomidil, and Valium. "If you have to go to work," he said, "take one of these Valium." Maybe I ought to get a job in a different parish, I thought. What would be the pros and cons? I sat by the window, staring at the snow-buried car, and drew a line from top to bottom of the notebook page. Pros on one side. Cons on the other.

Mama had written:

Dearest Chris—
Mary Jane was our HAPPY daughter—always seeing the brighter side of everything. Chris seems to be happy but filled with frustrations and NOT always finding the brighter side.... I don't think you have two

personalities. ... It is just because your lot in life has changed, and you have lost your old SECURITY and you are trying to do what you think is best for those whom you feel need your help, but you hit a solid wall every once in a while.

People have made a terrific mess of God's word here on earth and straightening it out is not going to be easy. The old security is gone – some folks (including us sometimes) play ostrich and try to pretend things are the same, and we can ignore the problems—but they don't go away. In a way, you are still one of the lucky ones. You KNOW the job you have to do, and you are well equipped for it—you can think and articulate on your feet, and be a great inspiration to those who come to you—and come they will, more and more of them. God gave you this talent, and you have his grace—don't cast it aside because some people oppose you—maybe this is part of the game—success is not supposed to come easily.

You sound really frustrated in this last letter which we got at noon today. Daddy just left to go back to the airport, and I was to follow in my car, but after he left, I decided to write to you NOW or it wouldn't get written and I can't afford to telephone you this month—if I did, I would be using money which should be paid to someone else on account.

Mama thought I could do this, but I wasn't so sure, at least it seemed I could not do it here, in this parish, with this priest, and this terrible, terrible war going on among the parishioners.

During some of the worst of it, while I was eating virtually nothing, Pat Kelly drove down from St. Cloud to whisk me away. He'd arranged for me to speak before the combined faculty of St. John's and St. Ben's colleges. Under the circumstances, with all my anxiety and frustration, you'd think this would be the worst thing in the world. I've no idea anymore what I was supposed to lecture on, or how I might have been considered an authority on anything of interest to them. You'd think I would have been overcome with fear. Instead, just a few miles north of St. Paul, I began to feel better. The closer we got to the College of St. Benedict, the better I felt, and once there Pat and I joined a small group of faculty members at a pizzeria. We shared stories, drank beer, ate pizza, and I didn't feel sick at all.

It was a Friday night. The workshop for the combined faculty would take place the next day. Pat drove me from the pizzeria to a little house by the college where two students lived, and where I could spend the next two nights. "You'll like them," he assured me. One of them had just left the Poor Clare Monastery. He made that linkage, the convent connection. We went up the shoveled path and knocked.

I remember them as exotic. Words come to mind: burnished, sultry, earthy, smelling like incense. One had long wavy dark hair; the other's hair was short. She'd been the Poor Clare, and just out from under her veil. They lived in the way I supposed hippies must live, with very little furniture, lots of candles, strings of colored beads for doors, and mattresses on the floor covered with Indian cotton spreads. They sold Shaklee products for survival money and went to St. Ben's on scholarships. I don't remember their names, but they were equally exotic—names like Deirdre, like Imogene.

Usually I would have been uncomfortable in a strange place with strange people, but not with these two, and not in this house. Let's say that Deirdre was the former Poor Clare. She'd found her way out of there, she told me. Yes, she loved her sisters. Yes, she had had dreams. But the dreams could not come true there, in the convent. It was too tight, too firm; she was too locked away. Maybe her dreams could come true here in a wider world. I believed her. I wanted to stay with her; I wanted, even, to BE her. Maybe I could walk barefoot on cold wooden floors, each step jingling because of the ankle bracelet from India. The other one—Imogene or Kara or something—laughed a lot. She came across as someone completely amused with the irony of the world, as though all of it might be a silly dream she was having—or that all of us were dreaming together, dreams from which we would eventually awaken. They told me I was way too thin, and gave me Shaklee protein to drink. "You should take some home with you." They gave it to me. "We get it cheap," they assured.

I slept on the mattress. A little candle flickered inside a glass.

The next day I stood before the combined faculty of the two colleges and gave whatever talk it was that I gave. I remember their faces—intent, respectful. They sat in a semi-circle several rows deep. Maybe we were in some kind of theater or lecture hall, because the rows seemed to ascend. The other image I have is of a game room with large colorful blocks of varying heights where people perched, smiling, leaning towards me, listening. Afterwards they asked questions. They engaged not only me but one another. They'd been having some

223

arguments they hadn't been able to resolve. Old vs. new. What? Structures. Programs. Procedures. It must be the same thing everywhere. Here, though, it didn't threaten me as it did back in the parish. The very things I found so frustrating back there, here at St. Ben's stimulated me to creative thinking.

I remember some faculty members that went away grumbling about me. What could I know? I'd never taught in a college. Others gathered around me to continue the conversation. It didn't seem to bother me either way. The grumbling as well as the adulation felt separate from me, having to do with ideas only and not with the frustrations I was experiencing in my life.

What if I were to leave my life, like Deidre had—sell Shaklee products, burn incense, sleep on a mattress lying on the floor in the corner of a room? What if there could be a way out? Of what, though? Parish? Convent? The old church? The new one? The world itself?

One morning, not long after the lecture at St. Ben's, the telephone woke me. Again I hadn't gone to my office at the parish, and was sleeping late (probably depressed, though I didn't have the words for it back then). My bedroom at the Bidwell house was located in the basement. It had been Bob's daughter's room and was decorated for an adolescent girl, with a single bed, frills, white and powder blue paint, a shag carpet, and a little glass covered stand with an old-fashioned telephone. No one else was still home. I answered.

"Sister Christin?" It was the voice of Sister Marie. She'd tried to call me at my office, but when she couldn't reach me there, she inquired about me at the convent, and Sister Vivienne told her I'd stayed home that day. I figured she might be calling about an upcoming meeting, a "Kick-Off" for a congregation-wide renewal. I'd been telling people that I wasn't planning to attend. When I answered the phone she asked me if something was wrong.

I acted like an upstart and told her I figured I wouldn't benefit from it because the format of our renewal meetings never had any lasting results. Hurt buried deep in me had smoldered over the years and turned to anger. I must have wanted to punish her for letting me go so easily.

"Well," she said, "why not come over and help us plan?"

This was a turn of events I had not expected and could hardly believe.

"Pardon me?"

"Why not help us? I know you are good at what you do in the Archdiocese, and we really want this renewal effort to be life-giving for the sisters. Often we *do* flounder in our efforts because of lack of things like communication skills. We really would appreciate your help."

All my desire to be one of this community of women flooded me. I could hardly believe it. Marie wanted my help. Wait—could it be a trick? Maybe. But I would be wary. If I were wary I would not get hurt again. Could they have forgotten their rejection of me? Maybe they had decided I was true to them despite my relationship with Pat. I felt myself rushing towards her like a river breaking through the ice in spring. Be careful. Be careful. But I couldn't stop.

"We've heard about the good work you are doing for the Archdiocese, and also about the workshop at St. Ben's." She said. She went on to state the obvious: I was out of the loop where the congregation was concerned. "We don't know if you'd like to be more involved." Wait a minute! Wasn't my lack of involvement their choice? I said something like "I didn't think you wanted my involvement."

She affirmed that the administrative team hadn't been convinced of my loyalty, but they had discussed it, and they thought they would test this doubt. That is, if I were willing. They had an event coming up, at our high school, where Paulette taught. It was right down my alley—the very thing I planned all the time in my work, an event requiring a mix of theology, process, and ritual. All our sisters from the convents in the Twin Cities would attend, and later they would repeat the event up in Crookston. The other provinces in our congregation would hold similar events as a kick-off to congregational renewal. "Are you interested?" She asked.

I said yes. My desire for the closest possible connection with this religious community had grown in proportion to the pain of rejection I'd felt. Now their sudden acceptance felt magnetic.

Dear, dear Marie, right there on the phone. I'd thought I lost her. She'd been my mentor, the woman I'd once loved, or thought I loved, as much as—even more than—Mama. I'd attached myself to her, walking like her, talking like her, wanting to think her thoughts, hoping one day to BE her. (Why did I always want to be someone else? Why didn't I try to be myself? *Mary Jane was our HAPPY daughter,* Mama said.) In these past years in West St. Paul, though, Marie seemed distant. When I did see her, she always was kind. But she also seemed to exist across some vast gulf, and she didn't reach out to me. I didn't reach out to her, either, but why should I? That's how I thought. It didn't occur to me that I felt angry over the loss of her, that when I stepped out to the edge, I lost many things I held dear.

In her letter, Mama had said, *Anyway, Sweetie, brace your shoulders, stick out your chin and double up your fists and get right in there and fight and don't let words from people discourage you. When it comes to WORDS, you are away out in front in your usage—words are your stock in trade—go ahead wherever you can and do Christ's work as it is spelled out.*

Then I got caught up in a flurry that made me forget my troubles at the parish. I felt almost as though I weren't working there anymore, as though I could be on automatic with the youth retreats and the adult discussion groups and the weekly religious education classes and the archdiocesan involvements. I hardly thought about the pastor. My list of pros and cons had led me to the decision to find a position in a different parish. Both Diana and I submitted our resumes to the archdiocesan religious education office that, at the time, was acting as a kind of employment agency for all the parishes. We wanted to be hired as a team. In the meantime, I brainstormed ideas with Sister Marie and Sister Ruth—ways of giving every sister a chance to speak her mind, talk about her dreams for the religious community, sort out the customs she hoped to keep and those she hoped to change.

We met on a Saturday in a large room at Brady High School. We'd seated the Sisters at round tables where they were grouped diversely—young with elders, professional with those who cared for the rest of us by cooking and keeping the house, teachers with nurses and social workers. We started by listening to John Lennon's "Imagine." Now I almost laugh. Just imagine that! "...and no religion, too." I remember holding my breath, wondering how they would react, if they would "get it," thinking I did—get it. We brainstormed, organized, reported to the total group. We laughed and sang. We came up with some good ideas. We joined in prayer, a ritual I created especially for the occasion, like so many rituals I put together back then connected with the parish work. They were smiling, seeming joyous with the day and with their own individual and communal dreams. With their imagining.

At the end of the day one of the administrative team, maybe Sister Ruth, told the group that the whole congregation, three provinces—Crookston, Cincinnati, and New Orleans—would be setting up a steering committee for renewal. A kick-off meeting would be held soon in New Orleans. Two administrative team members from each province would be present, plus one sister at large. One of them. Someone not in administration. The response was immediate.

"Sister Christin!" They said. "It should be Christin who goes."

Who would have believed it? Certainly not I. It dizzied me. Where was I, anyway; at the edge or at the center of this religious community? In all my life, I'd never been so stunned.

The next week I would be in Crookston to repeat the process with our sisters in the northern part of the province. That group would concur with the sisters in the Twin Cities that I should be their representative in New Orleans. Apparently I didn't tell Mama what was going on, because she writes:

We have been informed that you will be in Crookston for an all-out Congregational meeting— EVERYONE will be there, I hear....so this will go by special messenger.

Monday is a national holiday, so guess you will have a little time to rest (maybe?) after your trip. Hope I can be let in by someone as to what it is all about....your mom is always so curious, you know.

Love— again & always,
Mama –

I'd hit a wall, just as Mama said. But this time it seemed to be the wall that crumbled and fell.

NEW ORLEANS JAZZ

In all these years of dad's aviation career, no one in our family had ever flown in a jetliner. Boeing had, at the time, just introduced the 747, while Dad grumbled against the whole idea of a "jumbo jet." Shouldn't be that many people in one airplane, he thought; it's too much of a risk. Thank God, his daughter would be on a 707 or similar equipment for the Lore Family's maiden jet-flight.

I flew along with Sister Marie from Minneapolis to Chicago, and then on to New Orleans, and my fascination was with the lightning. Flight held no fear for me; I'd been flying with my dad since I was three years old. I can still recall that first flight, seated on Mama's lap, crying "Go back down," while at the same time peeping over her shoulder out the window of the Cessna at the spaghetti-like roads and the toy buildings of Omaha down below where Dad built B-29s for the war effort. Fear and fascination held me in thrall. Finally we'd landed, and I'd laughed through my tears, begging, "Do it again, Daddy!" all my fear of flying completely dissolved.

Lightning held no fear for me either, just beauty. I didn't consider then that the steel tube in which I sat could attract it. I still see the clouds, clear as though I were, at this moment, peering out the window of the plane. Clouds piled atop each other—grey, purple, mustard yellow, rose, powder-white. I think, now, we might have been flying directly through the storm, not above it, as I don't remember any clear blue sky. Lightning streaked from cloud to cloud, often several flashes simultaneously in different sections of the sky. The plane trembled, dipped up and down the air pockets. Sister Marie gasped. Some people cried out. The turbulence didn't bother me either; I was used to riding with Dad in small planes over Lake of the Woods where air pockets were common. The whole thing was so beautiful that my heart burned with it.

Our New Orleans sisters picked us up at the airport and drove us to the big convent on Mirabeau Avenue. This beautiful building, located in the lowlands, would be destroyed years later by Hurricane Katrina, and the remaining sisters, including Sister Marie, would escape to Baton Rouge just before the worst of it hit. She would take only what she could carry. They would not rebuild. So what my memory holds is all I'll ever have of it.

Others for whom the Mirabeau convent was home probably remember it much differently than I do. Memory presents the inner and outer landscape as one image that shimmers like a desert mirage. Emotional heat alters what is seen. Probably I no longer know at all how the convent really looked, how it would appear in a photograph taken at that time. In fact, if someone were to show me such a photograph, I probably wouldn't recognize the place at all. I'd probably have to ask, "What's that?"

Even before we arrived there in the car, while we drove through the neighborhoods leading to the large grounds on which the convent was located, I was struck with how flimsy all the construction looked. I'd never been out of the Midwest where every house has a basement, where the windows are double-paned to keep out the winter chill, where many have brick or stucco siding, and all of it looks safely solid. These New Orleans houses seemed built so that air might blow right through them. And, in fact, many of them were built just that way, to catch the breezes on hot sultry summer days. Of course, we weren't driving through the Garden District. No. The convent had been built where the sisters worked, among the poor.

The convent also had been built to accommodate the breeze, some of it without walls at all. I think there was a sort of cloister walk and a large porch-like room enclosed only by screens. We ate out there one evening. Someone had brought the sisters a gigantic catch of crabs which they boiled in a huge kettle like those I would later see in Fish Creek, Wisconsin, at a fish boil. They spread the brilliantly colored, steaming crustaceans on long paper-covered tables and taught us northerners how to crack the legs and extract the sweet meat, dip it in butter, and feast on it. I'd tasted shrimp before, and even lobster, but nothing quite like this crab meat—a sort of mirage of crab shimmers in memory with the laughter and singing that accompanied the eating of it.

I remember long hallways and a dormitory upstairs with what now seems to me floor to ceiling windows. The beds, I think, were enclosed by white curtains, and I'm quite sure it was in this room that I slept. I'd been assigned to a young sister about my age who would stay close by so I wouldn't get lost in the enormous building. She also had been chosen, as I had, to be on the Steering Committee for Renewal. She'd spent what seems now like a relatively long time during the past

229

year in Chicago at the Ecumenical Institute, learning the process for evolving cultural systems and societies. She'd been radicalized, and would be sharing her insights with the rest of us. A lively woman, she was filled with humor, often blunt, beautiful with dark eyes, and compelling in a way and to an extent I'd rarely experienced before. Her name was Sister Helen Prejean. She would become famous years later for her work with death row inmates, her book, DEAD MAN WALKING, and the Academy Award winning film that would follow.

The meetings on the first day were restricted to elected administrators of the three provinces of the congregation. Helen needed to stay at the convent because they intended to call her in to present her plans to them. They'd be setting up our schedule for the coming discussions. I would be free to do as I wished, and an older sister, Sister Pauline, offered to show me around the city. She'd lived there all her life and had the inside story on most everything. We drank coffee with chicory at *Le Monde*, while eating little round donuts, still hot, out of a brown paper bag. We stood in Jackson Square, people ambling past this way and that, and she told me the history of the French Quarter. It was her history, also, and the history of our Sisters there in New Orleans. She wove into her stories a thread of her own wisdom, binding me to her as a daughter is bound by the story of the past, the interconnections between people and events, the precise place where the daughter is knotted into the fabric. I'd been out on the edge; now I was fastened to the center as well. I could feel the knitting inside me, frayed threads coming together, binding, holding.

The next day I sat with the others around the table in a large room at the convent. Sister Helen stood beside a large easel, magic marker in hand. We each had a sheaf of papers in front of us describing the process she'd devised. Her work is my most vivid memory of the meetings. Her description of the vision held by that Ecumenical Institute—how she had improvised from their vision to design a plan specifically for our renewal process. It was ecumenical in every way— meaning universal or of a scope to apply world-wide. It was essentially socialistic in that no one would be set above anyone else. This pattern of equality extended to the planning of every event. It was believed that everyone was equal, with equal talent in everything. The "recognized lecturer" would no longer be considered as such. Anyone could lecture. In fact, the perspective of one not accustomed to such tasks could well give stunning insight and wisdom otherwise unavailable. The duties would rotate. At one event you might be the cook, at another you might lead discussions, at another you might lecture or do janitorial work. All were equally important. We could have no hierarchy of tasks or talents.

Would it work for us? We decided we could try it. Helen's plan would provide the blueprint for our renewal meetings back in our own provinces—at least for the coming year while we were preparing for the General Chapter in 1972 when changes would be presented and voted upon. We set our sights on that goal, and we called the process in which we would engage, "Vision `72".

I felt knit into the leadership of a community in which we were about to abolish leadership—or rather, where we were about to share leadership with everyone in such a radical way that the very word would cease to have meaning. The radical sound of all this appealed to me in such a fundamental way that I felt very nearly ecstatic with this new role I had of—well, of dissolving all our roles.

That night a group of us went to the French Quarter. We walked down Bourbon Street, Helen in the lead. We were headed for Preservation Hall. The street was filled with French sailors on Liberty. They flirted with us as we passed. We laughed. I was surprised to find that Preservation Hall was just that—an old union hall that looked more like a garage than anything. We sat on rough benches, right in front, so close I could have touched the slide on the trombone. Sweet Emma played the piano and sang in her gravelly voice. The trombone player locked eyes with me, playing right to me, or so it seemed. Jazz. What an intuitive act of union within a group. Feeling the thread of music in another player, winding your own music around it, weaving something new every time. Building on each other's sound, each other's soul, the musicians murmured "Umhum," and "Take it, Emma." I got lost in it, picked up on the sound, woven in and out. The trombone player smiled and passed the sound on to the clarinetist.

It was what we'd been up to all that week. It was the same. Something new in me had come alive and felt like music, felt like lightning zigzagging through the clouds, felt like something knitting itself together in my heart. It suddenly felt possible to be on the edge AND at the center, both at once, and the secret of it lay in ... how to say it? The secret was a consciousness that approximated music, love that wove a thought through many minds and hearts into a communal expression. The secret with the power to bind me back into this religious community, at that moment I felt sure of it—the secret: I was hearing it. It was New Orleans Jazz.

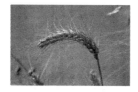

REMEMBER THE FALL

- Remember that you refused to believe it would come to this.
- Remember the separations: self from self, self from others, self from God.
- Remember a different perception of the world in which both truth and beauty are questions instead of realities.
- Remember the taste of hope turned to ashes.
- Remember the death of dreams.
- Remember the vertigo, the edge, the endless fall.

THE EDGE OF TENDERNESS

A LETTER FROM MAMA
It is my destiny
September 1, 1971

On the day following her sixty-first birthday, Mama wrote another letter that she never sent. It was included in the manila envelope filled with papers. On the outside she'd scrawled:

For Mary Jane
Please understand me.

These are the pages, saved over the years, of feelings, experiences, ponderings too close to her heart to be shared when she wrote them. Sometimes she was too filled with joy; at other times too anxious or guilty or nearly crazed to dare being seen so naked in her words. But in the end, ultimately, she wanted nothing more than to be understood.

This day I was to understand her happiness—never far from, actually the flip side, or maybe shot through with her anxiety. *"My head is filled with thoughts this morning. Deep thoughts, shallow thoughts, loving thoughts, thoughts of gratitude, and last and now are the thoughts of anxiety.*

Not anxiety in the painful way, but anxiousness to get at the work which must be done and which I have promised myself for years and years that I would do—in fact, it is my destiny to put it all down on paper, since in taking stock of others of my generation who know and remember the things I know and remember, I realize that none of them will attempt to leave a record for those who have and will come after us.

Over the years she tried again and again to write her memoir, but the present moment always intervened. She left scraps of the past, fragments of narrative, and these letters that now are themselves far past. But I do recognize her sweet anxiety, because I bear it too, that same impulse to preserve and pass along the stories of our lives.

But.... and along comes the intervening present moment. (it is wrong to begin a sentence that way, I think, and even more ungrammatical to head a paragraph with such a word—except that in this free generation in which we now exist, a little thing like a misplaced conjunction is a very minor matter—so there it is) first of all is my "right now" attempt to begin a long narrative of past events in the lives of those who were a part of the Anton John and Elizabeth Friesinger Klimek family and household (because that is what this part of my tale is going to be dealing with mostly) I must begin with the present which has only passed into ONE yesterday.

And off she goes, using up what time she has set aside for writing on that ONE yesterday, her sixty-first birthday which had turned out differently from what she'd anticipated. What we believe to be our destiny is sometimes, maybe even often, not. As she directed her intention over and over to this destiny, and then said, "But...," so also did I. While she wrote letters she would never send, many of them switching back and forth from the family story she felt compelled to write, to the moment she was living—I, too, was living between what I thought to be my own destiny, and a profound intervening conjunction.

By the spring of 1971 Sister Diana and I had signed a contract with a group of rural parishes in the Minnesota River Valley to set up a regional religious education program. Our offices would be in a storefront in the largest of the towns, New Prague, and our home would be in a different town, twelve miles away, in Montgomery. The move would not take place, though, until after a summer packed with courses at St. John's, a trip to Cincinnati, and an experiment in a different sort of "retreat" at our community's vacation spot—The Pines.

In a scrap of a letter, undated, Mama writes to our little Bidwell community: *Soon now, school will be closed for you there and you go more or less your separate ways again—but you will have your memories of Bidwell (and also Courthouse Road—and you will meet occasionally, but you will have that one winter in your hearts and minds as being separate from any other.*

We took pictures of the five of us that last morning at the Bidwell house or I would not remember leaving there. My mind had focused on a future in which I would fulfill my destiny as a Sister of St. Joseph. Since the time in New Orleans, I felt I'd finally found my way. My mind filled with ideas and plans for renewal, I rode a wave of excitement and not a little grandiosity because of the acceptance and recognition I felt I'd finally received from the other sisters. One could not call my motivations generous and unselfish.

The pictures show us sitting around the kitchen table at breakfast, some of us with our hair up in rollers, toasting one another with glasses of orange juice. Another picture has us grouped by the cars in front of the house just before the first of us, Emilie, leaves. There memory stops. The future was calling us; in my mind we already had arrived.

Why does memory block out whole sections of time, then focus in detail on a week, a day? The only thing I remember about Pat Kelly from that summer, for example, is that he was supposed to join a group of us at The Pines for one day during our retreat, and he didn't come. He was in the hospital, and Diana and I visited him after the retreat was over. How grey he looked. We stayed only a moment. I have more vivid memories of the drive away from that hospital when we stopped at a park somewhere between St. Cloud and Montgomery to eat a lunch of sandwiches and fruit. It was late August, just before Mama's birthday, and the tree branches hung heavy over the waters of the Mississippi.

Reconstructing, not remembering, that summer's session at St. John's, I realize that my attention was on Vision '72 rather than upon my courses of study or any social life with the other priest and sister students. Was I completely unconscious that summer? Now I think I might have been at least almost unconscious. Now I see that I was already well down a dangerous slide into dark impossibility. But I didn't know that then. In fact, I'm quite sure I felt just the opposite— that I was rising towards a life of possibility as a Sister of St. Joseph.

I did go to Cincinnati with Sister Marie for a steering committee meeting, and I took a week's leave from the summer session to do it. That had been permitted because my work in community renewal comprised one of the three thesis projects in my Master's program. All my planning of Vision `72 folded neatly into my theology degree. Whatever we did in Cincinnati, though, was lost in my plunge towards unconsciousness. All I remember of Cincinnati now is Sister Somebody's pink dress. I begged her for the pattern so that I could make a similar one of my own.

What in heaven's name was I up to?

I do remember the retreat at The Pines, and I remember some of it vividly. While I'd been at St. John's, Sister Diana had been in Seattle at a new program designed for Directors of Religious Education. From what I could tell after she returned, her first summer there had been much like my first summer at St. John's. She'd been transformed by possibilities. She'd met smart and articulate and forward-looking people including some of the biggest names in contemporary American Catholic theological trends. She'd spent late evenings on Elliot Bay with these people, sitting around bonfires, dreaming the future. They envisioned a new sort of religious community, one made up of both men and women. We needed this complementarity, a kind of wholeness of vision that we'd concluded could not be achieved within communities of one gender. One priest she met must have been assigned close to the Twin Cities, because we drove him up to The Pines with us. Ideas flew around the car. Wild ideas. Now I see them more clearly, and they were impossible ideas. But what a marvel it all was! We thought such things could come true. Diana's eyes sparkled.

There was a separate cabin at The Pines where our male guests would stay. It was some distance down the shore of the lake, and a path to it led through the woods. Everything was rustic—outhouses and a jerry-rigged shower inside a shed. The property had been inherited by the Congregation some years before, and the sisters had used it every summer as a place to hide away and relax in the most beautiful environment one could imagine. The two cabins used by the sisters sat atop a rise over a secluded lake just south of Bemidji, Minnesota, outside a tiny town called Shelton. Leaving Highway 2, we turned onto a graveled road marked only by a commercial sign advertising a business in Bemidji. The road ambled past the farm of some people who took care of The Pines in winter, when it was mostly snowed in, and who provided us with gifts of produce from time to time. It was a three-generation farm, with a succession of houses to accommodate everyone. The present manager of the place was a burly woman whom I mistook for a man in her coveralls and cap and with her husky voice.

After passing the farm, we turned onto another road, less wide, and then onto another with wheel paths separated by tall grasses that brushed the underside of the car as we drove over them. Finally we emerged into the clearing that was The Pines, named thus because of several gigantic Norway pines at the top of the hill that whispered a sound that mesmerized. Amidst the trees the sisters had erected a large bell that could be rung to call us back from our hikes or our languid drifting on the lake in the rowboat. I loved the place. I'd spent time there every summer since the year I first entered the convent.

At The Pines secrets were told and memories sculpted because of a freedom not possible back at the motherhouse. Here we circled around a bonfire at night, dancing the Zorba dance and then wandered the dark path down to the lake, sat in the wild reeds at the shore watching the stars. Here we woke early, took the rowboat to the center of the lake where mists swirled and the loons woke one by one to dance. Here we gathered moss for the Christmas manger scene, exquisite miniscule flowers of deepest green. Here Sister Innocent and I once drew bows and shot arrows at a bulls-eye target. We rode bicycles down the gravel road as fast as we could, our veils flying behind us, our long skirts wrapped up around our waists and pinned, our laughter and shouting unrestrained. Who would hear us? God. God might hear and might be laughing too. "I still know how!" I shouted. "I still know how to ride a bike." Here I sat all day in the rowboat with old Sister Philomena who liked to fish, and I read to her while she lifted her fishing rod up and down in a motion she thought was guaranteed to attract a trout or sunfish. It was Miles Connelly's book *Mr. Blue,* about the man who didn't fit into this world because he gave all his money away, played a trumpet from the top of a skyscraper, and gathered together those he called "the Spies of God."

"I like that Blue," Philomena said, pulling in a sunfish. "I like him a lot."

Something about this place held the essence of my love for religious life, or maybe not. Maybe it only seemed that way because I was a sister when I was there. Maybe, really, it held the essence of my self, a life that had little or nothing to do with my vows, a life that was my own.

The retreat was by invitation. The sisters who attended were all about the same age, separated by only about ten years from youngest to eldest. All five of us from the Bidwell house were there and several more I knew well. A few of the sisters I knew only slightly

238

because they had entered the convent while I was in college, and I'd never lived in the same house with them.

Two of the sisters, Eva Mary and Lydia, had spent the summer developing counseling skills, and this brought them into what was then known as Sensitivity Training. I think it was Eva Mary who suggested we try the methods of that process among ourselves. She said she couldn't lead the process, though, as she didn't consider herself qualified, so someone invited the priest who did a lot of counseling with sisters in the Crookston diocese. We all knew him; many of us had either worked with him or been counseled by him at one time or another. I'd worked with him while I taught at the academy and he was the student counselor. He'd never been my counselor. I didn't really want a counselor, and if I had I wouldn't have chosen him because something in my gut said not to trust him. I didn't know exactly what it was, and thought maybe it was just aversion to his mannerisms. He struck me as so circuitous as to seem double, dubious, duplicitous. Such an aversion seemed unworthy, and I attempted to ignore it or make my choices despite its presence. Nonetheless, I felt uncomfortable when he was around. Years later, during the priest sex scandals, he would be implicated and would end up leaving the priesthood.

Our session with him happened on the last night of our retreat. We sisters had experienced inspirational times together during those days at The Pines, and I believe we felt bonded. We crowded around the long table in the main cabin. Maybe we were eager; maybe we were apprehensive. But all of us were there. The process, as I recall, was simple. We'd be under scrutiny, one by one, while the others told us first our strengths, then our weaknesses. It shouldn't be anything new for any of us. Our superiors had been telling us these things from the moment we set foot on the convent threshold. Eva Mary warned us that it might be more difficult than that, but how?

We started around the table. The priest kept pretty quiet, more a witness than a moderator. The first few sisters on the "hot seat" had it easy, but once we got the hang of it, the time we spent on any given sister increased. What we hadn't counted on was the explosive combination of how well we knew each other from years of having lived so closely together, mixed with the reserve we'd all been taught. We'd lived with each other's faults, keeping quiet, overlooking what annoyed us. But after a few hours of sensitivity training our tongues were loosed. Faults and weaknesses began to pile up in front of certain sisters. Tears fell. The priest-moderator kept silence. It was beyond him; I see that now. I don't remember what they said to me. Maybe I was one of the first, before our reserve shattered. I do remember that fear tightened my chest and restricted my breathing while it was Joanne's turn. I knew I couldn't have borne the weight of all that we were piling on her. It was almost midnight by then and we were not even half finished. It seemed we had more and more to say to each sister. For a moment we paused to assess.

Most of the sisters believed it would be destructive to stop the process before we were finished. A few of us thought the process had been destructive enough already. The majority believed that you had to get through it, come out on the other end—you know, like death and resurrection. You couldn't just run off and leave the group in the midst of suffering. You had to finish it. And you couldn't just pick it up the next day. Probably we'd never get ourselves back into this cauldron, never again reach this peak of intensity. And anyway, the next day was our final day of retreat. We had to believe we could come through this and be better because of it.

I still don't know if I was wise to leave the group, or merely a coward who hated confrontation. I did know that I couldn't be part of doing to anyone else what we'd all just done to Joanne who still was wiping tears away. Where was her resurrection? We'd decided that those who couldn't stay awake or didn't feel right about staying could leave.

Until that night I hadn't realized how alone all of us had been—how alone I had been throughout all my convent years. Just imagine how much we all contained and how explosive such containment could become when it continued over years and couldn't be shared in little bits throughout the moments of our lives. It doesn't take a convent to do that to a person, though. I knew that. But in the convent it had been institutionalized and supported by a holy rule. Yes, it was changing, but was this the right way to do that? Reform, yes. **But**—should it be like this?

Right there, exactly at that moment, came that intervening conjunction. I excused myself, left the group and climbed the hill to the other cabin.

I lay in bed on a screened-in porch at the other cabin listening to the night sounds. Moths fluttered their wings against the screen. Mice scurried through the long grass. Women's voices drifted up the hill from the main cabin. I kept expecting them to finish and get some sleep. I drifted off for a while and then woke again to the sound of voices closer now. An argument. A cajoling voice. The sound of people walking just below the window. Murmurs growing more distant. I went back to sleep.

The next morning several of the sisters were gone. "They left before sunrise," Diana told me. The sensitivity training had been too much for one of them. She didn't want to be there anymore. "I think she's going to leave the community," Diana said. Or probably she just said, "She's leaving." We all knew what it meant. And she did—leave. She had climbed into the car early that morning and just kept on going. I never saw that sister again.

Within the next two years all but three of the sisters at that retreat would have left the congregation. Diana would stay. They didn't leave because of the retreat, but the retreat does seem now to have cracked open the container that up until then had held us. Maybe it all really does have to do with destiny. Mama thought she knew her destiny, but real life, the life of the moment kept intervening and compelling her to live it. Those of us at the retreat thought we knew our destiny also. We even vowed ourselves to it, thinking to create an unbreakable container of destiny. But it shattered. Maybe that night was real life breaking forth. Maybe I couldn't stay that night because I wasn't ready yet to have my dreams shatter. Maybe Diana and the other two women who remained in the convent all their lives had never formed the clay of their dreams into a vessel of destiny. Maybe their dreams were made of more flexible stuff than clay, and it was their flexibility that preserved them through the process of renewal.

Diana and I put our suitcases into the car later that afternoon and drove south, stopping in St. Cloud to visit Pat Kelly, and at the park to eat our sandwiches. Then we continued on to the Minnesota River Valley.

241

Mama sat at her Smith Corona, her thoughts about her birthday breaking through her resolve to fulfill her destiny of writing the family story:

Yesterday, August 31, 1971, I was sixty-one years of age. When I put it into words, it seems I am writing of someone other than myself. I CAN'T be that old! Why, the past is so close—the memorable past, that is. I can recall not long ago looking forward to an age such as this and thinking that being in the sixties would be an age of senility and quietness born from a final location like a rocking chair. Not so, let me tell you!

Let me tell you about my yesterday which is so vivid and so dear in my mind and in my heart. I had decided not to think about this birthday at all. I was in my sixties and should forget about frivolous excitement and gifts and a birthday cake and such. I would treat it as any other day and had, in fact, mentioned to George that he was not to purchase a gift as the intended remodeling of our guest room with birch paneling to cover the scarred walls would be my birthday gift when the work was finally competed...and I meant it from my heart!

When George awoke to go to work, he tucked the covers close around me and said "Happy Birthday, Mama! You stay in bed and get some more sleep." So I did just that—until 9:10 a.m. when the telephone rang and on answering came another "Happy Birthday" from the one person who apart from my family offers me the greatest consolation and friendly warmth and security (except from our divine Father who offers this to all who entreat Him) of all within my circle of dear ones. Her cheery and optimistic chatter made the day start out as though it were truly for me. Throughout the remainder of the morning I communed with myself and at noontime looked forward to George's arrival.

He arrived—and so did the postal mail. Two large envelopes, identical in size (7 ½ x 8 ½ inches); one white, the other a gorgeous lavender. Since the lavender one was on top, I opened it first. Exotic! A lavender framed shadowy feminine face, light reflected to show only one side and her black hair surrounding to the black-night shadows so the remainder of the face was in darkness—and a faint blue inscription "I'm sending you all my love on your Birthday—(the card opens to a complete lavender double page)—that may not seem like much of a present....but it's what I have the most of—" signed simply "Liz."

That is our Liz, christened Elizabeth Ann, called Betsy throughout infancy, childhood and high school years—then, by her own choice, she adopted "Liz" and grew to womanhood.

The other large card, in a white envelope, came next. Sweet and simple—a tiny child's hand placing into a mother's hand a small bunch of tiny daisies—the hands and daisies light against a shadowy black background—and inside the inscription, "Thanks for being there when I need you."

On the other side a very personal, "Happy birthday, Mama—This card seemed so perfect, what with the tiny daisies and the inscription and all. As I sit here trying to find words to be a gift to you on your birthday—I discover only that what I would want to say is either too deep to have words, or too common to warrant them. Since the deep cannot be spoken—but I want to say something, I will resort to the common and hope that you will hear all that these words contain.

   I love you, Mama— Live forever,

    Mary Jane"

You can see why my birthday was a great one. Do I feel loved? After so many years, I am overwhelmed. Thank you, all of you. and especially the man in my George, who reneged on our—or rather, MY decision, and casually set before me during the afternoon a gift-wrapped package containing delightful perfume and bubble bath. A beautiful day!

So much for the prologue, she writes then, and goes on to begin the work she sees as her destiny, the family history. She writes two paragraphs and stops midway through a description of her brother, Peter, *OH, how I loved him and throughout our growing up years he added much to my happiness and self-assurance.*

I sit back in my chair and stare out the window at the clouds swirling around the mountain tops, here, this day in my own seventy-fourth year. Destiny, I think, seeing her back then, interrupted by something in her present moment, and afterwards not writing another of these "understand me" papers until the next March, and then not one that concerned her family history. Destiny. What is she teaching me about my own life? Maybe that both of us had placed our dreams of destiny too far out and not paid sufficient attention to the clues about love that called to us in every moment. On that day she felt so loved, was that not her destiny? Even when she visited the past for the space of two paragraphs, even then she focused on her love. She fulfilled her destiny despite herself, willy-nilly, just living out her life and writing when she could. I was not so wise. I held tightly to that convent destiny of mine until the day, not long away, when it shattered like the container of life which it had become, and left me lying in the mess, trying to pick up the pieces of my broken dreams.

A LETTER FROM MAMA
"In a hurry—so must be snappy!"
September 3, 1971

Mama's hurrying to the airport before Sister Carol Ann arrives there to pick up peg board and fittings. It's left over from her Store of Lore gift shop, and she's agreed to donate it to Sister Diana and me for use in our storefront religious education center. *Went through a tangle of fittings and picked what I thought you could use for displaying brochures, etc.* Her paragraphs are short and breathless.

We both must have been breathless. *I realize you are busy— BUSY—hope everything went well at St. B's.* This comes at the end of a paragraph reminding me that it is her 37th wedding anniversary that very day. I guess I failed to send a card. *—know that you are also thinking about it—we are a close family—know each other's big days and it doesn't take cards and such to know that each is remembering.* I do hope my card was in the mail, and I hadn't actually forgotten to send one.

But apparently I'd been part of some sort of event at the College of St. Benedict, and would soon be participating in a Vision '72 weekend in Park Rapids. *Have prayed for your success at the meeting in P.R. —will get a report on it from C.A.* So that was why Carol Ann was hauling the peg board—to make a transfer from her car to ours in Park Rapids.

The entire year rushed by like this. All of Mama's letters after this one are missing, though I remember getting about two a week the whole time that Diana and I lived in the apartment above the dentist's office on Main Street. I left too fast, I guess, when I finally did leave. I must have abandoned more than just one box of things. I abandoned a lot that year—lost much that I had treasured and loved.

At the beginning, though, I was sure that I'd finally found my place professionally as a director of religious education, my place vocationally as a Sister of St. Joseph, and my place for living on this earth. For the first time in all my convent years I was back to living in a small town. For the first time since leaving my own small town of Baudette, I felt I could breathe free. Cities didn't agree with me, but I hadn't known that until September, walking up and down Main Street,

245

knowing that I could contain the design of the town in my mind, that I could know where I was and not get lost. You could drive in any direction and reach the edge of the town in two minutes. Surrounding the town were the farms, fields of corn and beans. We scooted past them daily in our leased red Maverick, driving from town to town to the parishes in our region. Some of the giant brick or stone churches weren't actually in a town, but were set down amidst the fields by immigrant farmers who had designed them to resemble the churches in Europe.

What a good place to begin my life anew. No more priest trying to fire me. No more stifling convent atmosphere. No more, even, being possessed by one single parish as one of their own iconic group of praying sisters. We set up our storefront office with Mama's pegboard on its walls, with desks and filing cabinets and typewriters provided by the six churches we served, and with a lively secretary named Caroline who talked constantly about Elvis Presley. I wrote a weekly column for the local newspaper, an inspirational/informational piece titled, "We're Open," but I don't recall anyone ever just dropping in. (We'd anticipated that people would.) The only people who dropped into our religious education center were the two young assistant priests whose focus was on the adolescents of the region, and a neighboring director of religious education who offered to join us, collaborating in teacher training and youth events. I think her name was Dottie. She played a wicked banjo, told amazing stories from her southern culture past, and was a theological wizard. She also liked a snifter of cognac to follow all our meetings and educational events.

Busy, busy, busy, Mama rightly said, and I found it invigorating, or possibly distracting. Besides the regional work—creating an education program for several parishes rather than just one, and the renewal work for the congregation which seemed to put me on the road to meetings at least one weekend a month, there were discussions with archdiocesan leaders who saw what Diana and I were doing as innovative and a unique opportunity to pilot new programs with youth. What a heady time it was. I felt important, powerful. Suddenly it seemed I knew exactly what I was supposed to do, and it was important work. Those I considered leaders were nodding their heads in my direction and saying "Yes."

Was I blind? What should I have cared for the acceptance of hierarchical leaders by then, so intent upon renewal as I claimed even to myself that I was? Was I dazzled? Was I seduced? If so, I hadn't realized it yet.

Our little apartment felt nothing like a convent. The kitchen and living room windows looked down on Main Street. When we first moved in, the weather still was warm enough to open them wide and let in the street noises and the breeze that billowed the curtains. We entertained, making fondue and buying wine to serve our guests—often the two young priests and Dottie. We soaked the labels off the bottles and decorated the window at the top of the stairs with them while listening to Neil Diamond sing "Cracklin' Rosie." on our stereo. We watched *The Dick Cavett Show* and *Laugh In* on TV whenever we didn't have meetings to attend. We also watched Walter Cronkite tally the body counts from Viet Nam, and afterwards we discussed Eric Severeid's commentary. We saved up our personal allowance of $20 a month and bought hip huggers and wide belts and Joan Baez LPs. I played the guitar and we both sang, Diana's voice weaving around mine in contemporary-sounding harmony.

Pat Kelly, fully recovered from his surgery, visited. He came the first time not long after we moved in and took Diana and me to lunch at an old hotel that served German food. We showed him our storefront office, and afterwards he came with us back to our apartment where we discussed the sorts of things we always discussed with him: church and world politics, his work at the college, our work in the region and with the congregation. He was troubled by aspects of all of this, but especially by his attempts to get the college administrators to recognize that as chaplain Pat was on a par with the college president. In his mind there was the spiritual dimension of the community and the educational dimension—both equal. The two leaders should work hand in hand, but the president believed that he ought to be head of everything, including Pat. He was a layman who practiced a lay version of Benedictine spirituality which he believed gave him an edge at a Benedictine College. Pat chafed under this secondary status even while he both respected and enjoyed the president as a personal friend. Imbued as he was with the theology of

247

Vatican II, Pat found himself caught in paradox. His new ecclesiology balanced on the three principles of collegiality, subsidiarity, and accountability, all of which justified for him the struggle he undertook to establish equality between the educational and spiritual component of Catholic education. But the struggle was also one for leadership of the college. Still rooted in his seminary-trained psyche was the notion, inculcated in clerics from the time the church was still young, that the ordained priest held a position between the people and God, and was an *alter-Christus* who acted as a mediator between human and divine. To my mind he never resolved this paradox.

Pat rejoiced in the sisters' new acceptance of me, and although my community involvement meant we would have less time together, we both believed that finally it would assure our continued commitment. But the community of my sisters wanted all of me, and something in me wanted to belong completely and only to the community. Something else in me held fast to Pat. I began to feel split as I never had before. Unable to withstand the tension, my body gave in to exhaustion.

As the weeks went on, Pat showed up every Sunday Diana and I were home. He'd finish his Sunday morning masses, get in his car and drive to southern Minnesota. He'd sleep on our sofa in the living room, take us to breakfast on Monday morning, and then drive back north to the college. After a few months of this I began to notice something different about myself: I wished he wouldn't come.

My long attempt to balance two loves began to fail, and I teetered between them. When Pat was present I clung to him, and when he was absent I clung just as desperately to my sisters. All the while I tried to maintain a calm front, a self-control, assuring everyone that I was fine. I just had to get my health back, slow down, rest. Maybe when the renewal project was completed…maybe with summer.

He didn't fit into this new life. In many ways, of course, he'd never fit, but in the past he'd been a source of freedom and companionship for me. Now my life felt free in itself and I was utterly involved in it. As a consequence it was Pat who began to seem like a hindrance or even a danger. I didn't reason this out at the time. It was a feeling, a flicker of "oh no," when he called to say he was starting out and would arrive at such and such a time. But I never said that. We always welcomed him. We fixed spaghetti or fondue or a creamy chicken casserole and he brought wine. We talked about the war or the church or his latest struggles at the college.

One weekend Diana and I drove to the Twin Cities to see the movie, *Cabaret*. Watching it, I identified with the individuals caught up in a tide of social change just as I had with the movie *Dr. Zhivago* which I'd seen years before. Both movies appeared as *pentimenti* through which to view present times, both cultural and ecclesiastical. My struggles for personal meaning and individual identity were taking place within a much larger context and could not be called unique. The struggle that had seemed so particular to me, I now glimpsed as the struggle of an era in which I was but a miniscule part. *Zhivago*, filled me with longing, while *Cabaret* left me with a kind of desperation. It was the yearning and desperation of history to resolve the paradox of the human need for simultaneous freedom and belonging. I watched and listened in fascination as Nellie Bowles belted out her hope that maybe this time she'd win. Win what, though? Love. Belonging. Me too, I thought. Maybe this time the world will change. Maybe finally I'll find the way. "I'll be home at last." Maybe...

Then she sang the naughty, dismissive, breaking-out-from-barriers song: "Bye-Bye, Mein Lieber Herr" and I thought of Pat...now it's over. My mind split open. I hummed the music and words all the way back home. Had it been a fine affair? Could it even be called an affair? I'd made promises to him. "I love you," I'd said. For years I'd held him in a separate place in my heart, along with my desire for freedom and the coming of a new world. He'd said I was his Lara, and I'd believed that. He said we were soul mates and I believed that also. In little ways, visit by visit, for six years, our lives had been weaving themselves together. He asked me to stay by him as a companion, to hold his hand when he died. I'd agreed to that.

Impossible! It was exactly what Steph had been talking about when she told me all about "the third way." But I felt increasingly suffocated by it. I needed the open air. I'd substituted him for my freedom. And he was surely better off without me.

These thoughts came in spurts over the next few weeks as I walked around humming the music from *Cabaret*. I developed a stomach ache that wouldn't stop. I'd started with a series of other illnesses too. A terrible sore throat that took my voice away. This led to a bout of

249

mononucleosis, though I knew of no one else who had that disease, so where did it come from? While trying to heal from mono I got the flu and then viral pneumonia.

I didn't want to see him.

Once I was well enough to resume my duties in the region, I began to stay after our wrap-up sessions to talk with one of the priests about my concerns, about this relationship with Pat. I see now that I wanted the priest to say "Stop!" I had six year's worth of stories, all leading up to this binding of my heart and mind that I now was struggling to loosen. All relationships touch places in ourselves we wish that we could hide. They question our essence. Of their very nature they set ultimatums. We had used each other as a doorway into a new life, not thinking that once we had crossed the threshold we would leave the other one behind. I wanted my freedom from him, and I told his secrets to the young priest.

"You'll have to break it off with him," the young priest said. To him it seemed so simple. But once he'd said it, the other side of my dilemma kicked in—the good things. The glory of the man—his mind, his spirit that yearned towards the future, his dreams of a utopian world to come, his urging that I be part of that, his laughter, the way he could whistle any tune, his priesthood and the elegance of his presence celebrating the Eucharist. My guilt at having handed him over to the young priest broke me open and I burst into tears.

"I can't," I said.

"You must," he insisted.

I'd just upped the ante. I walked down the dark street from the church to the apartment, hearing the voice of the young priest echo in my mind. You must. He didn't understand, I argued with myself. It's about promises. This was the first I realized what I'd done. I'd made contradictory, irreconcilable promises—to God through my religious vows and my religious community, and afterwards to Pat. I thought the promises could not only coexist, but could coincide. I once again brought up St. Francis and St. Clare; how did they make their relationship work out? Maybe they didn't make the same promises. Maybe life had planes or tiers of evolution, and the saints were on a higher plane than I was. Well, how silly; of course they were. Maybe they'd reached Teilhard's "Omega Point." Maybe my sense that the

250

promises could reconcile and exist together was true, but on a different plane, a plane of convergence that neither Pat nor I had reached.

Pat feared coming to the end of his life and dying alone. He spoke of it often as the most dreaded consequence of his vow of celibacy. Very early on I promised him that I would be there. I would hold his hand. I would step right to the threshold of eternity with him. I promised that. It might have been right after the murder/suicide of the young couple in Crookston, or it could have been several years later, and it probably was several years later, but I connect the two in my memory. He told me the story of an old priest who died alone upstairs in his rectory while his housekeeper worked in the kitchen downstairs, completely oblivious to the old man's passing, not really wanting to be with him anyway. Nobody wanted to be with him, he was such a grouch. He'd been alone too long. He'd said too many awful things to his parishioners. They yearned for a new voice. They wished him gone. They prayed God to take him to heaven. Soon. Pat was there as administrator while the old priest died, and the darkness of the dying man's abandonment seeped into Pat's soul staining it with fear. "Hold my hand when I die?" And I promised.

Lots of other promises followed. I promise I'll be here to comfort you when you need comforting. I promise to stand by you when you are struggling. I promise to walk beside you into this new world we anticipate and work towards bringing it about. I promise to be your companion in this life.

How do you just break that off?

Much as I wished Pat would stay away, much as I wished I'd not made those promises, here I was. The promises had been made. The religious vows had been made. Marriage seemed to be the only way to keep my promises to Pat, but he definitely didn't want to leave the priesthood and get married, and I didn't want that either. I wanted a coalescence of promises, a different sort of world where I could have both. But that was a dream, a childish fantasy. In this world they crashed head on, and I felt caught at the point of impact.

A LETTER FROM MAMA
Ramblings of a disturbed mind.
March 19, 1972

Mama's hidden "Please Understand Me" letters read like a series of wracking sobs. I'm stunned, as I read, that both she and I felt caught in a riptide at the same time. Secretly, secretly, because we'd both decided to keep the tearing of our minds private while we attempted a normal appearance, each of us was losing her moorings and being swept away.

At home—Noontime—Fixing dinner to take to airport—

I have come to a decision (for what it is worth—may change my intention tomorrow but at the moment it seems the only way left to us).

Am I becoming less than normal in my thinking? What am I doing to George? I am pushing him—and PUSHING and <u>PUSHING</u>! Being a man who has been my leaning post for over 33 years, does he feel that I am trying to remold him NOW?

Do I still love him? I think I do. I remember easily when he was my life—even now—could I exist without him? I doubt that I could and maybe at this stage of life, that is what is making me run SCARED! I am pushing and PUSHING—WHY?

He loves to fly—he is the MASTER—THE AUTHORITY on flying— has flown more hours and years than anyone in this area—he should be the authority. He does NOT want to retire—I see visions of retirement and years of compatibility and a chance to relax and communicate with each other and re-unite occasionally with our family—and his family— and not have to worry about keeping ahead of the governments (State and Federal) with regulations, taxes, fees, deadlines for filing, inquiries into payrolls, and insurance risks which sit like wolves at our door just waiting for something to happen which will take away all he has worked for in one big attack because someone erred and the result is LAWSUITS!!!! (Is wanting security wrong?)

Why does he drink ??? (Not excessively but definitely it seems wrong and threatening to our future for him to indulge steadily during the daytime and then there is always the risk that he will fly. (Last night I swear he had more than a couple while he was getting the power

252

steering fixed at Erickson's—and less than an hour later he backed the car into the gas storage tank and damaged the rear fender and bumper...which he NEVER would have done had he been COLD SOBER— or am I just suspicious and see his every error as a sign he has been drinking. Am I all wrong? He says he doesn't drink! I find half-consumed FIFTHS—He says he knows nothing about where they come from. Could he be telling the truth? Am I JUDGING? I have pleaded—threatened— argued—cried. Where do I go now?

I am fond of liquor—have tried to guard against it—should I follow the route? Maybe if I start using funds which we owe to others— buy plenty of it—drink all we want to—the business will suffer—he won't work—both of us drink and sleep—a common euphoria—forget— laugh—FORGET—let Jesme and Anderson run the airport—they both find it exhilarating. Why not?

Eventually, it will cure us both or we will die together! DIE—that is the "be-all of the end-all."

Am I sane? "All the world is queer save thee and Me—Sometimes even thou art a little queer." I feel I am the sane one and must come up with a solution, but maybe I am wrong. Where do I turn? Wild, isn't it? WHERE DO I TURN????????????

Do I leave—just vanish? Would he care? I think he would, but I don't know for sure— (I wouldn't want him to suffer)—(I want things as they were—understanding—communication between us —where has it gone??)

Dinner is ready—must take it to the airport. He likes my cooking and this meal is wild goose, wild rice stuffing, baked potato, creamed wax beans, cranberries.. I enjoyed fixing it for him—he will enjoy eating it—but he will fight against my pushing him—I only want him to NOT drink in case he must fly. Is there an answer?

The ramblings of a disturbed mind???? Who knows? I, the writer, do not know! What am I?

I wonder now: did the pain in my dad's face ever go away? His pulverized cheek bones. His squashed nose. He only said it had been left numb, dead-feeling. Did he drink to relieve physical pain? He always tolerated alcohol well, never appearing to have had too much. Or was he also enduring emotional pain, seeing the end of his aviation career looming ahead of him, wondering if he would want to live if he couldn't fly. And Mama kept reminding him, fearing that the business would wreck their marriage. All of us seem to have been standing at the stark edge of the known world, caught between opposites we couldn't reconcile.

It wasn't long after I revealed Pat's secrets to the young priest and was told to break off the relationship that Diana and I drove north to Park Rapids again for a Vision '72 meeting. I'd be presenting some ideas, as it seemed I often was asked now to do, and conducting some interactive sessions. This town, located on the edge of Itasca State Park and the source of the Mississippi River, was accessible to our sisters across the state, and we had a large hospital there where everyone could stay.

A winter storm system was moving down from Canada, but we could make it to Park Rapids if we started out early. It would pass while we were there, and we'd have clear weather again for the trip back home. We drove up past the rolling farmland of Stern's County into the lake district and the evergreen forests of Itasca. Arriving at the hospital we were caught up in a swirl of laughter and hugs and chatter of the sisters. Under the swirl, I realize now, was a deeper current of politicking. The proposed changes to our religious culture excited some and worried others. We mixed and mingled, conversation changing from friendly "how are you" to serious strategizing, depending upon the composition of a particular circle of women.

I don't remember when it started, but I'm pretty sure it was during my talk. My fingers still can feel the slick 3x5 cards on which I'd typed cues for myself. "Be a new man," we sang one of the newest guitar hymns being used at some Masses in those early years of renewal, "a new day's on its way." My theme, wasn't it? The new world, the utopian world to which I'd committed myself—with Pat. And here also—with my sisters. It didn't bother me that we were encouraging one another to be new *men*. My introduction to feminism would be several years off. I still thought of all the masculine words as being gender inclusive.

I gave my presentation, stumbling more than usual over the words, suddenly unsure that my words were honest. Here I stood in front of all my sisters, as though I knew something, was an authority on something, while guilt churned in my belly. Here I was, talking

254

about new ways of ministering together as sisters, about our congregation's essence—the work of reconciliation within ourselves, between ourselves, and flowing from our commitment out to the divided, ruptured situations in the world we served—and I was the broken one. I could barely finish.

Instead of staying for the small discussion groups afterwards, I went down the hall in the hospital and found a phone booth. I called Pat on his private office phone, collect. It was an arrangement that we had, since I had virtually no money of my own. He answered. My stomach sank. He sounded so excited, asking how the meeting was going, how my talk went, and the more I sensed his pride and confidence in me, the worse I felt.

I confessed that I'd betrayed his secrets to the young priest.

His tone changed immediately. "He knows who I am?"

"Yes."

His tone turned colder than the winter storm that had already blown in. I don't remember what he said to me. Surely he told me that he could never trust me again. This ought to have settled things for me. "It was a fine affair...now it's over." But I became frantic, turned wild.

"I have to see you," I sobbed.

"I've nothing to say to you." He said. Cold. Cold. Cold.

"I can't stand this."

"You betrayed me."

"But I want to make it right."

"That's impossible."

"I'm coming to see you," I told him and hung up the phone.

I went back into the meeting room and motioned to Diana. My face was streaked with tears. "I have to go to see Pat," I said. "Something terrible has happened."

"Now?" she said. She knew I was asking her to drive me, that she always drove the car, that I didn't have the experience to drive myself in such a storm.

"I have to go." I couldn't stop crying.

"It's already too late to drive down there, take care of whatever it is, and then drive back." Always reasonable, that Diana.

"I'll stay. You can just drop me off and then come back here and go to the meeting tomorrow. You can pick me up in the afternoon and we can go home."

"Overnight? Where will you stay?"

There would be a place, I was sure of it. Maybe those exotic hippie girls still were there.

She told me it was storming too hard for her to risk coming back alone. She'd ask Sister Andrea to join us.

And we left. They sat in the front seat, I curled up in the back. Outside the snow cut through the coming darkness. Diana tuned to a music station on the radio. "American Pie." It was the first time I'd ever heard it...this'll be the day that I die. One way or another, I thought, that will be true.

Pat and I talked most of the night. I cried a lot. I'd hurt him irreparably, he told me, but he'd give me a chance to earn back his trust. He still sounded cold when he told me he needed sleep. I should sleep in the bedroom attached to his office. No one had seen me, and no one should in order to maintain propriety. He'd go down the hall to the room he used when he was sick—a guest room kept available, and one he often used anyway because it was in a quieter part of the building.

I lay awake the rest of the night, angry with him the whole while for the hold he had on me and not really understanding why I'd run to him so frantically to mend the rupture I'd caused—probably with the intention to loosen that hold. I could smell his scent in the bed on which I lay. My stomach turned. I'd left my sisters in the middle of an important meeting, endangering two of my dearest friends who might or might not have reached Park Rapids safely, and for what? To mend something I didn't really want mended. I'd left my sisters and maybe my future with them to run to this.

Wild isn't it? Mama was writing in her private letters. *Where do I turn?*

As the weeks went on my anger grew into a fury. It began to seem that his secrets and not my revelations to the young priest were the real problem. I write this now with the realization that I still am keeping those secrets, still trying to keep him safe. They were human secrets, ecclesiastical secrets, insignificant had Pat not been a priest. Similarly, my father's drinking would not have been as significant a problem had he not been an aviator.

Pat visited as always, but he must have felt my anger seeping out sideways. I never unleashed it on him directly, though that might have been a better thing to do. It may have been impossible for me since I wasn't clear whether he was actually the object of my deepest anger. It might have been the hierarchical church. It might have been the convent. It might have been confusion over the differences between Mother Celine and Sister Marie that led to a deep set confusion in my own identity as a sister. It might have been all the changes in the culture and from Vatican II which I had welcomed and which seemed so unsettling now. It might simply have been me. But I pushed at *him,* now I know, to go away. He lost his coldness as he felt his hold on me becoming tenuous.

Paul Tillich maintains that faith is the position we take in the midst of ambiguity. Caught in the tension between seeming opposites, faith requires us to remain there, enduring the situation which really is the human condition at all times. When we aren't aware of that, we are living in illusion. Temptation comes in the form of "easy" faith—eliminating one side of the paradox and taking refuge in the other side as though the ambiguity did not exist. In God all the opposites are reconciled.

I have a picture of Pat taken on the day I think I broke him. It's hard to believe the cruelty of which we are capable when our backs are against the wall. He wanted me to take his picture, several pictures, He wanted his eyes to express how much he loved me, had forgiven me—even that. His eyes begged me. He'd been having such a hard time, he said, at the college. His tiff with the president had grown worse and several of his closest friends and colleagues had taken a stand against him in a meeting about (I think) the restructuring of the system's patterns of authority. He couldn't stay. He'd very nearly been broken by this, and so few years after he'd left Crookston. Where was he to turn if not to me?

How can one not feel sympathy, but I didn't feel it. I took the pictures. Surely I told him I was sorry, though. I must at least have done that. All I remember is how weak and supplicant he looked. And now I see I feared this far more than his anger. I could barely breathe. His need for me would suffocate my life.

He'd have to go, I told him, because I had a dinner to attend with the religious education team, and I needed to dress and leave in a short while. He wanted to join us. How often had I joined him and his coterie of priests back in Crookston and then at St. John's? But I said it wasn't the same. It was to be just the regional team and he'd feel out of place.

Oh well, then he'd drive to the Twin Cities to visit a friend of his, a Lutheran pastor, who was back in town from Texas. Fine. And he left.

We'd just ordered prime rib at the Thunderbird Hotel when Diana came back from the women's lounge.

"Pat Kelly's out there," she announced. "He's with Jonathan and Mona. He wants to know if they can join us."

The young priest looked at me. I shook my head. "No," I said. "Please tell him no."

"Don't you want to go out to the lobby and see him?" Diana asked.

"I can't." The waiter brought my prime rib. I looked down at it and started to cry. Tears dripped into the juice of the rare meat. It looked garish to me, disgusting. I couldn't move or speak. Something odd seemed to be happening to me. The voices of all the team members around the table mingled, becoming unintelligible. I was peripherally aware of chairs sliding back. Of the waiter removing my plate. Of Diana putting her arm around me to take me to the women's lounge. Of the young priest going out to speak with Pat, to tell him to leave me alone, or whatever he told him.

But whatever it was, a long, long time passed before I saw or spoke with him again.

258

A LETTER FROM MAMA
I am two selves
March through May, 1972

Diana convinced me to make an appointment with a psychologist, one who was under contract with our congregation to help us learn to improve our community interactions and decision making. Besides working with our community as a whole, he also saw some sisters as individual clients. What a renovation this was! Up to this time our sisters had seldom had this sort of opportunity unless they became dangerous to themselves or others as Sister Innocent had during our college years. But our struggles with community life and our difficulties with our vows didn't fit that category. They were seen, I think, as hurdles encountered in our spiritual growth as sisters, to be dealt with in conferences with our religious superiors. I came to see that this former view may actually have been the better one, if our religious superiors had been appointed for their spiritual guidance skills. Unfortunately they were mostly good administrators rather than spiritual guides. And anyway, by 1972 the superiors could well have been as confused as anybody else, since the whole structure was folding in and collapsing under us.

So I made an appointment to see the psychologist. He ordered a battery of tests which I took home, laid out on the kitchen table, and completed one by one. The MMPI, the Myers/Briggs, and a few others I don't remember. "Does your soul ever leave your body?" I laughed. Are you kidding? Not even imagining that the test might be pointing to that time of dissociation and then denial that I experienced in the Thunderbird Restaurant.

I began to feel better. Spring was coming. I hadn't heard a peep from Pat. Diana and I had visited a consignment store in the Cities, and I'd bought a new outfit for Easter with money I'd been saving up since Christmas. Surely it was the most elegant outfit I'd worn since we stopped wearing the long habit and veil. I was tall and slender and the pants and top fit like a kidskin glove. A calf-length flowing vest finished the costume. I felt so chic. It didn't occur to me to question whether chic was a feeling appropriate to a sister.

In the meantime Mama continued to collect her ramblings in the manila envelope. She and Dad had talked, and she was also feeling

259

a bit more stable. She used her Smith-Corona as a therapist, trying to sort out her feelings:

What will the day bring? Hopefully, I can remain my controlled, more or less stable self. At the moment I feel that THIS IS OUR NEW DAY! (We have talked this morning, George and I—quietly and meaningfully— and we shall both make our supreme effort to work for all good—in business and in home relationship—and I feel our love for each other will carry us through. Next week is Easter week and with the Resurrection, we too should start a new life, beginning today.)

My March 19th ramblings have proven one thing to me now when I just re-read what I wrote. I am two selves. (They say everyone has two selves but the OTHER self does not always get a chance to come forth,.. and right now I have my other self—ME. I guess I shall refer to the suppressive one as "Sadie" (for reasons appropriate—she has thoughts of sadism, suicide, cruelty, etc.). She is born, generally, of my hypertensive self—when things get to the point where I can't reason or find my way out, Sadie comes and takes over—and HOW she takes over! She plots gleefully and wildly—unlike anything I, Alyce, can condone or understand. Things like—"I'll show him" (She takes it out on George whom I love so much that I would die FOR him—but not Sadie. No, her way is just the opposite.) Listen—"I'll take double my pills and knock myself out! He'll be sorry;" or "I'll quit taking my blood pressure medicine and hope I have a stroke and then I'll be a freak and he'll have to take care of us! THAT will show him;" or "I'll buy more booze and I'll show him what drinking <u>really</u> is! I'll become an alcoholic like no one ever saw before. I'll take what money is left and disappear and leave him to run his business alone!"

As I write this, I become so ashamed that such thoughts could take hold of me. Fortunately, I guess God comes to my aid, and Sadie loses out—and I try to remember what happened to make me feel as I did. Then I get SO TIRED and exhausted, but I soon feel normal again after a night's sleep.

We MUST pull together to get our business out of the mess it is in—we owe more than we earn unless we make every day count and every hour productive. I feel energetic now after our morning talk and good resolutions— so—if I can keep Sadie-girl in her place, I can win the race—or we, George and I, can win the race.

Each of us experienced periods of relief from the chaos of disintegration. She was way ahead of me, however, since she'd analyzed quite astutely what was wrong, and I hadn't. I still was in flight from those powerful, hidden impulses, nowhere near giving that part of myself a name as she had done. Nowhere near claiming it as part of me. I didn't realize that the Sadie in me had broken from the essence of my self, and wasn't anything bad or evil, but a part of me that was crying out to live while I attempted with all my might to kill her off. She didn't fit the life I thought to be my destiny. She never had fit there. She was actually not Sadie at all; she was Mary Jane fighting for her life.

Right after I took the tests, but before I met with the psychologist to discuss the results, Diana and I had driven to the country home of a parishioner for dinner. It was a big family, as I recall, and the children were fussy at the table. Diana and I were discussing parish matters with the adults when I heard an awful scream. I thought it was one of the children screaming, and looked around the table to see what was wrong. Nobody was screaming. For a brief moment I thought they had hidden a child in a room, and it was that child who was screaming. Everyone was ignoring the sound. But then, almost instantly, I realized that no one else could hear it because the scream was inside of my own mind. I touched Diana on the arm, leaned over to her and said in a low voice, "I'm feeling sick. We need to go home."

She was intent upon the conversation she was having and told me we'd leave as soon as dinner was over. But I thought if I stayed any longer I might black out. "No. We have to go now!" I said.

On the way home to our little apartment I described the scream I'd heard, and how afraid I was. It was a good thing then, she said, that I had an appointment with the psychologist soon.

That weekend she went to a Vision '72 meeting while I stayed home. In the middle of the night I woke from a nightmare. The room seemed to pulsate with something evil, an energy or atmosphere I'd never felt before, and it terrified me. It seemed to be everywhere, permeating everything. It had started in the dream and continued into my waking state.

261

I dreamed I was in total darkness at the motherhouse in Crookston where an evil wind blew. I went looking for someone who could tell me how to get rid of it and found one of the three members of the administrative team, Sister Ruth, who told me we had to go to the source of the wind. Still in total darkness she took me in the station wagon on the road leading into the woods to the place we used to build bonfires and watch the stars when we were novices. "This is the source of the wind," she told me. We turned a corner and suddenly I saw a burst of light. It came from a house made completely of glass. Inside the house, stunningly visible, black hummingbirds or devils flew against the windows. I cried out "THE LIGHT," and woke up in my apartment bedroom.

My teeth were chattering. My whole body trembled uncontrollably. I went into the living room and turned on all the lights, waiting for the trembling to stop and the sense of evil to disappear. I waited there until morning.

I couldn't fathom what the dream meant. For years afterwards I tried to decode it, always getting more confused because how could the evil be at the motherhouse? It seemed such a paradox. I thought being a sister was my destiny. Consequently, I determined and failed to protect myself from every instinct that threatened that destiny which I'd thought was essentially connected to the motherhouse itself. But I was taking it all too literally. It seems clear now, as I revisit those times, that the powers of destruction, for me as well as what could be called my destiny, resided at the center of the convent itself. Because of the Vatican II renewal, convent life itself was on a cusp, divided against itself. I'd chosen the side of change, but none of the sisters knew yet how to implement changes that remained vague at best. All of us were on the edge of a fundamental crisis of opposites. We were caught between worlds and between identities. We'd been trained to be sisters in a disappearing world, and we hadn't yet envisioned the world to come. I had to go all the way back to my time of training—the choices I made at the time I was a novice—to find the source of my own disintegration. It was perfectly clear, like a glass house filled with light to illumine the threat—that the danger for me lay in having chosen and then having clung to an impossible life—one divided against itself. The irony would be that neither my understanding of past traditions nor my vision of the church's future could save me. No longer could I be Sister Mary Christopher. And I had no idea who Sister Christin was supposed to be. Some of the sisters would make it through the fault lines on our path into their new world. I'd let too much go too swiftly. I'd slipped on loose stones. I'd envisioned too much that never could come true. I'd concocted too many fantasies to make those visions seem real. I'd mistaken the mirage in front of me for the eternal city. I teetered on the edge. Soon there would be nothing beneath me. No house. No church. No world. The dream of the glass house belonged to Mary Jane. She was at the edge of a broken path, clinging for her life, willing to do anything to save it.

The psychologist motioned for me to sit in the chair opposite him. He was an imposing man, tall, powerful looking, with dark hair and eyes. I knew him a bit already because of the workshops his team had conducted with our sisters. He wore a white suit, like a guru.

I sat down. Well, I had some problems, he told me, that showed up in the tests, The Myers/Briggs, for example, showed quite a bit of ambivalence, and he wanted me to be tested a bit more. A Rorschach would be good. He'd set up an appointment. But why not just tell him my story? What was going on and why did I feel it important to come to him?

So I did.

Did I want to remain in the convent? He wanted to know.

Of course I did. I was very involved. I was on the steering committee for renewal, I told him proudly.

Was there anything else I wanted?

Maybe I'd like to be a priest, I said. I'd heard there was a program at an ecumenical seminary in New York that was educating Catholic women towards that end.

Hummm.... well, he thought I could probably be anything I wanted to be. I was an intelligent, dynamic woman. I'd be really powerful once I had straightened out in my mind the path most consistent with my personality.

Maybe I'd look into that ordination program then, I told him.

He nodded slowly, almost stereotypically. "And what about this Father Kelly?" He asked.

I think I told him Pat was out of the picture now.

Well, that's good, because he wouldn't be a good match for me. He knew this because Pat had been to see him too, because of me, because Pat had heard that I had sought counseling and wanted to be supportive. "That's why Pat *thinks* he came to see me," the doctor said. The implication was that Pat wanted to stay on top of this—keep in control.

"If you were here for advice about whether or not to marry Pat, I'd counsel you not to do it."

"You would?" Nobody had ever put it on the line like that. I wouldn't let them. Whenever anyone would talk about Pat and me, I always had a whole "Francis/Clare" explanation worked out. He'd always be a priest. I'd always be a sister. We'd work together for the coming of a new world and a reformed church.

"Yes." He pinned me with his dark eyes. "You'd need a powerful man. You'd walk all over a weak man like Pat. You'd need someone you considered your equal, not someone who falls back every time you exert your individuality."

This notion stunned me. "I thought *he* was the one with the power."

He laughed. "Well, Sister, you thought wrong."

Mama's struggle with Sadie wasn't over either. Two days later she was holding her at bay again. Mama tried listing everything she was worried about—two pages of Smith Corona text, and then:

STOP IT! I must NOT let Sadie take over—Alyce, keep steady. Look at what is written; is it all so bad—George has big problems too. Maybe he does see the symptoms I worry about but he won't discuss it— refuses to admit things are bad—but maybe he is trying to spare me. But I can't be fooled. Things are bad.

My left leg is tingling—nerves—will I have a stroke one of these days? That would make things worse—Why can't I relax and control my tensions? I do NOT want to have a stroke—I remember my father and I especially remember Paul. This is the 8th year since Paul died and 8 years before that my mother died and 8 years before that (all in the fall of the year) my father died. Will I go this year? I MUST get things all in order just in case. I hate to leave this conglomeration in my house for the girls to set straight—such a mess. I cannot see George getting along without me—I want us to be together as we grow old. Our needs could be meager and we could look after each other, but the business is like a demon which comes between us—I say things (actually Sadie does) which I know hurt him and I don't want to hurt him. Maybe I'm wrong in one thing—maybe he would be better off without me.

I have forgotten Jesus—remember Him—must have faith—.

LATER: feeling better now—after an hour of other involvement, telephone calls, etc., I feel like I can keep on top. Worry seems to have receded—Sadie is gone—bright and sunny day—I'm going for the mail now. Maybe good news is coming our way, like some checks on account – or letters from the girls ………

I'm pretty sure I was home with Mama and Dad that spring because I have a vivid memory of lying on the grass above Wabanica Creek by Uncle Frank's cabin. It was actually a property bequeathed to the sisters by a local bachelor who was grateful for the care he received from them when he was old. We used it as a little retreat, like The Pines but much smaller. In memory I am alone there. I've spread out a blanket and am lying on my back with my eyes closed. Light flickers through my eyelids as the breeze rustles the leaves of the tree above me. I've written some poetry and the pages are lying next to me, secured by the edge of a book. Wabanica Pines is a place almost sacred to the Mary Jane part of me, a place of tenderness and young love, a place that calls forth my pre-convent self. It was here that I spent many hours with John Weber, the young man I loved in my senior year of high school, but left when I entered the convent. He was my first true love, something surprisingly far beyond any adolescent crush that I'd called love before. I'm sure that he was there with me that day, his young spirit still whispering on the breeze. I know I'd kept vivid memories of him all my years of convent life, even during those ambivalent years of Pat's presence. If my destiny had been different, I always thought, I might have married John Weber. I can imagine now that I thought tenderly of him that day, lying so close to the place where we spent long afternoons beside the creek that emptied into the Rainy River, speaking of our love, holding carefully our innocence, always knowing ourselves on the verge of goodbye.

That afternoon in late May of 1972 I was considering my options. I'd been seeing the psychologist for a few months, and now I needed to decide whether or not I would be going back to the summer session at St. John's. Pat would be there. I could do that if I chose, but it would be difficult. I had other options. I could skip that summer session, going back when I felt stronger—probably the next summer. I could continue having therapy sessions once a week and let strength return slowly as my understanding of my life deepened. Or I could admit myself into a program connected to a hospital. Not your usual psych unit. I'd been told this was more like a resort. Nice grounds. Pleasant rooms and surroundings. I could spend the time away from all that had caused me so much stress. And best of all, I'd probably have it all worked out by the end of the summer and could go back to work with Diana at the regional religious ed. center. Or, and the doctor tossed this one off as a sort of after-thought—I could just do nothing and see what happened.

I knew I wanted to "get myself together." That's how Mama would have said it. I'd heard her say those words a thousand times—blending Alyce and Sadie, I guess. Oh, that day it felt so good to be Mary Jane. How could I ever have let her go? Maybe I should just have stayed there for the summer. I'll bet the sisters would have let me use Uncle Frank's cabin. It would have been better. Maybe I could have stayed there and learned to fly airplanes. Daddy had wanted to teach me back when I was sixteen, but I was too busy with whatever a sixteen-year-old girl is busy with. Maybe in a flight through the sky above the lake all my selves would have found their place again, binding together in a supreme and glorious act of individuation. Maybe I could have stayed, helping Mama and Daddy with those crushing bills, working together to envision possibilities and open our hearts to hope. Maybe I could have stayed there in the tenderness...

But in the end, I chose expediency.

On the "Old Journals" shelf of my bookcase a ragged plastic-covered day planner is tucked in between more acceptable blank books from the years that publishers first began to sell such things. My first journals, the ones I kept from convent years, are simply loose leaf notebooks. Then this one. And after it are the bound books with golden edges, or simple black books, or the ones from the Minneapolis Institute of Arts Gift Shop that are bound in silk and contain paper so thin and fine that I felt enticed to write in them just for the experience of drawing out a line of ink on the page. But this one—this day planner—it's almost as though it didn't exist for me all these years. As I take it down from the shelf, I think how like Mama's hidden journal pages it turned out to be. It is from 1972, the very year I've just tried to remember, knowing all along, somewhere way in the back of my mind, that I'd already hidden most everything right there. I'd written it and turned the page, never returning to look at it again because it simply was too haunting and hard.

Well, if you're looking at your life, you're looking at your life! I pull it from among the other books on the shelf and open it for the first time in all these years. The back of the day planner is broken because of the letters I'd stuck in among the pages. A few of them are from Mama. Mostly they are from the young priest who had counseled me to discontinue my relationship with Pat. I read a line here and there in the letters, remembering how new to priesthood he was back then and how intent he was that I would get past this struggle, get well and take up my convent life again.

Suddenly I am curious. Did my memory of those months match my real-time description of events? I pause for a moment. Will it be fair to the memoir if I consult this on the spot documentation? Are there rules about this? Who cares! I open it and read.

The style's the same, my writer's mind critiques as I delve into the entries for 1972—a little ragged, maybe, and with a patina of romance. Now I can detect every evasion, all the places in my mind that I'd been hiding from myself. I squint at some of those descriptions; it was almost as though I'd been writing in code, hieroglyphic sentences that I might have hoped I could still decipher in these later years, in case I ever wanted to come back to dig up my reasons for - - - all of it: Pat, convent, renewal, and (I'd forgotten) the frenetic style of my life that year as though I couldn't bear to look at it as it flew past.

If this were someone else's journal, my writer's instinct would insist that its author was pretty much creating her world as she went along. I lean back in my chair and stare at the shade I've pulled over the window to keep out the sun's glare. "But I'm sure that I thought back then I was telling the truth," I say to myself. My feelings as I wrote them and my thoughts and my interpretation of events all sound mercurial, changing form even as I tried to hold them still. My heart aches for who I was. My world had crumbled. It had emptied out into a kind of nothing. If I were to continue on, I had to create a different world to fill up the empty space.

It was at Uncle Frank's cabin that I confronted my emptiness. Folded between the pages are the poems, written that day on spiral notebook paper, small, 3 x 6 inches. In the day planner I wrote, "I lay in the sun for a few hours, but the quiet, the sort of vacuum, made me sick to my stomach." Now I meditate on those words, putting myself back into that time as best I can, and I think that for those moments, in that place that represented all the freedom of my pre-convent youth but was owned by my community of sisters, I must have experienced the fundamental contradictions of my life, and my constructed world crumbled away. When is nothing everything?

One of the poems is addressed, I think now, to Pat:

Now that I have died
You walk around within
My empty house
To pick up memories
I have scattered here or there
And holding them,
To cry some.

I wish that you would also die
And waking from death,
Find me in a new house
Where every room would be
A place that we could fill
With shining,
And every day
Might be clear enough to see
A more humble you,
A gladder me.

For years afterwards I dreamed of the sister part of me, and in the dreams she was simply "the woman I killed." In my journal I wrote: "I have killed you. In the locked room three steps up, the walls are covered with blood and only I know—violence, pain, then the escape, the locked door. I live in fear of being discovered by everyone who knocks. I live pretending there is no bloodied room three steps up. In yet other dreams I have killed you and hidden you behind the furnace, under the workbench, buried in the garden. I distract the others as they walk through my dreams. I smile. I hold their attention with words, with songs, with drama, achievements, titles, degrees. If I can be engaging enough they will not miss you. I have hidden you for twelve long years against the discovery that I killed you for your inheritance, for the life you promised and withheld. I killed you in self defense, but also with violence, in order that I might live. I loved you and I tried to choose us both, to let us both live. But I cannot deny what you did to me: the slow suffocation, the blindfold on my eyes, the gagging rag in my mouth, the tying of my hands, paralyzing of my feet, the attempt to stop my heart. I remember now the struggle for my life, the almost letting go to you, the almost ceasing to exist, and then the fatal blow and it was *you* who died; and I was wild and in flight crying 'I am' into the wind."

I thought I could succeed in making a choice, eliminating the ambiguity, living more simply and maybe honestly, but really—I'd walked into emptiness. I looked for myself and found no one. I looked for the sister in me and could no longer find her. The prairie on which the motherhouse stood now seemed dry and barren. The woods had become a wilderness, a chaos, demonic at its core. The meadowlark's song had died. The circle of women was broken, the finely woven threads of the web that once connected me to them had been ripped apart and set adrift on the wind.

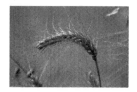

REMEMBER FROM THE CLOUD OF UNKNOWING

- Remember where you are.
- Remember spaciousness, lack of sensation, relinquishment of theories.
- Remember calling out. Remember the nature of your cry. Remember your faith in God:
- Remember that when you call God "Darkness," you are led into the night.
- Remember that when you call God "Fire," you taste ashes on your tongue.
- Remember that when God leads you into the center, you fall through.
- Remember that when God holds you, you feel nothing.
- Remember that when God calls you Beloved, you sense only the breeze.
- Remember that around God is stillness and you are flying in a whirlwind
- Remember that if you cry out in humility and truth, God answers, "I Am"
- Remember that if you whisper, "Beloved," God whispers back, "amen."

ASHES AND SMOKE
Summer, 1972

Ten minutes after I entered the treatment center, I knew I'd made a terrible mistake. Liz and our friend, Kath, had driven me there and were waiting in the lobby, If I turned from the inquiring eyes of the intake secretary I could have seen them, still sitting on the red imitation leather chairs, waiting for me to be finished giving information to the most condescending woman I thought I'd ever met. "It says here you are clinically depressed."

What? Who said that? I'm not depressed; I just have to work a few things out is all. I have to make a decision. Can you just cross that out?

They had to have a diagnosis or they couldn't admit me. This was a common diagnosis. What kind of medication was I on? She looked at me in that objectified, supercilious way that has the effect of stripping away individuality, even humanity. I felt like a lab rat. "When did you first notice the symptoms?"

Maybe I should just leave, go back to Liz's apartment with her and Kath.

"I'm not taking any medications." It was the truth, but I'd have to be careful here. An instinct told me that the more I told her, the more of me would disappear. Suddenly I thought of Sister Innocent. Good Lord! Why hadn't I thought of her before I agreed to this?

"They think I'm depressed," I told Liz and Kath a little later, back in the lobby, waiting for the nurse to take me up to my room. What does she know? one of them consoled. She's just a clerk. Their eyes were sad. "You can change your mind," Liz said. But it didn't seem as though I could. "I'll be back to pick you up on Friday—you can last until Friday." This was the program in which I had enrolled. Monday through Friday at the center, then the weekend with Liz in her little apartment on Cedar Avenue. Probably she was right; I could make it until Friday and then I'd just quit if all of this had been a mistake.

The nurse came. I left them sitting on the red chairs.

Up the elevator. Past the nurses station. Down the hallway. A private room—bed by the window. Reclining chair. Desk against the wall. Closet. Bathroom. Outside the window, manicured grounds.

Leave a urine sample. Someone will be in shortly to draw blood. Please don't leave your room.

Why do I have to have those tests? I'm not sick.

It's what is done. A requirement. It has to go on your chart.

I did as I was told. When the technician left with my blood I hung my clothes in the closet and lay down on the bed. It's a mistake, a mistake, a mistake. I started to panic.

The phone rang. "Sister Christin? How are you doing?" It was the psychologist. I broke into tears.

A nurse social worker came to take my history. I complained that all of this intake procedure was enough to make a sane person crazy, and wasn't it supposed to be the other way around in a place like this? She laughed. She had a sparkle about her combined with nonchalance. "You don't have to tell anybody one thing you don't want to tell them," she assured me. "We do this so often that sometimes we forget we are talking to a human being!" She handed me a clipboard and suggested I write my own history when I felt like it. No hurry. When I was finished—today, tomorrow, whenever—I could just take it to the nurses' station and they'd put it into my folder. Later I would be supplied with a ream of paper to keep a journal, which would also find its way into my records. Each day the pages would be collected off my desk and I'd not see them again. Nothing would be private here, nor would it be of much use to me once it was gone.

The psychologist showed up at my door in his white guru suit. I was lying on my bed having another good cry, and he sat beside me, encouraging me to give this at least a week. Once I was adjusted he was sure I could make good use of the program. It was all mine, after all. Completely for me. I could stay here and leave everything else— convent, Pat, my work, my family (except for Liz, of course, because I'd be with her on weekends—and that might be really good also because she'd be sharing her life with me, and hers was the life of a young professional woman. So good for me to experience, didn't I think so?) I tried to calm down. I felt so small, insignificant, intruded upon, skinned alive.

Just before supper the nurse who'd left the clip board came again to my door to tell me there was someone she wanted me to meet.

We walked together down the hallway to the double rooms and she introduced me to a woman about my age named Suzie. Suzie could show me the ropes, take me down to supper with her, maybe be a friend. She'd been in the program for a few weeks already. She smiled and looked normal, not like someone who needed to be in a treatment center.

We sat at a round table for two in the dining room, a bright place on the main floor with large windows and glass doors that opened onto a patio. After we ate, she said, we could go out there and walk around the grounds. Maybe sit for a while on the lawn chairs. We just had to be back on our floor by nine.

Suzie had a round pleasant face, pretty, with even features, dark welcoming eyes and pixie-cut hair. She seemed more poised and self-contained than the nurses. What in the world was she doing here? I voiced that, and she laughed. "I attempted suicide," she said, "and I didn't even know until afterwards what I'd done. I sure didn't want that to happen again, so here I am."

We were suddenly like two friends who had met at a café. She said that she'd just had a baby, only a few months before, when she found out that her husband was having an affair. She'd taken the baby with her in the car to town for supplies, still stunned by what seemed the breakup of her marriage coming on her so suddenly. She was driving down the main street of the town when something took her over, some force against which she had no control. She crashed the car into a telephone booth. "I could have killed us both."

Suzie and I aren't all that different, I thought that evening. The worlds we'd each dreamed up for ourselves broke right down the center, and we each felt the fissure someplace so deep in us that it was beyond rational control.

Dr. Benson would be my doctor at the center—a psychiatrist with a Rogerian style. He just sat there in my room, across from me, twice a week. If I'd never said a thing it would have been alright with him; he had amazing tolerance for nothingness. I didn't. I kept trying to pry from him what it was he wanted me to do in order to get well and out of that place.

Do you think I should contact Pat? The sisters? My family?

Do *you* think you should?

273

Gads! It drove me nuts. The convent mode was to ask permission for everything. It didn't matter that in recent years I avoided doing this—even refused on some occasions. The requirement remained steady; it was something I could count on, a boundary of sorts that I could either accept or batter myself against. This Dr. Benson was more like the Void. Push against him and I'd just fall into the darkness of myself. He must think I shouldn't contact them, I conjectured when faced with that void. I had no idea yet that it was I who thought that.

He wrote some orders on my chart. Two hours of group therapy in the morning. Two hours every afternoon in occupational therapy. Twice a week with him. Write that journal for my records. Did I want medication to help with depression? I didn't. So that was fine. How about sleeping pills? I didn't think so. Well, if I found out I needed them he'd leave an order to that effect. Sometimes people started having nightmares, and the pills could help with that.

I'd never encountered such a bland, unreadable person in my entire life.

I decided not to contact Mama while in the hospital after she confessed in a low voice her fear that if I left the convent she'd lose the rest of the sisters, her close friends, since I would no longer belong to them. That whole family of sisters had seemed to her like daughters of her own, like sisters of her own, like mothers—the older ones who had been generous in sharing their wisdom with her. Her fears pulled on me so hard that I felt tempted to make my choices based more on her needs than on my own. She and I would need to endure this part of my life separately, I decided. If I hadn't been so fragile right then, I might well have seen the situation differently. Both of our hearts were broken. Both of us might have been more quickly healed had I been willing to join our broken hearts together. But that's not certain, even now.

Of course, she didn't share her brokenness with anyone either, but continued to tap it out in words on her Smith Corona and stuff the pages into the brown manila envelope. We were two of a kind.

Some other people at the hospital seemed in really bad shape. A skeletal woman sat in a wheelchair—I'd never seen anorexia before.

She frightened me. The loss involved; the long slow killing. A nurse brought her food to the unit. The woman couldn't enter the dining room because the abundance of food down there was too much for her to bear. That's what I thought, anyway. But maybe that wasn't true. Maybe she simply had become too weak.

A woman who did come down to the dining room reminded me of the Madwoman of Chaillot. She actually wore a feather boa, long dresses, and garish makeup. I feared her also. I feared and kept away from anyone who reminded me exactly where I was and the depths to which human beings can plunge once they begin to fall.

I avoided the TV room where people on massive doses of medication sat staring at soap operas. I went instead to the music room with a young man named Steve who was barely out of his teens and who told me he worked for the CIA. He'd seen too much, he said, over in Viet Nam. He was an assassin for the government. I shouldn't tell anyone, though, because all of this was top secret. He was only telling me because I was a sister and could be trusted. Were you really? I wanted to know. And he grinned and said, "Of course." I liked sitting with him in the music room listening to the Beatles and Judy Collins.

Most of my free time, though, I spent with Suzie and her new roommate, Claudia. We sunbathed, lying on towels in the grass just beyond the patio. I'd borrowed Liz's bikini—a totally risqué bit of clothing made of what looked like shiny brown leather held together over my hips and between my breasts with white plastic loops. I looked shameless—and, the other two assured me, terrific! Suzie wore the most modest suit, while Claudia's had a design more like mine/Liz's. We talked about our lives, lying there, laughing at the men who approached us with a "hey girls, when we all get out of here, how about a date?"

"He has no idea you're a sister," Claudia grinned. "That's something I could never be." She'd just been moved over from ICU after a suicide attempt that almost succeeded. She'd tried suicide before, but told us she really meant it this time. She had red hair that gleamed in the sunshine, and was the mistress of some big executive with connections to organized crime. She'd had a child with him, and he kept her on a short leash. But the man she really loved was a

275

Londoner, a rather poor bloke in a simple flat. She wanted to go to London and marry him, but was stuck here, knowing all the secrets of the executive mobster who would have had her killed if she tried to get away. Killing herself had seemed easier somehow. She hadn't counted on failing and ending up in ICU. She wouldn't have attempted it if she'd known she would fail. Terrible place, that ICU—worse than jail.

"You're damned lucky, honey," she said to me. "All you've got is your convent and some harmless priest. I'd say dump the both of them!"

Friday afternoons Liz always was there waiting to drive me to her apartment. She was twenty-two. She filled weekends with short trips to one of the Minneapolis area lakes or to Minnehaha Falls where we crossed the safety barriers and climbed the rocks close to the spray. We hiked the paths all the way down the creek to the sandstone cliffs where it emptied into the Mississippi. Some evenings she and Kath argued politics. It was the summer of the Watergate break-in, but nobody had much noticed it yet. We watched Mark Spitz win five gold medals at the summer Olympics. I'd never paid the slightest attention to the Olympic games before those weekends. Everything we did felt far removed from my convent life.

Each night Liz washed her hair, let it partially dry, and then wound it into a tight knot on the very top of her head. I watched her, from my side of her queen-sized bed. Something about that simple action calmed me. Repetition, maybe. Ritual. The other side of the freedom I'd been seeking. Maybe a person can place herself in a situation of too much freedom and end up adrift. Liz bound her hair each night and in the morning she let it fall in long waves down her back. Binding and loosing. I watched her without thinking of all this, but learning from her actions.

I had no sense of my own rhythm. Mama could slam out of the house and escape, but she knew when to return. Even in her desperation, she knew the rhythm of binding and loosing, of fixity and flight, of what must be kept and what could be surrendered. I hadn't learned that yet. Liz bound her hair. She bound *her own* hair. She loosed it in her own time, when she was ready. She made her own rhythm. No rule commanded her or cared for her or saved her from danger. She'd found that rhythm on her own. I'd subjected myself to a different rhythm, one outside of me. When I no longer subjected myself to that convent rhythm, I didn't know how to be. The first task was to find my own binding and loosing. Nothing apart from me could give me freedom. Flight could not free me. I'd done a terrible injustice to myself for all those years. I'd let all of them—the convent, the Vatican council renewal, Pat, even the young priest and the psychologist—bind the strands of my life when I needed to have bound them myself, in my own time, according to my own rhythm. I needed the confidence that when I chose to unbind those strands they would fall gracefully, beautifully and shining into my new life.

I'd almost forgotten that at St. John's the summer session of the Master's program was well underway. One of those weekends I got a call from Felicity, a Dominican sister in my class who had become a good friend. She and a priest companion planned to be in Minneapolis the next weekend, Saturday night, and would I be able to go do dinner with them? I felt a pang of loss, of missing the summer. Of course I was available and would love to join them.

Felicity was in love. I could see it. This priest was courting her and had come up to St. John's from Michigan so they could spend some time together. We sat in a carousel restaurant at the top of a skyscraper hotel, looking out the windows at the city lights. I had my first taste of escargot. They'd decided to marry. Lots of things needed working out, of course, before either of them could be dispensed from their vows. And yet it all seemed so possible for them, even easy.

"Pat's really missing you," Felicity said. "I don't think he's doing so well this summer." He'd been spending a lot of time talking with her, exploring ways to get back in touch with me. "He wanted me to tell you," she said.

"I can't see him," I told her. "Tell him not to try to contact me."

I don't remember my feelings. Maybe I went back the next week and told Dr. Benson. Maybe I told the therapy group, but I doubt it, because I didn't feel safe with them. I spent a good deal of my time trying to protect myself, being careful not to say too much. It felt a lot like sensitivity training at The Pines, and I knew the sort of result that came from that. It didn't take too many sessions for me to conclude that I'd get more help from Suzie and Claudia than I'd ever find in that group. A sense of the danger of depression had begun to grow in me, however, culled from the stories I heard about suicide attempts. It hadn't just been Suzie who didn't know what she was doing. A man in the group said he hadn't even known he was depressed. Then one morning while looking in the mirror, shaving, he cut his throat. His wife had found him almost immediately, or he would not have survived.

Didn't you know you were doing it? several of the group members asked. He thought he'd been in a kind of trance. Something took over. Something slit his throat. Some of the quieter members nodded. That happened to me, too, one after another of them said.

I should stop using the convent as a cover, the facilitator told me. I was hiding behind the veil, he said. He also said that he could tell by the way I talked to him that I hated men. And since I was quite sure that was not true, I dismissed his other assessments as probably off the mark. But I'd leave there with snakes in my belly, never knowing what those snakes might tell me if I, like Eve, were willing to listen. She got herself into a heap of trouble. Did I even entertain the thought that I'd already listened, and fallen right into the squirming center of that heap?

I would have stayed in Occupational Therapy all the time if it had been possible. Nobody talked to me unless I wanted conversation. I didn't need to weave baskets or paint by numbers. I had free creative reign. I worked with clay, making bowls and sculptures, loving the feel of it in my hands, trying to form in the pliant earth an image of the feelings I held inside. Then I worked with oils on a slab of wood to create an image of the dream that continued to trouble me, the one of the glass house in the clearing at the motherhouse.

One afternoon I saw a 3x5 foot piece of birch leaning against the wall and asked the therapist if I could paint on it. The grain of the wood intrigued me, reminding me of a Judy Collins recording of Leonard Cohen's song, "Joan of Arc." It had haunted me all summer and now, looking at this grainy wood I was seeing *the ashes of her wedding dress.*" I wanted to take oils, thin grey-white to a ghostly texture and highlight that grain, veiling it. The wood's pattern would appear through the veil.

Of course I could use it. That's why the materials were there to be used by patients in whatever way would help us.

I painted slowly with the words and images from the song swirling through my imagination, taking on the contours of my convent destiny and what was happening to all my dreams that summer. The God I'd gone into the convent to find thirteen years before had become a divine fire. Now I painted the veil turning to ash in that flame.

The place through which Joan was riding felt completely familiar. I was in that place, surrounded by that smoke. This dark world had no edges, no boundaries, and seemed to have no end. I'd sought help from men, and had plunged even more deeply into the darkness. There really was no man, was there? No one had been helpful, though several had tried to help. It wasn't that I hated men, as the therapist had suggested. I simply found them powerless. How could they do anything here in this internal world of my mind and heart, maybe my soul, with its tangible darkness—the precise night of my dream, but now with no evil wind. There existed only darkness, the smoke, and the unquenchable fire of divine love that followed, followed.

We'd been called the Brides of Christ. I thinned the white oil paint—how could I paint this? There were five of us in May of 1959, waking up at dawn the morning we were to receive the black and white habit of Sisters of St. Joseph. I remember standing by the window the moment I sprung from bed. "Rosy-fingered dawn," came first to mind, and then "Awake lyre and harp! I shall awake the dawn." from the psalms. For the ceremony we would dress ourselves in wedding dresses—not in the flouncy, lacy style of contemporary brides, but in the simple elegance depicted on Greek statues. Dresses of flowing white nylon, long full sleeves, white cincture around the waist. We would walk down the aisle carrying tall beeswax tapers, carrying fire. "You are now the Brides of Christ," the bishop would intone according to ritual.

Since the Vatican II reforms the bridal metaphor had been discouraged as a poetic conceit, a mystical flight of fancy that could be easily misunderstood. I dipped my brush in the thinned paint and began to paint the wedding dress. It had been difficult to let go of the image, but I had. I'd traded it for "church reformer," and the new identity, while it excited me, hadn't the same power to move my soul. Church renewal and reformation had become a war, and I was sick of it, even made sick by my part in it.

I wasn't seeing this clearly yet, but feeling it strongly as I painted the wedding dress and veil on the slab of wood. As I painted I began to feel my convent destiny dissolving, began to feel that the divine fire for which I'd yearned could not be found there, especially not since Vatican II and all the changes I'd been working so hard to bring about. As I listened to Judy Collins sing Leonard Cohen's lyrics, and as I painted the flames, the wedding dress, and the spirit in the smoke, I started to remember just a little bit what I had left my home in Baudette to find.

On the journal pages that ended up in my patient chart, never to be seen by me again, I started writing poetry. When the Joan of Arc painting dried I brought it up to my room and set it up like an icon on the desk. It reached almost to the ceiling, and I gazed at it every night before I went to sleep. I heard the music behind it, within it, under it, blazing. The voice in divine fire spoke to my heart.

All this time, throughout this internal war in the midst of ambiguity, I'd never really been alone. I still didn't know what to do, which choice to make, how to live from here on. It still was a riddle. But I felt I'd touched on something that might finally bring me through the smoke and darkness. I just needed to give myself to the fire. I went to the music room and listened to the song again and again. I stared at the picture.

I cried each time I heard Joan's final words because they seemed branded upon my heart as well. I, too, longed for love and light. I, too, found love too cruel, and the light too bright.

During my last session with Dr. Benson I asked him if he thought it would be better for me if I were to leave the convent.

"Is that what you think would be better?"

Well, I didn't know. Five weeks earlier I would have said absolutely not. Now I wasn't sure of anything but my own longing.

I had time, he finally said. I could do whatever I wanted whenever I knew what it was. It might be difficult until I figured it out.

He gave me a prescription for Stelazine—just in case. If I got depressed or anxious I could take it and it would help.

He was right about one thing, I think now as I write this—no one else can tell us what is best to do with our lives. Somehow I got the Joan of Arc painting to Liz's and then to the big old empty rectory designated as the place where Diana and I would live and work during the coming year. I walked in through the front door and stood alone in the middle of the living room. Light splashed in through all the windows onto the hardwood floor, highlighting the grain. I took a deep breath and sat down on the floor with the light around me everywhere.

I AM
August, 1972

In the old rectory I began to set up my office for the coming school year. It was a small room at the front of the building, just to the right of the front door across from the living room. Probably it had been an office for the pastor who used to live there, as a desk remained. Somewhere I located a stash of bricks and some boards with which I constructed a bookcase. Someone had hauled things like the stereo from the apartment to this house, and I set that up also. I drove to the city in the leased red Maverick and bought colorful material on sale to decorate the walls and windows. I set Joan of Arc against the wall in my little bedroom under the eaves. The window faced the back yard and caught a stream of morning sunshine.

Diana hadn't yet returned from the summer session in Seattle, and another sister, Sister Judith, would join us that year to coordinate the elementary program of religious education for the region. But she hadn't yet arrived either, so I was alone. A few parishioners I'd come to know quite well during the previous year invited me to dinner at their homes. One family had a bicycle for sale, a restored Schwin that looked much like the one I had as a child. Twenty-five dollars. I bought it. The next day their thirteen year old daughter came by the old rectory and handed me a pair of very short shorts. "For when you ride the bike," she said. She'd bought them for me with her own money.

"But these are too short for a sister." I told her, holding them up. It's one thing to wear a bikini at a treatment center, and quite another to wear short shorts in the little town where I was a director of religious education.

"They'll fit just perfect!" She countered. "Everybody's wearing shorts like these."

I wore them. I wore the short shorts and a T-shirt and took the bike to the country roads at the edge of town. I felt sixteen. Sometimes I rode with the young girl who gave me the shorts. Mostly I rode alone, the wind in my hair that had grown long, the August light filtering through the leaves, the endless rows of corn.

It's strange to me now that I never had the sense of being watched, though the people must have been watching me. That's the nature of small towns. There's that new sister, they might have said. Looks like a strange one. Not like any sister I've ever seen before.

Though it seems in memory that I was there alone for a long time, it wasn't long. Two weeks at most. Diana and Judith were scheduled to arrive around August fifteenth. It was, for those of us who had entered the convent in the years after the Second World War, the anniversary of our entrance day. For me it was the fourteenth anniversary. I thought I looked forward to seeing them. Maybe others would come for the night – we could have a celebration, a party. We'd light candles, play music, sing together, tell the stories of our summer.

They walked in the door and I panicked. I felt like a hunted animal who's just been captured in a net. It will pass, I thought, trying to control myself. Both of them were filled with stories of the motherhouse where they'd just been for a retreat, of Vision '72 and all the politics surrounding the renewal. Maybe I should take a Stelazine, I thought, but pushed the thought away.

I had filled the prescription and begun to take the pills right after leaving the treatment center. In a very short time my legs had begun to ache with a severity that required me to stretch them out on a footstool every time I sat down. One of the parishioners who had befriended me during these few weeks was the wife of the local physician. She had invited me to their home in the country for dinner one evening, and I'd asked for a footstool because of my aching legs. Her husband, who knew about my summer, asked me if I was taking any medication. It hadn't even occurred to me that the ache in my legs might be related to those little pills. "As long as you are taking that Stelazine," he said. "your legs will ache." I never took another.

Pills were a temptation that afternoon, however, when the sisters flung that net back over my life. And the temptation became even worse two days later when Diana drove me into the city to see Pat Kelly. I've no idea anymore how that came about—whether he arranged it with me or with her, and she was the one who convinced me to go. "To settle things," is what I seem to remember she told me. She dropped me off in front of a Perkins Pancake House. Fear gnawed at my belly. It must have been that he arranged all this with Diana, because I now can look at myself standing there and know that I hadn't seen or spoken with him since that fateful night he tried to see me at the Thunderbird Restaurant. It seemed a lifetime had passed since then. I opened the door and went in.

That fear—I'd felt it often in my life and it always puzzled me. Now I recognize it as ambivalence. It was fear of making the wrong choice when I was trying so hard to discover which choice was best. It was fear of being trapped in a situation in which betrayal seemed certain—I would either betray the other person or I would betray myself, and I could see no way out.

I went through the door. Pat was seated already in one of the booths by the window. He looked as nervous as I felt. I slipped in across from him.

"You aren't wearing the ring I gave you," he said after we'd said hello and how are you and how was your summer.

I looked at my ring finger. "It irritated my finger," I said, and that was partly true. The other part, not said, was that the ring had become symbolic of my ambivalence, and it relieved me to have it shut away in my dresser drawer. I'd removed it that summer sometime, long enough before so that I was surprised when he mentioned it. But I knew the implications behind his comment. What about the promises you made? Is our relationship over?

We skirted the issue. He said he was in St. Paul now, at the U of M Newman Center. He'd left St. Ben's and joined the Newman Staff. He had lots of ideas and plenty of freedom to implement them.

He told me about his study at St. John's that summer. He'd written a paper, a sort of ontological study of God and the presence of evil. What had happened between us, he said, created the impetus for the study. He'd felt oppressed by so much suffering, so many questions, such disbelief. How could a good creator God allow for the presence of evil in the very creation he'd flung forth? He wasn't going to cop out by invoking free will—that argument had been done to death. He'd located the source of evil in the very essence of the being of God.

I was relieved that he'd taken the conversation to such a heady place, a realm beyond feeling. He laid a copy of his thesis on the table and pointed to sections of it as he spoke. It's because God is infinite, he explained. So in creation He had infinite possibilities for the form and structure of the universe. But God had to choose only one form. If God wanted to create, then God had to limit Himself.

Pat grew excited. So you see what that means? God spun out this one finite universe, but all the other possibilities remain. All of that infinity of possible universes still exist within Him—and sometimes they break through. When that happens they are inimical to our time-space continuum which is the form of this universe. So they destroy our universe a bit. We call that breakthrough "evil." But from God's perspective it's simply a completely different paradigm for creation, and as good as any of the infinity of paradigms that God contains. It's just broken through into the wrong place, is all. To our way of seeing, it is an absence of being, a void, a nothingness, a destruction of what we call "good."

I half expected him to say, "And that's what has happened to you and me, don't you see?"

But he folded up his paper and placed it in my hands. "I hope you'll read it," he said.

We'd managed not to talk about ourselves very much at all.

We left the pancake house and he walked me to the car where Diana was waiting. To her he said, "Why not drive over to the Newman Center? The three of us can take a little walk around Dinky Town."

Diana looked at me. I think I shrugged. She said OK, and off we went. As we walked the streets of Dinky Town—the little section of shops and restaurants then frequented by college students—I began to feel exhausted. Pat talked and talked. He took us into shops that sold posters and T-shirts. He pointed out a particular poster "Life is not a problem to be solved but a mystery to be lived." At least it was something like that.

"That's what we are up to," he said to me and smiled.

I told Diana that I needed to get back home. We left the shop and walked back to our car where we said goodbye to Pat. "I hope we can get together again," he said to me. Maybe I smiled.

"It was too long a time to be with him," I told Diana once we were on the road.

"I was afraid of that." She said.

"I hope this was the last time." I said.

By the time we arrived at the old rectory, I was trembling uncontrollably. Would this never stop? I thought it had stopped. I thought I'd figured it out pretty well that summer. I was fine until the other two sisters came back, and now here was Pat and it all had started up again.

It must have been a Saturday night because Diana asked if I wanted to accompany her and Sister Judith to Mass, but I couldn't. I watched them from the dining room window as they walked across the lawn to the big brick church. Then I went upstairs and curled into a fetal position on my bed.

The old priest came for a visit the evening of August 22nd. He was the one who formerly had lived in the rectory, but he suffered from MS, and in recent years had lost the ability to climb the long staircase. The parish had purchased or rented a different house for him, one with no stairs, and set it up so he could get around easily. He was a tall, gaunt man with white hair and a perpetual smile who loved opera and the telling of tales. I thought how kind he looked as we were seated around the round oak dining room table with its majestic chairs which he'd left in the house when he moved. No room for it in the new place, he'd said.

Only a few days had passed since my visit with Pat, but it seemed much longer. Diana, Judith and I had spent most of the afternoons planning the calendar for the teaching year, entering monthly dates for Regional Council meetings, adding Vision '72 events, sketching out workshops and adult education programs, and so forth. Whenever I had some mental task, a problem to solve, a lecture to prepare, I seemed fine. It was only when I came down out of my head that I began again to feel the ambivalence begin to churn again in the pit of my stomach.

We sat around the table listening to the old priest's stories. Diana and Judith laughed sincerely. I laughed obediently. The old priest beamed and started another story. Suddenly I felt myself slip into that strange dissociation I'd experienced at the restaurant. It wasn't as bad as before, but it felt pretty much like the same thing. I wanted to catch myself, turn around before I began crying or something equally uncontrollable. I pleaded tiredness and left the table. The staircase went up directly out of the dining room. I held to the ornate banister and climbed the stairs. The old priest finished his story and the two other sisters hooted. What a funny tale. What a great joke.

Maybe I'd never laugh again. Maybe this void was endless. I walked down the hallway to the end where my bedroom was, and sat down on the edge of the bed. God, what should I do? This terrible feeling—I hadn't counted on it coming back. Maybe I should leave the convent. But when the thought came it trailed a host of fears. Who would I be if I weren't Sister Christin? How could I get along? Could I even get a job? What did I know about supporting myself? Nothing! I didn't even now how to write a check. Where would I live? How would I find my way around the Twin Cities? My sense of direction was terrible. I was sure to get lost. Please God, don't let me get lost.

But if I stayed I'd surely go insane. This feeling in the pit of my stomach would conquer me. It would eat me from the inside. Even if I stayed I didn't know who I was. I was nobody. I wasn't the Sister I'd dreamed I could be. Maybe this wasn't my destiny after all. How could I stay? I'd be no one. How could I leave? I'd be no one then as well. Christin and Mary Jane were canceling each other out. I felt like the essence of evil—exactly what Pat had described. Where being had been, I felt only absence. Where God once had been was now only this hellish void.

There on the dresser in front of me was the almost full bottle of Stelazine. Maybe I should just take them, all of them. I was nobody anyway, so why not? I couldn't think of any other way to get out of the crush of my ambivalence. Suddenly I thought of Claudia and her suicide attempt. She'd failed. So had the man who slit his throat—failed. That would be just like me, wouldn't it? Take the Stelazine and fail to die. I'd end up in ICU worse off than I already was.

I put on my nightgown and crawled under the covers. I'll figure it out in the morning, I told myself, and I went immediately to sleep.

I awoke. The morning sun streamed through the window and lit on the painting of Joan of Arc. Outside I heard a bird singing "I am." Over and over the song: I AM. I AM. I AM. Then in my mind the words from the Easter liturgy surfaced, "I am risen and am still with you." All of my ambivalence was gone. My stomach felt fine. I knew immediately and with certainty that it didn't matter which choice I made. God, the *I Am that I Am* had freed me.

"I Am." I said aloud. "I AM!"

I got up and went downstairs. Sister Judith was at the kitchen table drinking coffee and she offered me a cup. "Feeling better?" She asked.

I told her the whole story.

"What will you do?" She said. There was not even a hint of judgment in her eyes.

"I'm leaving," I told her, only realizing that it was true as the words escaped my lips. "I've decided to leave the convent—today."

MY SISTER LIZ

I returned to the secular world through my sister's doorway. She'd been so little when I left for the convent fourteen years before, but on August 26, 1972, the day she welcomed me into her Minneapolis apartment, she seemed to be the elder one. The confidence I'd felt during the "I Am" experience of the previous day had all but disappeared. Even though I was pretty sure that God had no preference whether I was in the convent or out of the convent, I'd been trained since girlhood exactly how to be a religious sister. As for being a woman in contemporary society without the cloak of sisterhood around me, as for how to be myself in the way Liz was herself, as for that—I didn't have a clue. I was a raw egg cracked open, its shell discarded. I'd never felt so vulnerable. Even in the hospital I'd felt identified as "sister." Even when I wasn't behaving or thinking like a sister, I still carried that identity. The minute I walked through my sister's door, that identity sloughed off. I wasn't even Mary Jane. The egg isn't such a bad metaphor for what I was, except that I had no womb to protect this fragile, floating, unrecognizable thing.

Liz was perfect for me, the sister I'd longed for during most of the nine years of my life during which I'd been an only child. She'd been wished for on stars and birthday cakes from the moment I knew what wishes were. Once she was born I doted on her, sang lullabies, told her my favorite stories, fed her Gerber's strained carrots and apricots with her little silver spoon, changed her diapers, gave her baths, showed her off to all my friends. One evening when she was three or so she gave me the moon. She'd been standing at our big

289

picture window in the living room gazing into the twilight when she cried out, "Look, look, look!" She was pointing at the sky. I went to her and looked. There was the new moon, the slenderest of fingernail moons, with Venus balanced just off her tip. "Sissy's Moon," she looked at me and grinned.

Sissy's Moon never fails to bring her back to me, even though she has preceded me past the stars.

When we were young and Mama owned the gift shop in town, Liz/Betsy spent days with her there, but she became my responsibility once the school day was finished. I was her little mama.

In 1972 the tables turned, and she became a little mama to me.

Because of the weekends I'd spent living with her and Kath during that summer, my sudden reappearance in her life wasn't a complete surprise, though it was unexpected. We had expected me to get better as time passed, and for all of us getting better meant that I would readjust to convent life, embrace my professional duties, and I'd soon be normal. But there I was, standing at her door, grateful that when I'd called her to say that the convent wasn't working out after all, she'd immediately said, "You can stay with me."

Somehow Liz knew what to do with me. She went about her business, putting no pressure on me at all. She let me panic. She let me flounder. Each morning she went off to work while I lay in bed, in such a well of fear and loss of myself that it took me until noon to face the day. Then I would move from the bedroom to the living room couch, watch daytime television and write in my journal.

"The days begin in nausea. I have spent my time fighting to climb into a space of hope. I should have kept writing, but often a feeling of such helplessness comes over me that I cannot write. At this point in my life I can do nothing else but set out along the pathless way to new life. If I let the future hit me all at once I am afraid, but if I can just remember that it comes on me a moment at a time—one moment can be handled by anyone." (*Journal:* August 30, 1972)

Liz became my safe place—a kind of emotional womb of protection for what seemed an endless time, but was actually only two months. Sisters and friends visited and encouraged me. Marie wrote:

"How are you? Yesterday afternoon the council met for a short time and Margaret had your letter. Everyone appreciates your searching as you move towards a decision."

After only two weeks I applied for a parish position in religious education, and by the end of October I felt ready to move from Liz's apartment into one of my own.

She remained close. Though I was older in years, she and I looked about the same age, and she had far more experience that I did negotiating the social and cultural life of a young woman in the 1970s. During these months we forged a bond that would remain strong our entire lives. We hadn't really grown up together, so we hadn't experienced normal sibling rivalries. During my post convent time and her time of establishing herself as a professional woman, we met as equals, each of us able to fill up what was wanting in the other's development. For the rest of our lives we would go to one another with complete confidence that whatever need we might have would be filled by the other as far as she was able. Love and understanding always was there in abundance which could make up for whatever might be lacking of other resources. My sister became the most important person in my life.

DISPENSATION
February 1973

Six months after Liz had opened her door to me, Sisters Margaret, Ruth and Marie sat on the sofa in my efficiency apartment in Minneapolis. They had brought the official forms from the Vatican for me to sign, dispensing me from my vows as a Sister of St. Joseph. They reminded me, though I didn't need reminding, that the church could not actually take the vows away as if they never had been spoken. I would live the remainder of my life as a woman vowed to God, but what the church could do was to release me of the obligation to practice those vows as a sister in a religious community. Somehow I would need to develop ways to practice poverty, chastity and obedience as a single woman and perhaps later as a married woman. These were evangelical councils given to every Christian, but I had vowed myself to fulfill them. And this vow remained though its observance would change. Did I understand?

I said I did, and I thought it was the truth.

Then came the financial arrangements. They'd decided that since I'd been employed for three months at a Minneapolis parish and had not sent part of my check to the motherhouse, justice required that I leave with them the $2000.00 dowry I'd brought with me fourteen years before. Was that acceptable to me?

It was. They had given me far more than money. I still couldn't believe this was taking place. I'd never intended to leave the convent, and I remained convinced that God had called me to that life. But now God was calling me to something else, a different life, and had been calling for years while I refused to heed. Even this little legal ceremony felt unreal. I looked at the three sisters, lined up on the sofa, backs straight as they'd been taught, and I realized that none of us really were there. The deepest part of each of us had not been allowed into that room. It was a formality none of us wanted but all of us were required to endure.

One of them handed me the papers.

I signed.

Under my name each of them placed her own.

On that long past morning in 1961 I'd knelt in the motherhouse choir loft after holy communion to make the offering of myself to the merciful love of God. As I understood it, this offering turned me over to God to be used in whatever way needed to bring divine love into the world. It was to the very essence of love, the person, the divine being, Love itself, that I was vowed. I wanted to embody this love. In whatever way people needed the love of God, I wanted to become that love for them. I felt I'd failed completely.

It never occurred to me that love itself could summon me to a life outside the convent, and for many years I interpreted that summons as a temptation. I tried instead to make the convent a kind of life that was open and free enough to accommodate my response. My misinterpretation led to failure. Probably I was meant to fail. I needed to lose that life, to feel it slipping out of my mind and heart, to know the emptiness I would experience once it was definitely gone.

In the end I returned to my beginning. "In other words, through the Law I am dead to the Law, so that now I can live for God. I have been crucified with Christ, and I live now not with my own life but with the life of Christ who lives in me. The life I now live in this body I live in faith: faith in the Son of God who loved me and who sacrificed himself for my sake. I cannot bring myself to give up God's Gift. If the Law can justify us, there is no point in the death of Christ." (*Gal.* 2:19-21)

God will not be made an idol – even if the form of the idol is the church or the cloister. God will be worshipped in the holy solitude of a human heart. We do not choose the form of our offering nor the suffering we will endure to hold it up and have it received. We fly from all else, naked of soul, past all understanding, in the name of love, simply to do God's will.

Life would continue on, like the Red River of the North, though the pond would dry up in the lowland where a red leaf once caught on green moss under ice more fragile than glass. The motherhouse would be sold and the sisters scattered. But Marie still would write to me and I would eventually realize how deeply she had always loved me and I, her. One day I would come across the folder of her letters and begin to read them, as years before I'd read those other letters from Mama, and one of them would bring me to tears. I would hold it in my hands for a long time, staring at the words straight from my Sister Marie's heart:

In some mysterious way you have never left us.

And I would know that to be the truth.

A LETTER FROM MAMA
Flight Home

Here's the letter I opened to in the beginning. Ah yes. And I smile. The apex moment is just that, a moment, then the spiral of experience begins again. You can feel the slight tip as the world you know begins again to rotate. You hold on, not even thinking what you're up to. You feel the slippage, the tilt. You sing; you maybe dance, ignoring what you already know—life is motion; it never stops.

In January, 1973, Mama had been named Mrs. Aviation for the State of Minnesota. She took the award, smiling, and stepped up to the microphone. I don't remember what she said, but she seemed composed. She seemed like the Alyce that most of the people in the audience had met at one time or another in the airport office. She knew their names. She knew the call letters of their airplanes. Did she think, even for a fleeting moment as she accepted her award, of the hidden letters? Of Sadie? Of her fears and her longing for Daddy to retire? Of the fact that they couldn't even afford this trip? As she felt the weight of the award in her hands, did she wonder if it was worth it?

How could she not think those things? But even thinking them, how could she not at the same time feel both happy and proud? This was a moment of convergence. Her whole family looked up at her where she stood. We loved her and were proud.

Three months later Mama's Holy Week letter in red would be written, Easter would arrive, and then May and the closing of my religious education office for the summer.

Memorial Day weekend Liz and I drove from Minneapolis to Baudette for the traditional parade, Dad's fly-over to drop wreathes of poppies in the river, and a fishing excursion with Bill and Alice Delaney who always visited for that holiday. Alice tied all our blouses up bolero-style so we could tan our midriffs. We caught our limit of Walleyed Pike and ate them dipped in egg and flour and pan-fried.

The next morning Liz and I waved, climbed back in the car, and started back south. Everything seemed fine except for that nearly imperceptible tipping of the world, the one no one was noticing except for maybe Mama who had written in her red-typed letter that even after her award that winter as Mrs. Aviation, and even despite her gratitude over the honor of it, she still wanted to sell the business. She wanted to finally take a vacation with Dad, maybe go south for a few weeks that coming winter, *I'm not going to let George wait until we are too old to enjoy it.*

Liz dropped me off at my apartment around dinner time, and I drove my own car to the church where a parish board meeting was scheduled. It was late when I finally got back home—after ten, I think. The phone was ringing. I hurried to unlock the door. I dropped my briefcase and answered the phone.

A man's voice: "Is this Christin Lore?"

"Yes."

"This is officer (I don't remember his name) from the Minneapolis Police Department. I'm a friend of Bill Delaney. He's asked me to get hold of you to tell you that George Lore has suffered a massive heart attack and you need to call home immediately."

The earth plummeted. Did I ask him to repeat? Did I say thank you? Probably not. Maybe he asked if I understood. The next thing I knew I was dialing home. Bill answered. I think he's the one who explained what happened. But maybe it was Mama. Or maybe she was at the hospital. It's strange to me that I don't remember the details. By this time the plummeting world was spinning, and nothing appeared clear except that Daddy was still alive. "They don't expect him to survive though," the person at the other end of the line said. "We can't reach Betsy. Can you try to reach Betsy?"

A night flight had been chartered for Liz and me as soon as we could reach Shakopee's Flying Cloud Airport. We should get there as quickly as possible. Courage. Hurry. A pilot friend of Daddy's was already waiting for us and the plane was gassed up and ready to go.

I hung up the phone and began to tremble. My teeth were chattering. I held out my shaking hands and looked at them. So far I hadn't cried, but I was also not quite right in myself—not balanced—and as the seconds passed I felt myself becoming more shaky. Could I stand up? Would my legs support me? My breath came in gasps. Might I hyperventilate? How could I drive? I had to get to Liz's apartment. I tried to call her. It was hard to get my fingers to dial the right numbers. Then she didn't answer. I simply had to get there. Luckily I hadn't unpacked; I could just take the same suitcase back to Baudette. My heart pounded in my chest. My hands wouldn't stop shaking.

Someone would need to drive me to Liz's. But who? It was eleven o'clock. Who could I call at eleven o'clock?

Pat. He was the only one who came to mind. I'd been awful to him—really, we'd been awful to each other—and hadn't seen or spoken months, but somehow I felt certain he'd do this. I dialed his number. When he answered, my voice broke as I explained what I needed. In twenty minutes he was carrying my suitcase to his car.

My cousin, Marilyn, wrote not long ago with the idea that maybe God is not rational—at least not in the sense that we think of ourselves as rational. I laughed. I'd been writing this story with all its twists and turns in which intention rarely yielded expected results. God's ways, it is said, are not our ways. Sometimes I've thought that it wouldn't have mattered what choices I made, I'd have ended up in the same spot, doing not what I intended, but what God intended anyway. "God writes straight with crooked lines," said Paul Claudel about the paradox of human choice.

Against all reason, I called Pat, and he came.

We hurried up the stairs to Liz's apartment and Kath came to the door. She'd just arrived home and finally had answered the phone had been ringing off and on all evening. Liz had been sleeping with the bedroom door closed, and Kath woke her just before we arrived. I saw her crumpled in upon herself, collapsed on the floor by the phone, holding the receiver to her ear. She just had been told the news and was crying.

"She didn't hear the phone." Kath explained.

Pat drove the two of us to Flying Cloud Airport where an 8-seat turbo prop plane was set to go. He walked with us to where two men stood on the tarmac, and gave my hand a squeeze, helping me up. "Go with God," he said. "If you need me, call. I'll be here."

I bent to enter the small plane. At some time or other we must bow down. Life's never as organized as we pretend. All people are both strong and weak. We do what we can and sometimes it ends in broken promises, in betrayal, in lost dreams. God holds us through it all. God holds us up. Don't conclude that I know what all this means. Of the gods C.S. Lewis writes, "Whatever can be said clearly cannot be said truly about them." People enter our lives for a reason. I have only faith to substantiate this, and a long life to observe it all play out in retrospect. The only adequate answer to the ambiguity in which we constantly live is to bow down, to let it be, to be within it faithfully.

The engines roared and I thought of Daddy, of all his flights. I hoped that this night would not mark the last of those flights. I could not imagine life without him. He seemed the one still thing, and regardless of the flaws he carried through his days, he was what we counted on for steadiness. He kept us from crashing. Or if we started to go down, we knew he'd bring us in alive. How could he die?

Out the window of the plane the sky was clear and layered with stars. "Good to go," the pilot said, and the roar of engines increased as we started down the runway back towards home. I've had some flights of my own, I thought as we lifted off, different sorts of flights from those that Daddy made, flights to and from my life—often not knowing in which direction I might be heading. Maybe someday I'd know better, or maybe not.

Only now can I see from more than forty years in the future, the place to which this flight and every flight of my life would lead. Right now, this moment, I realize where I was headed, but I couldn't know it then. Then I couldn't even have told myself what future years would make clear: You start out in this life, most of us do, as an overflowing of tenderness, and after that you mostly travel in the dark. The turns you take often lead to edges, uncharted cliffs, endings unplanned. Promises turn out to be like fine glass; attention wavers for an instant; they fall, shattering on stones below. You wonder if perhaps you shouldn't have made that promise in the first place. Perhaps it was a promise needed at the time but held too long. Hands sweat or cramp up. You stumble on the edge. Glass slips. Away it goes. No amount of tears can bring it back. Maybe that glass held all the water you could get to stave off thirst. Maybe you can live without water, but you don't think so. You'll make another promise, carry another fragile glass somewhere you didn't plan to go, on a different journey, a further flight.

You'll finally make it through. You'll finally make it to the place that you were seeking all along, and you'll stand on that edge of tenderness where you will see dawn burgeoning like divine fire on the horizon. And at that moment, in the fullness of your time here on this earth, everything you've been and done will have been preparation. Everything will have been good. And you'll fly towards that holy fire, arms wide open, heart completely exposed, voice singing, eyes filled with glory.

The plane leveled off. Below us my sister and I could see the blackness of lakes and forests interrupted only from time to time by patches of light marking the presence of a small town. At dawn I'd take Mama in my arms. How often in past years had she waited at the airport to take me into hers? Those agonizing times in my early convent years that I called her and she sent Daddy flying south so I could make the flight from Crookston, home. Now she still would be there waiting, but this time she would be the one held. I could do that—hold her, hold Mama. If she needed to cry, we could combine our tears. Maybe I could sing her lullabies. "Goodnight Sweetheart," my dearest Mama—I could sing the song to her now. Maybe I began to hum the melody as I gazed through the window of the airplane at the stars. "'Till we meet tomorrow...sleep will banish sorrow." Mama would be waiting at the Baudette Airport, and I'd run to her and take her in my arms.

For now there was only the journey, this night flight home.

THE EDGE OF TENDERNESS

Daddy lived two more years, a stick man, like a winter tree, brittle in body as his spirit communicated increasing compassion. His last Christmas after we'd said goodbye I snapped a photo through the picture window into the house where he stood. A reflection of his winter world on which he looked each day almost concealed his image while revealing something deeper and more mysterious. He appeared ghostly behind reflections of trees and snow. I caught my breath, later, when the pictures were developed. I thought I was seeing him through the scrim of death. He died on a sunny day the following May. He and his friend, Roy, were sitting together at the airport, talking, when suddenly Daddy exclaimed, "What the hell?" and fell off the chair onto the floor. Not the finest of last words, according to Mama, who suddenly worried for his soul, as though at the moment of death, he'd actually seen the shadowlands.

Not so, I thought and told her so. For this man of few words, that was a phrase he invariably used to express surprise. It could have been the Eternal Light he'd seen. He could have noted the stoppage of his heart. He could have passed into a realm so beautiful that the man of few words had to utter something, and his habitual expression of surprise emerged.

Mama crumbled physically under the stresses, first of his illness and then of her grief following his death. Six months after his first heart attack she discovered a malignancy in her breast which was treated with radical mastectomy. She seemed to place her own health in secondary position to her unceasing efforts to keep him alive. I don't believe it was a sacrifice on her part, but rather a natural and spontaneous outcome of her love and their commitment to each other. Her body was aware, though, of the emotional and psychological agony that, except for her few "please understand me" letters, she hid from her everyday awareness. Not long after he died, she suffered a massive cerebral hemorrhage, brain surgery, and a convalescence that lasted sixteen years. She left us slowly. Every time I visited her in the care center less of her remained. Nothing I could do could stop this certain slide towards oblivion and finally death.

One of Mama's final letters, probably in 1985, was written to her friend Evelyn. It never fails to break my heart. Bits of it read:

I received your lovely card which I received a week or ten days ago AND NOW TODAY, MAY% (5?) I must get this letter off to you but I hope I manage to find a STAMP for the envelope...

I shall PRAY each day and spend time in our CHAPEL HERE in the NEWLY enlarged Saint Therese HOME and I no longer have an apartment of my own...

MY typing is readable and I won't mind if at times it makes you laugh.

My BRAINsurgery resulted in failure and I cannot EVER recall my past (at all)

DO recall that I shall pray each evening in our chapel where we have DAILY MASS and ROSARY.

My writing is poor and I am brooding over my failing health.

and I realize you cannot know what I mean.

She and I had spent our lives dancing on a fault line. I'd formed my life based on patterns created in my soul by her original disappearance just after I was born. Most of what I am today is the result of each choice I made to keep myself safe from ever again needing to experience a loss as drastic as that original loss of the Mother. And Mama was dying. She would be lost again, and I would keep on dancing.

During this difficult time I wrote: I expect that the separation caused by Mama's tuberculosis gave Daddy the time he needed to figure out the practicalities of being a married man as well as to form himself into the protector he must have thought this frail, wispy, sprite of a woman—this exotic, volcanic, theatrical woman—needed. And even though his protective spirit sometimes came close to suffocating her, she came to understand it as his love. She believed she needed his love. She was willing to sacrifice anything for George's love and not to find it a sacrifice at all. Whatever pain his protection caused her she attributed to her selfishness. To do this she sometimes needed to twist her own reality around, turn it upside-down. She denied herself, worked to quench the fire within her. She often said the opposite of what she felt, hoping, I think, that anyone who really loved her would see through her subterfuge and do what she wanted regardless of what she said. She hoped to be caught in her lie.

I recall a time when she was in her early seventies and still suffering from the decreased self-confidence resulting from her brain trauma. I invited her to accompany me to some friends' thirtieth wedding anniversary party at their home outside of Clearwater, Minnesota. I thought she would enjoy the people and the fifty acres of paths through the woods and alongside the Clear River in front of their house.

"Oh, I couldn't," she whined, "I'd just embarrass you."

Ordinarily I would have attempted to convince her that she absolutely would not embarrass me, that the people would find her charming, that she looked just fine, that I really and truly wanted her to come. But over the years I had learned that this kind of talk elicited only a further argument from her and further frustrating attempts on my part to convince her that she was okay. So that time I nodded thoughtfully and said the unexpected:

"Well, Mama, I'll tell you what; if you embarrass me I'll just take you out to the car and lock you in there until it's time to go."

She laughed, delighted, I think, to have been found out, thrilled that I had finally figured out her game. She came with me to Clearwater and every time I sought her out she was laughing and talking with someone. She walked in the woods with friends of mine, and they discussed religion. On the way home she said, "I think I'll just take a nap," and fell asleep with a smile on her face.

She tried to quench her fire. I wonder if this is the meaning of that childhood dream I had in which I felt responsible to keep her house from burning down. I wonder if the impossible task of quenching Mama's fire could have been passed on to me. I wonder whether the conflict I feel within myself is the conflict of my parents' voices: Mama's saying "Blaze, Mary Jane, blaze with the fire I could not permit myself," and Daddy's saying "Put the fire out or it will kill your mother; it will drive her crazy." In 1992, not long before her death, I wrote:

Mama's house is burning down
Lady Bird Lady Bird
FLY

        Mama's house is flame
        Burning flesh burning brain making bone
        Pure bone, fire bone, white
        White flame.

        What remains?
A WORD
        Fire and the word
LOVE.

        I watch as she shrivels, a tinder

303

A dry pine on a hill
Lightning! Crack! Flame!
White red blue the sky burns
She screams; she is silent
Her brain shines

A JEWEL

It explodes.

Where is her mind?
The sky lights up
I back away.

She lifts her arms
She dances on her death
She flies on tiptoe
She spreads wings like a firefly
She is a moth, a moon-moth
Drawn to flame and into fire and sticks
To the candle wick and burns and

BURNS

Oh Mama Mama Oh
I long for you

Your flesh—
But you are seared
And your flesh has melted off your bones

Your voice—
But it has turned to firefalls
And rains on me in notwords

Your arms—
But they are bones white hot singing searing
And you are firesong rising in the night

Nothing of you here is left for earth

Yet you burn.
I cannot touch you Mama
You are too red
Too hot too white red burning hot
Too much transformed to recognize
Too gone
Too not you to be who sang me lullabies
On warm October nights
While red leaves fell.

MAMA MAMA

Let the fire die.
Let me hold you once
Before you fly;
Be a bird in my hand
Resting Nesting
One again with everything
We ever hoped to understand
About our hearts

YOUR HEART
HIDING

In my too too frozen life.

I would continue to dance through each movement of my life's love song, dancing on the music's edge, dancing with my lost mother's ghost through three marriages and two widowhoods, through the church's evolution and devolution wrought by the Second Vatican Council, through every anticipation and through every grief, through life and loss...

Until now...

The other night PBS broadcast a bucolic documentary about a group of nuns who experienced none of this upheaval at all. They are a cloistered community of women with solemn vows in Missouri whose singing came to the attention of a Grammy Award producer. It helped, I guess, that the Abbess had been a college classmate of his. Both musicians. From what I could deduce, this monastery was founded only a few years ago, probably during the papacy of Pope Saint John Paul II. The median age of the nuns is 28. Their singing broke my heart, it was so beautiful. It was an image of all I wanted to be and to do with my life when I was that very age. And I lost it.

But then I realized something important: Back in those turbulent post-Vatican II years, the convent I'd dreamed of left ME, not the other way around. I've known, of course, that the times back then were both exciting and dreadful, filled with possibility and with loss. I was a pioneer of post Vatican II thought and the effort to put it into practice. But really no one knew how to make that thought part of the day to day life of a Catholic convent or parish. I believed in my own vision, perhaps too much.

These new nuns in Missouri could reach into the medieval past and draw out of those pre-Vatican II times the most beautiful of what had been there, while leaving behind the problems it contained. And surely they haven't experienced, and may never need to experience, that gulf, that edge between worlds that we experienced in the sixties and seventies.

My heart ached for love of them and for my own longing from many years ago—longing for the "More." Yet I know that the film makers had no way of going inside that convent, or into the hearts of those young women, to discover the agonizing purging of soul that happens to all who give themselves to that kind of life.

The following morning I woke with a realization: For me the convent/habit/veil was all about protection. My original experience was one of total vulnerability, about the loss of the ultimate protection (Mother/Self) in this earthly realm. In some real, but also symbolic way I went to the convent in the first place because of the veil/habit. As soon as I write those words, I am flooded with memories all the way back through my life to early childhood and the dichotomy of being wounded—naked to the bone, and being veiled. Nakedness is a kind of absolute danger—the edge of death itself. The veil is safety.

When the veil that covered the still raw wound is removed, even a breath can make it ache.

In the convent documentary a particular scene mesmerized me—a schola of six nuns singing with what seemed one voice. Both the chant and their bodies were a paradox of stillness. Their faces looked like statues or like a painting of absolute purity. The music rose in an unearthly way as if each were an ivory flute that no one fingered—and the music flowed through but not from them. Nothing about them interfered, even their lips barely moved as they produced the clean Latin syllables.

The apotheosis of virginity.

The antithesis of the wild.

Here was a moment of almost beauty, a glimpse of safety in the very heart of the wild. But it couldn't last, and must not. Not for me, nor for any one of us until we pass through this earth's density into a clearer, freer, more whole and integrated realm of being. We are not yet home.

We have not yet fully encountered God.

But we stand at the edge of tenderness.

ABOUT THE AUTHOR

Christin Lore Weber lives and writes with her husband, author John R. Sack, at Casa Chiara Hermitage in the mountains of Southern Oregon.

GRATITUDE

To Mama for her letters, for her love, for that incomparable genetic package with its respect for words.

To Daddy for his silences that required me to find the words.

To the Sisters of St. Joseph who surrounded me and imbued within me such a gift of life—its paradox and beauty, its love and resistance to love, its freedom and whatever is held captive, its suffering and surrender—that I can never express enough thanks. Nor can I ever weep enough tears at needing to say goodbye.

To Sandra Scofield for her belief in this story and her incisive critique communicated with confidence: "This is a beautiful manuscript, and I am in awe of it and of your mind and spirit." Who cannot, after such words, continue to the very edge of one's craft and beyond?

To all who read this memoir during the many years of its composition—you know who you are. Each of you in your own way urged me towards deeper truth.

To John whose love both humbles and sustains me.

Made in the USA
Columbia, SC
15 January 2018